french
DeMYSTiFieD

Annie Heminway

New York Chicago San Francisco Lisbon London Madrid Mexico City
Milan New Delhi San Juan Seoul Singapore Sydney Toronto

1 2 3 4 5 6 7 8 9 0   DOC/DOC   0 9 8 7

ISBN-13: 978-0-07-147660-7
ISBN-10:   0-07-147660-1
Library of Congress Control Number: 2006940164

Maps created by Douglas Norgord, Geographic Techniques.

This book is printed on acid-free paper.

CONTENTS

INTRODUCTION

You might be taking your first steps in French. You may be someone who has already climbed partway up the ladder but wants to refresh your memory of the language. Or perhaps you are studying on your own, or need a companion book for your French classes in college in order to review the subtleties of the French language, such as what verbs require which prepositions. Whatever the reason you're studying French, *French Demystified* will set you on the fast track to learning the language and developing your skills. By demystifying French, we mean taking the mystery out of the language so that it becomes clear and easy to learn.

French has a lot in common with other languages, especially English, and, as you will soon discover, the two languages share many words in common. In fact, one of the advantages of studying French is that not only do many English words have a recognizable French origin, but a number of English words have also been incorporated into the French language. Here are a few examples of words in French that are identical in spelling with English.

téléphone	*telephone*
différent	*different*
révolution	*revolution*
rare	*rare*
télévision	*television*

There are also many words that may be spelled slightly differently but mean the same thing in both languages:

forme	*form*
jugement	*judgment*
projet	*project*
naturel	*natural*
délicieux	*delicious*

Sometimes you can use letter substitution patterns to recognize cognates. Many French words that begin with **é** have cognates in English. Just change the French **é** to an *s* in English.

éponge	*sponge*
épice	*spice*
étudiant	*student*
état	*state*
étranger	*stranger*

Similarly, try adding an s in English after a vowel that has a circumflex accent in French.

fête	*feast*
forêt	*forest*
hôpital	*hospital*
île	*island*
pâtes	*pasta*

With this book, it will be easy to get rid of any anxiety in your French studies. No drama, no myths, nothing to fear.

How to Use This Book

Demystifying French goes beyond recognizing the similarities between French and English. This book will provide a clear and straightforward approach to understanding French grammatical concepts. This includes uncomplicated explanations of new material, a variety of examples that illustrate that material, and numerous vehicles for practicing what is learned. In this book you will also find vocabulary items presented both in short lists and in context.

French Demystified can be used in two ways. You can begin with Chapter 1 and work your way through the chapters in a linear progression. Alternatively, you can use this book in a modular way, using the table of contents and index to locate particular areas of French that you want to study.

This book features two kinds of practice exercises: oral and written. It's important to understand that one form of practice is not more important than the other. They are different in form but work together in the development of French skills. Language is basically a spoken entity; therefore, oral practice is obviously necessary when one is learning a new language. But written practice provides time to think about grammatical concepts and the meaning of words. It allows the student to think about and analyze what is being learned. This is the way people record knowledge and evaluate progress. Both exercises will be important for you as you proceed through this book.

Below is an illustration of how oral practice is structured. It is not merely a list of words or of random sentences to be practiced aloud. Instead, oral practice contains paradigms that illustrate a concept important to the language. Let's look at an example of oral practice in English which provides a student with paradigms that illustrate pronouns used as direct objects.

Practice saying the following list of sentences out loud.

I gave her a book.

She gave us advice.

We gave him a tie.

He gave them a box of chocolates.

You gave me a ticket.

She gave you a kiss.

Written practice will appear in various forms. In some instances, you will be asked to complete a sentence with new words. For example, an English exercise with pronouns changing from their subjective form to their objective form would look like this:

Rewrite the following sentence with the pronouns provided in parentheses.

Julia sent _____ a letter.

(he) *Julia sent him a letter.*

(you) *Julia sent you a letter.*

(I) *Julia sent me a letter.*

(we) *Julia sent us a letter.*

Other forms of written practice include verb conjugations, multiple choice exercises, and writing original sentences.

You will occasionally find *tables* in this book. They are used to highlight special information and to remind you of a concept that is important to keep in mind. For example:

French does not capitalize adjectives that refer to a country.

un étudiant américain	*an American student*
une voiture japonaise	*a Japanese car*
une danseuse russe	*a Russian dancer*

Each chapter ends with a *quiz* that will help you to evaluate your understanding of the material of the chapters. The quizzes are *open-book* quizzes, which means that you should use the content of the chapters as a resource for determining the correct answers. A good suggestion is to achieve a score of at least 80 percent before going on to the next chapter.

After every five chapters, you will have a *part test*. There are four parts to the book, and the part tests are, therefore, named Part One Test, Part Two Test, Part Three Test, and Part Four Test. It is suggested that you consider these tests *closed-book* tests in order to check your comprehension of the concepts in each part. You should get a score of 75 percent on a part test before moving on to the next part.

The last test in the book is a *final exam*. It consists of questions that are drawn from the four parts of the book. The final exam contains 100 questions; a good score on this exam is 75 percent.

At the end of the book, there is an Answer Key, which provides the correct answers for all quizzes, part tests, and the final exam. In the case of questions that require you to provide an original sentence as your answer, you will be provided with a sample answer for comparison.

No more myth, no more mystery. With *French Demystified* you'll be able to make your study of French an enlightening and fun experience. Have fun!

PART ONE

BASICS OF FRENCH UNDERSTANDING

CHAPTER 1

French Pronunciation

In this chapter you will learn:

The French You Already Know: Borrowed Words and Cognates

The French Alphabet

Pronouncing Vowels

Pronouncing Consonants

Syllabification

The Francophone World

The French You Already Know: Borrowed Words and Cognates

Starting a new language can be intimidating. But even though French is a complex language, you may already know more vocabulary words than you realize. This means that you also have a basic idea of French pronunciation.

French Demystified

French culture has a worldwide reputation, and French cinema, in particular, is a good way for you to get your ear accustomed to the sounds of French. Moreover, the Internet gives you access to French-language media, music, sports, and arts to a greater degree than ever before. So take advantage of the spoken French language environment around you, and you will quickly improve your pronunciation and comprehension.

BORROWED WORDS

English already uses a variety of French words. You may already have eaten *pâté* or *foie gras* for dinner, or drunk *champagne* or *cognac*. If you once asked someone for a *rendezvous*; if you once felt on the *qui vive* or *blasé*; when you remember nice *souvenirs*; then you're already putting your French to use. There are many other words, such as *apropos*, *cul-de-sac*, *pastiche*, *poste restante*, *sabotage*. Note that the spelling of some words is slightly different in the two languages: for example, the right French spelling for *rendezvous* is **rendez-vous,** for *qui vive* is **qui-vive,** for *apropos* is **à propos**.

In addition, English has a variety of words that have their roots in French, but which have been slightly changed as they have become anglicized. Many of those words are related to food: for instance, the English word *veal* comes from the French **veau**; *pork* comes from **porc**.

COGNATES

French and English share a number of cognates, or words that share the same linguistic root and are therefore similar in spelling and meaning. Some cognates in English and French are exactly the same; others are so similar they are unmistakable. Although they will be pronounced differently in French, you should be able to tell just by looking at cognates what their meanings are. Here are some examples. Can you guess the meaning of each?

Adjectives	Nouns	Verbs
capable	l'acteur	arriver
certain	la définition	calculer
différent	le dîner	changer
important	l'exemple	décider
intelligent	le fruit	divorcer
manuel	l'information	excuser
naturel	la nièce	imaginer
patient	l'opinion	importer

possible	la question	organiser
responsable	la température	respecter

Many French words starting with an **é** are very close to English, as long as you know you have to change the French **é** into an English *s*. Guess the meanings of: **épeler, épice, éponge, état, étole, étrange, étrangler, étudiant, étudier.** (Answers: *to spell, spice, sponge, state, stole, strange, to strangle, student, to study*.)

Also, most French words ending with the letters **tion** or **isme** are very similar in English; some examples are **abstraction, adaptation, collection, évolution, libéralisme, modernisme, paternalisme**.

FALSE COGNATES

False cognates are words that are written similarly in English and French but do not share a similar meaning. There are many false cognates in French and English. Here are some French words that look as though they would mean something else, along with their actual meanings:

French	English
actuellement	*currently*
affronter	*to face*
attendre	*to wait (for)*
le bénéfice	*profit*
le car	*bus, coach*
la caution	*deposit*
la chance	*luck*
complet	*full*
le grief	*grievance*
la journée	*day*
la librairie	*bookstore*
la nouvelle	*a piece of news or a short story*
le patron	*boss*
regarder	*to look (at)*
retirer	*to withdraw*
le roman	*novel*
le surnom	*nickname*
sympathique	*pleasant, nice*
travailler	*to work*
les vacances	*holidays, vacation*

Written Practice

Now that you realize you already know more French than you thought you did, try translating these sentences into English. If there are any words you do not recognize, take a guess by using the surrounding context clues to help you.

1. L'acteur est patient. _____.
2. Le dîner est délicieux. _____.
3. Valérie et Thomas attendent la nouvelle. _____.
4. Le patron prépare une réorganisation de l'entreprise. _____.
5. Sandrine travaille à la librairie. _____.

The French Alphabet

French pronunciation follows specific rules. Just as in English, not everything is spelled as it sounds or sounds the way it is spelled. English and French share many sounds, but French can have several spellings for the same sound.

You will find the French alphabet in a table below. The list includes the letters, their names (just as we say "jay" for the letter *j* or "zee" or "zed" for the letter *z*, letters in French also have names), the sound each letter makes, and example words. The pronunciation of each example word is in parentheses. In the next section, we will explore the pronunciation of some of these letters more in depth, but this list can act as a reference as you make your way through the book.

Letter	Name	Sound	Example
a	a	*a* in f*a*ther	**art** (*ahr*)
b	bé	*b* in *b*order	**billet** (*bee-yay*)
c	sé	*s* (soft c) in *c*entral before **e, i, y;**	**cime** (*seem*)
		k (hard c) in *c*offee before **a, o, u**	**café** (*kah-fay*)
d	dé	*d* in *d*ay	**dame** (*dahm*)
e	uh	*uh* in *a*lone	**le** (*luh*)
f	èf	*f* in *f*arm	**ferme** (*fehrm*)

g	zhé	*zh* (soft g) in plea*s*ure before **e**, **i**, **y**;	**gymnastique** (*zhim-nah-steek*)
		g (hard g) in *g*uarantee before **a**, **o**, **u**	**garage** (*gah-rahzh*)
h	ash	always silent	***h**ameau* (*ah-moh*)
i	ee	*ee* in m*ee*t	***i**ci* (*ee-see*)
j	zhee	*zh* (soft g) in plea*s*ure	***j**ava* (*zhah-vah*)
k	ka	*k* (hard c) in *c*at	***k**ilo* (*kee-loh*)
l	èl	*l* in *l*ight	***l**une* (*lun*)
m	èm	*m* in *M*onday	***m**alle* (*mahl*)
n	èn	*n* in *n*atural	***n**atte* (*naht*)
o	oh	*o* in r*o*ll	***m**ot* (*moh*)
p	pé	*p* in *p*earl	***p**iscine* (*pee-seen*)
q	ku	*k* (hard c) in *c*arry	**bar*q*ue** (*bahrk*)
r	èr	pronounced in back of mouth, rolled like light gargling sound	***r**êve* (*rehv*)
s	ès	*s* in *s*imple in beginning of word or before or after consonant;	**ma*s*que** (*mahsk*)
		z in *z*one between vowels	**ba*s*ilic** (*bah-zee-leek*)
t	té	*t* in *t*ask	***t**ennis* (*tay-nees*)
u	u	no equivalent in English; pronounce *ee* and then round your lips	***tu*** (*tu*)
v	vé	*v* in *v*alley	***v**ivace* (*vee-vahs*)
w	doobl vé	*v* in *v*alley	***w**agon* (*vah-goh(n)*)
x	eeks	*gz* in e*x*act; *ks* in e*x*cellent	**e*x*act** (*eh-gzahkt*) **e*x*quis** (*ehks-kee*)
y	ee grèk	*y* in *y*es	***y**aourt* (*yah-oo-rt*)
z	zèd	*z* in *z*one	***z**est* (*zehst*)

Pronouncing Vowels

French has six vowels: **a, e, i, o, u**, and **y**. French vowels often take accents:

- The acute accent (**accent aigu**): é
- The grave accent (**accent grave**): à, è, ù
- The circumflex (**accent circonflexe**): â, ê, î, ô, û

a The vowel **a** (*a*) and its variants **à** and **â** sound similar to *a* in f*a*ther. Practice saying these examples:

la (*lah*)	*the* (feminine)
facile (*fah-cee-l*)	*easy*
pâte (*pah-t*)	*paste*

e **e** is pronounced *uh* like *a* in *a*lone or *u* in b*u*rn. Practice saying these examples:

je (*zhuh*)	*I*
le (*luh*)	*the*
ce (*suh*)	*this, that*

NOTE: *Except in short words like those above, an unaccented* e *at the end of a word is usually not pronounced. Practice saying these examples:*

carotte (*kah-rot*)	*carrot*
argile (*ahr-zheel*)	*clay*
verre (*vehr*)	*glass*

é is pronounced like *ay* in d*ay*, but not drawn out (**er** and **ez** are pronounced the same way). Practice saying these examples:

thé (*tay*)	*tea*
vélo (*vay-lo*)	*bicycle*
carré (*kah-ray*)	*square*

è is pronounced like *e* in g*e*t (**ai** and **aî** are pronounced the same way). Practice saying these examples:

mère (*mehr*)	*mother*
père (*pehr*)	*father*
chère (*shehr*)	*dear or expensive* (feminine)

i The vowel **i** or **î** sounds like *ee* in b*ee*t. Practice saying these examples:

mari (*mah-ree*)   *husband*
vie (*vee*)   *life*
pari (*pah-ree*)   *bet*

o The vowel **o** has an open and a closed sound. The open o sounds a little bit like *au* in c*au*ght. Practice saying these examples:

bonne (*bon*)   *good*
sotte (*sot*)   *silly* (feminine)
vote (*vot*)   *vote*

o The closed **o** sounds like *o* in r*o*ll. Practice saying these examples:

abricot (*ah-bree-koh*)   *apricot*
sot (*soh*)   *silly* (masculine)
pot (*poh*)   *pot, jar*

u The vowel **u** has no equivalent in English, but you can make it by pronouncing the sound *ee* and then rounding your lips. Practice saying these examples:

tu (*tu*)   *you*
vu (*vu*)   *seen*
lu (*lu*)   *read*

u After the letters **q** and **g**, the **u** is silent in French. Practice saying these examples:

quatre (*kahtr*)   *four*
guérir (*gay-reer*)   *to heal*

Oral Practice

Practice saying the words in the list. Focus on your pronunciation of the vowels. Look at the transliteration to check your pronunciation.

French	Pronunciation	English
1. avis	*ah-vee*	*opinion*
2. métro	*may-tro*	*subway*

3.	Paris	*pah-ree*	*Paris*
4.	rose	*roh-z*	*pink, rose*
5.	image	*ee-mahzh*	*picture*
6.	cidre	*seedr*	*cider*
7.	modèle	*mo-dehl*	*model*
8.	sérieux	*say-ree-uh*	*serious*
9.	parole	*pah-rol*	*word*

DIPHTHONGS

Diphthongs are a combination of two vowels or of a vowel and a consonant and are treated as one syllable. There are many diphthongs in French.

ai or **aî** is pronounced like *e* in m*e*t. Practice saying these examples:

lait (*leh*)   milk
chaise (*shehz*)   chair
chaîne (*shehn*)   chain

au or **eau** is pronounced like *o* in r*o*ll. Practice saying these examples:

seau (*soh*)   *bucket*
veau (*voh*)   *veal*
château (*shah-toh*) *castle*

eu has two sounds. The closed sound is pronounced like *u* in p*u*t. Practice saying these examples:

peu (*puh*)   *few*
jeu (*zhuh*)   *game*
deux (*duh*)   *two*

eu The open sound is pronounced like *u* in f*u*n. Practice saying these examples:

bœuf (*buhf*)   *beef*
seul (*suhl*)   *alone*

er and **ez** at the end of a word are pronounced like *ay* in l*ay*. Practice saying these examples:

assez (*ah-say*)   *enough*
marcher (*mahr-shay*) *to walk*
garer (*gah-ray*)   *to park*

oi is pronounced like *wa* in *watch*. Practice saying these examples:

moi (*mwa*)	*me*
toit (*twa*)	*roof*
loi (*lwa*)	*law*

oy is pronounced like *wa* in *watch* + *ee*. Practice saying these examples:

voyage (*vwa-yazh*)	*travel*
noyau (*nwa-yoh*)	*pit, fruit stone*
loyal (*lwa-yahl*)	*loyal*

ou is pronounced like *oo* in *zoo*. Practice saying these examples:

jour (*zhoo-r*)	*day*
sous (*soo*)	*under*
vous (*voo*)	*you*

ui is pronounced like *wee*. Practice saying these examples:

bruit (*brwee*)	*noise*
nuit (*nwee*)	*night*
pluie (*plwee*)	*rain*

oui is pronounced like *oo* + *wee*. Practice saying these examples:

oui (*oo-wee*)	*yes*
Louis (*loo-wee*)	*Louis*

NASAL VOWELS

The syllables composed of a vowel and **n** or **m** create a nasal vowel sound, which is produced when air is expelled from both the mouth and nose. In French, a consonant **n** or **m** that follows a nasal vowel is not pronounced. In the word **France**, for example, we pronounce the nasal vowel **a** through the mouth and the nose but not the consonant **n.** Following is a chart of nasal vowels with examples:

French Spelling	Approximate Sound	Example
an, en	vowel in b*a*lm	***a**n*, v*e*ndre
em	vowel in b*a*lm	**emm**énager
in, ain, ein	vowel in m*a*n	v*in*, b*ain*, pl*ein*
im, aim	vowel in m*a*n	**im**berbe, f*aim*
ien	y + vowel in m*e*n	ch*ien*, b*ien*, r*ien*
ion	y + vowel in s*o*ng	pot*ion*, Mar*ion*
oin	w + vowel in m*a*n	c*oin*, s*oin*

on	vowel in s*o*ng	mais*on*, ball*on*
om	vowel in s*o*ng	c*om*pagnie
un	vowel in l*u*ng	*un*

If **i** or **y** is followed by a nasal vowel, it sounds like *y* in *yes* and is pronounced with the vowel in one syllable. Practice saying these examples:

passion (*pah-syoh(n)*)	*passion*
chien (*shyeh(n)*)	*dog*
étudiant (*ay-tu-dyah(n)*)	*student*

The combination **oin** sounds like the English *w* followed by the nasal vowel **a(n)**: **coin, foin, loin, moins, point, soin.**

A vowel + **n** or **m** + another vowel is not nasal. Practice these examples:

canne (*kahn*)	*stick*
semaine (*suh-mehn*)	*week*
aspirine (*ahs-pee-reen*)	*aspirin*
comme (*kom*)	*like*
amertume (*ah-mayr-tum*)	*bitterness*

The word **pays** (country) is pronounced *pay-ee*.

Oral Practice

Practice saying the words in the list and for each word, write down how many syllables it has. (It may help if you divide each word into syllables, using vertical lines.) Remember, a diphthong counts as one syllable, but two strong vowels next to each other count as two. Answers are in the Answer Key at the back of the book.

French	Number of Syllables	English
1. Aurélia	_____	*Aurelia*
2. alouette	_____	*lark*
3. sieste	_____	*nap*
4. cuisine	_____	*kitchen*
5. bruit	_____	*noise*
6. américain	_____	*American*

7. rituel   _____   *ritual*

8. boire   _____   *to drink*

Pronouncing Consonants

French consonants are mostly pronounced like their English counterparts, with a few variations and exceptions. The consonants **b, d, k, l, m, n, p, s, t, v,** and **z** are generally pronounced as in English.

Final consonants are usually not pronounced in French, except for **c, r, f, l** (consonants in CaReFuL). Practice saying these examples:

Unpronounced Final Consonants

vous (*voo*)   *you* (plural)

alors (*ah-lor*)   *so*

assis (*ah-see*)   *seated*

vas (*vah*)   *go* (second-person singular)

épuisé (*ay-pwee-zay*)   *exhausted*

Pronounced Final Consonants

avec (*ah-vehk*)   *with*

sec (*sehk*)   *dry*

œuf (*uhf*)   *egg*

bref (*brehf*)   *brief, short*

il (*eel*)   *he*

In verb forms, the final **ent** of the third-person plural is silent. Practice saying these examples:

(ils) achètent (*ah-sheht*)   *(they) buy*

(ils) marchent (*mahrsh*)   *(they) walk*

(ils) vivent (*veev*)   *(they) live*

In the verb form **est** (*is*), only the **e** is voiced. Practice saying this example:

est (*ay*)   *is*

c As in English, French **c** has a soft and a hard sound. The hard sound *k* sounds like the *c* in *c*arry. It occurs before **a, o, u**, and before a consonant. Practice saying these examples:

carré (*kahr-ray*)	*square*
d'accord (*dah-kor*)	*OK*
climat (*klee-mah*)	*climate*

c The soft **c** (*s*) sounds like the *c* in *c*innamon. It occurs before **e, i**, or **y**. Practice saying these examples:

cercle (*sehrkl*)	*circle*
cinéma (*see-nay-mah*)	*cinema*
cynique (*see-neek*)	*cynical*

ç ("**c cédille**") before **a, o**, or **u** is a pronounced like a soft **c** (*s* sound). Practice saying these examples:

français (*frah(n)-say*)	*French*
déçu (*day-su*) *disappointed*	

c + h The combination **c + h** is pronounced like *sh* in sun*sh*ine when followed by a vowel. Practice saying these examples:

chat (*shah*)	*cat*
chercher (*shehr-shay*)	*to search*
chaud (*shoh*)	*hot*

c + h is pronounced like **k** (or the hard *c* in *c*ut) when followed by a consonant. Practice saying these examples:

Christine (*krees-teen*)	*Christine*
chrétien (*kray-tye(n)*)	*Christian*

g The letter **g** has a soft sound (*zh*) and a hard sound (*g*). The soft **g** occurs in front of the vowels **e** and **i**. It is represented by *zh* and is pronounced like *s* in plea*s*ure. Practice saying these examples:

gérer (*zhay-ray*)	*to manage*
nager (*nah-zhay*)	*to swim*
juger (*zhu-zhay*)	*to judge*

g The hard **g** occurs everywhere else. It sounds like the *g* in e*gg* or *g*o. Practice saying these examples:

gai (*gay*)	*joyful*
griller (*gree-yay*)	*to grill*
guide (*geed*)	*guide*

gn is pronounced like *ni* in o*ni*on. Practice saying these examples:

Agnès (*ah-nyes*)	*Agnès*
vigneron (*vee-nyuh-roh(n)*)	*wine grower*
saigner (*say-nyay*)	*to bleed*

h The letter **h** is always silent in French. Practice saying these examples:

haricot (*ah-ree-koh*)	*bean*
habit (*ah-bee*)	*clothing*
hôtel (*oh-tehl*)	*hotel*

t + h The combination of **t** and **h** is pronounced like **t**. Practice saying these examples:

thé (*tay*)	*tea*
marathon (*mah-rah-toh(n)*)	*marathon*
Nathalie (*nah-tah-lee*)	*Nathalie*

j The French **j** sounds similar to the soft **g** sound, no matter where it is placed. Practice saying these examples:

Jacques (*zhahk*)	*Jacques*
éjecter (*ay-zhay-ktay*)	*to eject*
joli (*zho-lee*)	*pretty*

l The letter **l** is usually pronounced like the English equivalent, though with more vigor and distinctness. Practice saying these examples:

la (*lah*)	*the* (feminine)
allumer (*ah-lu-may*)	*to switch on*
lire (*leer*)	*to read*

ille and a final **il** are often pronounced like *y* in *y*es. Practice saying these examples:

vfamille (*fah-mee-y*)	*family*
travail (*trah-vah-y*)	*work*
pareil (*pah-ray-y*)	*similar*
veille (*vay-y*)	*the day before*

p French **p** is pronounced like English *p*, and the combination **p + h** is pronounced like *f*, as in English. Practice saying these examples:

poli (*po-lee*)	*polite*
phrase (*frahz*)	*sentence*
pharmacie (*fahr-mah-see*)	*pharmacy*

q The letter **q** (usually **qu**) is like the English *k*. Practice saying these examples:

querelle (*kuh-rehl*)	*argument*
qui (*kee*)	*who*
quarante (*kah-rah(n)-t*)	*forty*

r The **r** in French is very different from the English *r*. It is pronounced at the back of the mouth and is slightly rolled. Practice saying these examples:

arriver (*ah-ree-vay*)	*to arrive*
rire (*reer*)	*to laugh*
vivre (*vee-vr*)	*to live*

s The letter **s** can be pronounced in different ways. The doubled **ss** is pronounced like *s* in *s*ing. Practice saying these examples:

paresse (*pah-rehs*)	*laziness*
lisse (*lees*)	*smooth*
saucisse (*soh-sees*)	*sausage*

s at the beginning of a word is pronounced like *s* in *s*ing. Practice saying these examples:

sage (*sahzh*)	*wise*
sel (*sehl*)	*salt*
Simon (*see-moh(n)*)	*Simon*

s between vowels is pronounced like *z*. Practice saying these examples:

visage (*vee-zazh*)	*face*
fraise (*frehz*)	*strawberry*
valise (*vah-leez*)	*suitcase*

t The French **t** usually sounds like the English *t*, except when followed by **ion**: it is then pronounced like *s* in *s*un (same as **ss**). Practice saying these examples:

aviation (*ah-vya-syoh(n)*)	*aviation*
fiction (*feek-syoh(n)*)	*fiction*
rationnel (*rah-syohn-ehl*)	*rational*

x The letter **x** is pronounced with a *ks* sound, like the *x* in fa*x*, or a *gz* sound, like the *x* in e*x*am. Practice saying these examples:

maximum (*mah-ksee-muhm*)	*maximum*
proximité (*proh-ksee-mee-tay*)	*proximity*
exaspérer (*eh-gzah-spay-ray*)	*to exasperate*
exercice (*eh-gzehr-sees*)	*exercise*

Oral Practice

Practice saying the words in the list. Focus on the pronunciation of your consonants and vowels. Look at the transliteration to check your pronunciation.

French	Pronunciation	English
1. glisser	*glee-say*	*to slip*
2. haut	*oh*	*high*
3. quel	*kehl*	*which*
4. accès	*ah-kseh*	*access*
5. centre	*sah(n)tr*	*center*
6. casserole	*kah-suh-rol*	*saucepan*
7. agneau	*ah-nyoh*	*lamb*
8. temps	*tah(n)*	*time*
9. exagérer	*eh-gzah-zhay-ray*	*to exaggerate*
10. soleil	*so-lay-y*	*sun*

Syllabification

In French, syllables within a word generally end in a vowel sound. Compare:

French	English
pau-vre-té (*poh-vruh-tay*)	*pov-er-ty*
a-mé-ri-cain (*ah-may-ree-ka(n)*)	*A-mer-i-can*
com-pé-tence (*koh(m)-pay-tah(n)s*)	*comp-etence*

When several consonants come together in a French word, the syllables are usually divided between the consonants:

mar-cher (*mahr-shay*)	*to walk*
dé-ve-lop-pe-ment (*day-vuh-lop-mah(n)*)	*development*
pois-son (*pwas-soh(n)*)	*fish*

OMISSIONS

An unaccented **e** at the end of a word is usually not pronounced, with the exception of short words like **je**. Practice saying these examples:

Silent *e*

moule (*mool*)	*mussel*
glace (*glahs*)	*ice cream*
âge (*ahzh*)	*age*

Pronounced *e*

le (*luh*)	*the*
ce (*suh*)	*this*
de (*duh*)	*some*

In addition, an unaccented **e** within certain words is not pronounced. Practice saying these examples:

avenue (*ahv-nu*)	*avenue*
acheter (*ahsh-tay*)	*to buy*
samedi (*sahm-dee*)	*Saturday*

LIAISON

Many final consonants are linked to the vowel that follows. In a liaison, the consonant **d** is usually pronounced like a **t**, and the consonants **s** and **x** are usually pronounced like a **z**. Practice saying these examples:

ils-(z)-aiment (*eel-zehm*)	*they love*
ils sont-(t)-arrivés (*eel-soh(n)-tah-ree-vay*)	*they arrived*
c'est-(t)-amusant (*say-tah-mu-sah(n)*)	*it is amusing*
un grand-(t)-immeuble (*uh(n)-grah(n)-tee-muhbl*)	*a tall building*
Bon-(n)-appétit! (*bon-nah-pay-tee*)	*Enjoy your meal/food!*
deux-(z)-idées (*duh-zee-day*)	*two ideas*

Because the **h** is silent, this is also true when what follows the final consonant is an **h.** Practice saying this example:

dix-(z)-histoires (*dee-zee-stwar*)	*two stories*

When the indefinite article **un** (*a, an*) is linked to a vowel or **h** that follows, the sound is still nasal but the **n** is pronounced. Practice saying these examples:

un-(n)-ami (*uh(n)-nah-mee*)   *a friend*
un-(n)-éléphant (*uh(n)-nay-lay-fah(n)*)   *an elephant*

Elles-(z)-habitent dans-(z)-un-(n)-hôtel. (*ehl-zah-beet-dah(n)-zuh(n)-noh-tehl*)
     They live in a hotel.

Before a vowel, **il** is linked, sounding like the *y* in *yes*. Practice saying these examples:

un vieil-(y)-animal (*uh(n)-vyeh-yah-nee-mahl*)   *an old animal*
un vieil-(y)-homme (*uh(n)-vyeh-yom*)   *an old man*

SYLLABLE STRESS

In English, one syllable is stressed more than the others: *per*fect, prag*ma*tic. In words of several syllables, you may even have a primary and a secondary stress. In French, each sound is pronounced clearly and equally, with a mild stress on the last syllable of the word. Compare stresses on these similar words:

French	**English**
mod*erne* (*moh-**dehrn***)	*mo*dern
obser*vation* (*op-sehr-vah-**syoh(n)***)	*ob*ser*va*tion
pas*sion* (*pah-**syoh(n)***)	*pa*ssion
libéra*lisme* (*lee-bay-rah-**leesm***)	*li*bera*lism*

INTONATION

In French, the last syllable of the last word of a sentence receives a slight downward inflection. Practice saying these examples:

Je vais au thé*â*tre.   *I'm going to the theater.*

Il est huit h*eu*res.   *It's 8 o'clock.*

NOTE: *In these examples the last **e** is mute.*

The last syllable before a comma receives a slight upward inflection. Practice saying these examples:

En eff*et*, le climat est plus   *Indeed, the weather is milder in the*
   doux dans le sud de la France.   *South of France.*

Apparem*ment*, il est sorti.   *Apparently, he went out.*

The last syllable in a question receives a slight upward inflection. For example:

Viens-tu ce *soir*?   *Are you coming tonight?*

As-tu des nouvelles de *Marc*?   *Have you heard from Marc?*

The Francophone World

The French language is descended from the vernacular or "street" Latin of the Roman Empire. When ancient Gaul (France) was conquered by the Romans in the second and first centuries B.C., its inhabitants spoke a language called Celtic. This was rapidly supplanted by the Latin of the Roman rulers. In the fifth century A.D. the Franks, a group of Germanic tribes, invaded Gaul, but they too were romanized. Although modern French has several hundred words of Celtic and Germanic origin, its structure and vocabulary derive from Latin. The term *Francophone* refers to people whose cultural background is primarily associated with the French language, regardless of ethnic and geographical differences. The Francophone culture beyond Europe is the legacy of the French colonial empire. Francophone countries include France, Belgium, Canada (Quebec), Switzerland, Haiti and the French West Indies, and several countries in Africa and Asia that were former French colonies. These countries are members of the International Organization of Francophonie (francophonie.org), an intergovernmental organization of French-speaking nations that promotes the education and culture of French speakers as well as peace, democracy, human rights, and economic development in the French-speaking world. Francophone writers have produced a body of literature that is strikingly beautiful in its use of language and imagery.

QUIZ

Choose the closest approximate English sound for the letter or letters in bold in questions 1–5.

1. **boi**sson
    (a) *bwoo*
    (b) *bwa*
    (c) *bwee*

2. as**s**ister
    (a) *z*
    (b) *s*
    (c) *c*

3. **ho**rloge
    (a) *ho*
    (b) *o*
    (c) *au*

4. lou**p**
    (a) *oo*
    (b) *ouh*
    (c) *oh*

5. **nui**t
    (a) *noe*
    (b) *nee*
    (c) *nwee*

Identify the correct meaning for questions 6–10.

6. **un car**
    (a) une automobile
    (b) un autobus
    (c) une cabine

7. **actuellement**

    (a) réellement

    (b) à vrai dire

    (c) à présent

8. **une librairie**

    (a) un magasin de livres

    (b) une collection

    (c) une bibliothèque

9. **un patron**

    (a) un client

    (b) un protecteur

    (c) un directeur

10. **un poisson**

    (a) un animal vivant dans l'eau

    (b) une substance toxique

    (c) un élément pernicieux

CHAPTER 2

Naming Things

In this chapter you will learn:

Definite Articles

All nouns in French have a gender, either masculine or feminine, whether they refer to a person, an animal, a thing, or an abstract notion. While English has only one definite article, *the*, French uses **le** for masculine nouns and **la** for feminine nouns.

Masculine		Feminine	
le téléphone	*the telephone*	la maison	*the house*
le mouton	*the sheep*	la tortue	*the turtle*

Le and **la** become **l'** in front of nouns starting with a vowel or a mute **h**. A mute **h** is silent. The word acts as if it began with a vowel. The plural of **le**, **la**, and **l'** is **les**. Liaisons are done as if the **h** were not there:

les hommes	lay zuhm	*men*

Masculine		Feminine	
l'avion	*the plane*	l'Américaine	*the American woman*
l'hôtel	*the hotel*	l'huile	*the oil*

French Nouns and Gender

Although there is no fixed rule to determine the gender of a noun, its ending provides a general rule of thumb. Of course, once in a while you'll run into exceptions. It would be no fun otherwise.

Nouns ending in **age, ment, eau** tend to be masculine.

le paysage	*landscape*
le gouvernement	*government*
le manteau	*coat*

Nouns ending in **t, al, ail, eil, isme** also tend to be masculine.

l'objet	*object*
le cristal	*crystal*
le travail	*work*
le sommeil	*sleep*
le journalisme	*journalism*

Nouns ending in **ure, ence, ance, sion, tion, té, ouille, eille** tend to be feminine.

la culture	*culture*	l'exposition	*exhibition*
la différence	*difference*	la beauté	*beauty*
la tendance	*tendency*	la citrouille	*pumpkin*
la décision	*decision*	la merveille	*marvel*

Some nouns that refer to people can be changed from masculine to feminine by adding an **e** to the masculine form:

l'ami	l'amie	*friend*
l'étudiant	l'étudiante	*student*
l'avocat	l'avocate	*lawyer*
le Français	la Française	*Frenchman/Frenchwoman*

Nouns with certain endings form the feminine in other ways:

eur → euse

le chanteur	la chanteuse	*singer*
le vendeur	la vendeuse	*salesperson*

(i)er → (i)ère

le passager	la passagère	*passenger*
l'ouvrier	l'ouvrière	*worker*

teur → trice

le directeur	la directrice	*director*
l'acteur	l'actrice	*actor*

ien → ienne

le musicien	la musicienne	*musician*
l'Italien	l'Italienne	*Italian man/woman*

A few nouns have different meanings in the masculine and feminine.

le livre	*book*	la livre	*pound*
le tour	*trip, ride*	la tour	*tower*
le poste	*job; television set*	la poste	*post office*
le moule	*mold/form*	la moule	*mussel*
le poêle	*stove*	la poêle	*frying pan*

Now let's look at the changes from the masculine to the feminine in the words for family members.

le père	*father*	la mère	*mother*
le fils	*son*	la fille	*daughter*
le frère	*brother*	la sœur	*sister*
le grand-père	*grandfather*	la grand-mère	*grandmother*
l'oncle	*uncle*	la tante	*aunt*
le neveu	*nephew*	la nièce	*niece*
le cousin	*male cousin*	la cousine	*female cousin*

Asking Basic Questions

Let's see how to ask about someone's profession.

Quelle est la profession de l'oncle de Julie?	*What is the profession of Julie's uncle?*
L'oncle de Julie est pharmacien.	*Julie's uncle is a pharmacist.*
Quelle est la profession de la sœur de Jérôme?	*What is the profession of Jérôme's sister?*
La sœur de Jérôme est avocate.	*Jérôme's sister is a lawyer.*

Oral Practice

Ask someone's status or profession and then answer each question, aloud.

Qui est-ce?	*Who's that?*
C'est l'ami de Caroline.	*It's Caroline's friend.*
Quelle est la profession de Fabien?	*What's Fabien's profession?*
Fabien est journaliste.	*Fabien is a journalist.*
L'amie de Marc est indienne ou italienne?	*Is Marc's friend Indian or Italian?*
L'amie de Marc est indienne.	*Marc's friend is Indian.*

Fabrice est danseur ou chanteur?	*Is Fabrice a dancer or a singer?*
Fabrice est chanteur.	*Fabrice is a singer.*
Sabine est avocate ou dentiste?	*Is Sabine a lawyer or a dentist?*
Sabine est avocate.	*Sabine is a lawyer.*
C'est le fils ou le neveu de Rémi?	*Is that Rémi's son or nephew?*
C'est le neveu de Rémi.	*It's Rémi's nephew.*

Written Practice 1

Keeping in mind the rules of thumb we've given for determining the gender of a noun, use the following pattern to fill in the blanks.

fromage	*cheese*	le fromage
chanteuse	*singer*	la chanteuse

1. soleil   *sun*   _____
2. télévision *television* _____
3. gâteau   *cake*   _____
4. journal   *newspaper*   _____
5. nature   *nature*   _____

The Gender of Countries

Countries, continents, states, provinces, and regions also have a gender. In this context, for the most part, an **e** ending will be feminine. Other endings tend to be masculine, with a few exceptions. Here are some examples.

Feminine		**Masculine**	
l'Afrique	*Africa*	le Brésil	*Brazil*
l'Australie	*Australia*	le Canada	*Canada*
la Californie	*California*	le Chili	*Chile*
la Chine	*China*	le Colorado	*Colorado*
la France	*France*	le Japon	*Japan*

la Normandie	*Normandy*	le Languedoc	*Languedoc*
la Provence	*Provence*	le Mali	*Mali*
la Russie	*Russia*	le Sénégal	*Senegal*

NOTE: *Some countries and states ending in* ***e*** *are masculine:*

le Cambodge	*Cambodia*
le Maine	*Maine*
le Mexique	*Mexico*

Oral Practice

Practice saying the following sentences out loud.

Luc préfère la Suède ou la Norvège?	*Does Luc prefer Sweden or Norway?*
Luc préfère la Norvège.	*Luc prefers Norway.*
Yan préfère l'Afrique ou l'Asie?	*Does Yan prefer Africa or Asia?*
Yan préfère l'Afrique.	*Yan prefers Africa.*
Inès préfère l'Écosse ou l'Irlande?	*Does Inès prefer Scotland or Ireland?*
Inès préfère l'Écosse.	*Inès prefers Scotland.*
Marc préfère la Chine ou le Japon?	*Does Marc prefer China or Japan?*
Marc préfère la Chine.	*Marc prefers China.*
Zoé préfère l'Alsace ou la Vendée?	*Does Zoé prefer Alsace or Vendée?*
Zoé préfère l'Alsace.	*Zoé prefers Alsace.*
Léa préfère le Maine ou le Vermont?	*Does Léa prefer Maine or Vermont?*
Léa préfère le Vermont.	*Léa prefers Vermont.*

Written Practice 2

Answer, using the following pattern.

	Texas	*Texas*	le Texas
	Tunisie	*Tunisia*	la Tunisie

1. Bretagne   *Brittany*   _____
2. Allemagne   *Germany*   _____
3. Virginie   *Virginia*   _____
4. Pologne   *Poland*   _____
5. Venezuela   *Venezuela*   _____

The Plural of Nouns

To form the plural, add an **s** to the singular noun. In the plural, **le** and **la** become **les.**

le carnet	*notebook*	les carnets	*notebooks*
la bague	*ring*	les bagues	*rings*

If a noun in the plural begins with a vowel or a mute **h,** you need to make a liaison with a **z** sound.

l'idée	*idea*	les idées	*ideas*
l'assiette	*plate*	les assiettes	*plates*
l'homme	*man*	les hommes	*men*
l'hôtel	*hotel*	les hôtels	*hotels*
l'État	*state*	les États-Unis	*United States*

Nouns ending in **s, x,** or **z** do not change in the plural.

le pays	*country*	les pays	*countries*
la voix	*voice*	les voix	*voices*
le nez	*nose*	les nez	*noses*

Nouns ending in **eu** or **eau** usually take an **x** in the plural.

le feu	*fire*	les feux
le couteau	*knife*	les couteaux
le drapeau	*flag*	les drapeaux

Nouns ending in **al** usually change to **aux.**

l'animal	*animal*	les animaux
le cheval	*horse*	les chevaux
le journal	*newspaper*	les journaux

Do not be surprised if here and there you run into exceptions. Here are a few examples:

le festival	*festival*	les festivals
l'œil	*eye*	les yeux
le bijou	*jewel*	les bijoux
le pneu	*tire*	les pneus

Some nouns have different meanings when singular or plural.

la vacance	*vacancy*	les vacances	*vacation*
le ciseau	*chisel*	les ciseaux	*scissors*

Some nouns are used only in the plural form.

les mœurs	*mores*
les arrhes	*deposit*
les fiançailles	*engagement*

In French, no **s** is added to a family name used in the plural. You'll refer to Monsieur and Madame Chabrol as **les Chabrol**.

Oral Practice

Practice saying the following list of sentences out loud.

Aimez-vous les cerises?	*Do you like cherries?*
Oui, j'aime les cerises.	*Yes, I like cherries.*

Aimez-vous les fraises?	*Do you like strawberries?*
Oui, j'aime les fraises.	*Yes, I like strawberries.*
Aimez-vous les chats?	*Do you like cats?*
Oui, j'aime les chats.	*Yes, I like cats.*
Aimez-vous les films italiens?	*Do you like Italian movies?*
Oui, j'aime les films italiens.	*Yes, I like Italian movies.*
Aimez-vous les roses?	*Do you like roses?*
Oui, j'aime les roses.	*Yes, I like roses.*
Aimez-vous les épices?	*Do you like spices?*
Oui, j'aime les épices.	*Yes, I like spices.*

Written Practice 3

Answer using the following pattern:

| la langue | *language* | les langues |
| l'architecte | *architect* | les architectes |

1. le plat | *dish* | _____
2. le château | *castle* | _____
3. la clé | *key* | _____
4. le jardin | *garden* | _____
5. la maison | *house* | _____

Indefinite Articles

We have just studied the nouns using the definite articles **le, la,** and **les.** The indefinite articles are **un** (masculine singular), **une** (feminine singular), and **des** (masculine and feminine plural).

| un tableau | *a painting* | des tableaux | (some) *paintings* |
| un mois | *a month* | des mois | *months* |

une montre	*a watch*	des montres	*watches*
une saison	*a season*	des saisons	*seasons*

Oral Practice

Ask someone whether he or she has certain things or acquaintances, then answer each question, aloud.

Avez-vous un jardin?	*Do you have a garden?*
Oui, j'ai un jardin.	*Yes, I have a garden.*
Avez-vous un dictionnaire?	*Do you have a dictionary?*
Oui, j'ai un dictionnaire.	*Yes, I have a dictionary.*
Avez-vous un chien?	*Do you have a dog?*
Oui, j'ai un chien.	*Yes, I have a dog.*
Avez-vous un manteau noir?	*Do you have a black coat?*
Oui, j'ai un manteau noir.	*Yes, I have a black coat.*
Avez-vous des amis en France?	*Do you have friends in France?*
Oui, j'ai des amis en France.	*Yes, I have friends in France.*
Avez-vous des vacances en mai?	*Do you have a vacation in May?*
Oui, j'ai des vacances en mai.	*Yes, I have a vacation in May.*

Written Practice 4

Answer with an indefinite article, using the following pattern:

hôtel	*hotel*	un hôtel
amis	*friends*	des amis

1. avion   *plane*   _____
2. avocate   *lawyer*   _____
3. maisons   *houses*   _____
4. clé   *key*   _____
5. châteaux   *castles*   _____

The Cardinal Numbers Zero to Fifty

Let's start counting up to fifty. Although final consonants are generally silent in French, they are pronounced in the following numbers: **cinq**, **six**, **sept**, **huit**, **neuf**, **dix**. With **sept**, the p is silent, but the final **t** is pronounced. The final **x** in **six** and **dix** is pronounced like an **s.**

When the numbers **cinq**, **six**, **huit**, and **dix** are followed by a word begining with a consonant, their final consonant is mute.

zéro	*zero*	vingt	*twenty*
un	*one*	vingt et un	*twenty-one*
deux	*two*	vingt-deux	*twenty-two*
trois	*three*	vingt-trois	*twenty-three*
quatre	*four*	vingt-quatre	*twenty-four*
cinq	*five*	vingt-cinq	*twenty-five*
six	*six*	vingt-six	*twenty-six*
sept	*seven*	vingt-sept	*twenty-seven*
huit	*eight*	vingt-huit	*twenty-eight*
neuf	*nine*	vingt-neuf	*twenty-nine*
dix	*ten*	trente	*thirty*
onze	*eleven*	trente et un	*thirty-one*
douze	*twelve*	trente-deux	*thirty-two*
treize	*thirteen*	trente-trois	*thirty-three*
quatorze	*fourteen*	quarante	*forty*
quinze	*fifteen*	quarante et un	*forty-one*
seize	*sixteen*	quarante-deux	*forty-two*
dix-sept	*seventeen*	quarante-trois	*forty-three*
dix-huit	*eighteen*	cinquante	*fifty*
dix-neuf	*nineteen*		

Ordinal Numbers

Ordinal numbers, for the most part, follow a regular pattern, ending with **ième.**
Premier (*first*) and **dernier** (*last*) are exceptions.

premier	*first*	vingtième	*twentieth*
deuxième	*second*	vingt et unième	*twenty-first*
troisième	*third*	vingt-deuxième	*twenty-second*
quatrième	*fourth*	vingt-troisième	*twenty-third*

cinquième	fifth	trentième	thirtieth
sixième	sixth	quarantième	fortieth
septième	seventh	cinquantième	fiftieth
huitième	eighth		
neuvième	ninth		
dixième	tenth		

NOTE: *In France, **le premier étage** corresponds to the American second floor. The American first floor is called **le rez-de-chaussée**. For example:*

C'est la première fois que Jim est à Paris.

This is the first time Jim has been in Paris.

Béatrice habite au deuxième étage.

Béatrice lives on the second floor.

Oral Practice

Ask the following questions and then repeat the answers, aloud.

À quel étage est l'appartement de Léa?

On what floor is Léa's apartment?

L'appartement de Léa est au sixième étage.

Lea's apartment is on the sixth floor.

À quel étage est le bureau de Sophia?

On what floor is Sophia's office?

Le bureau de Sophia est au dixième étage.

Sophia's office is on the tenth floor.

À quel étage est la boutique Dior?

On what floor is the Dior boutique?

La boutique Dior est au rez-de-chaussée.

The Dior boutique is on the first floor.

À quel étage est le restaurant italien?

On what floor is the Italian restaurant?

Le restaurant italien est au troisième étage.

The Italian restaurant is on the third floor.

À quel étage est la terrasse?

On what floor is the terrace?

La terrasse est au trente-cinquième étage.

The terrace is on the thirty-fifth floor.

À quel étage est le salon de coiffure?	*On what floor is the hair salon?*
Le salon de coiffure est au neuvième étage.	*The hair salon is on the ninth floor.*
À quel étage est le cabinet d'avocats?	*On what floor is the law firm?*
Le cabinet d'avocats est au quatrième étage.	*The law firm is on the fourth floor.*

Written Practice 5

Write out the following numbers.

40 *quarante* _____

1. 38 _____
2. 11 _____
3. 42 _____
4. 16 _____
5. 9 _____

Written Practice 6

Answer the questions, following this pattern:

C'est la première fois? (10) *Non, c'est la dixième fois.*

C'est la quatrième fois? (2) *Non, c'est la deuxième fois.*

1. C'est la première fois? (8) _____
2. C'est la cinquième fois? (4) _____
3. C'est la deuxième fois? (10) _____
4. C'est la quatrième fois? (3) _____
5. C'est la deuxième fois? (1) _____

Days, Months, and Seasons

Making plans? You need to know the days of the week and the months of the year.

DAYS OF THE WEEK

The days of the week are masculine. They are not capitalized. The week starts with Monday.

lundi	*Monday*	vendredi	*Friday*
mardi	*Tuesday*	samedi	*Saturday*
mercredi	*Wednesday*	dimanche	*Sunday*
jeudi	*Thursday*		

The definite article is used with weekdays when an action is repeated on a particular day of the week. Here are some example sentences:

Laure étudie l'anglais le mercredi.	*Laure studies English on Wednesdays.*
Christian étudie l'italien le samedi.	*Christian studies Italian on Saturdays.*

If an action takes place once on a certain day, the definite article is not used. For example:

Téléphone à Odile dimanche!	*Call Odile on Sunday!*
Noémie arrive mardi.	*Noémie is arriving on Tuesday.*

MONTHS OF THE YEAR

Like the days, the months of the year are not capitalized.

janvier	*January*	juillet	*July*
février	*February*	août	*August*
mars	*March*	septembre	*September*
avril	*April*	octobre	*October*
mai	*May*	novembre	*November*
juin	*June*	décembre	*December*

SEASONS

The four seasons of the year are:

le printemps	*spring*	l'automne	*fall*
l'été	*summer*	l'hiver	*winter*

Here are some example sentences:

Vincent voyage en France en juillet.   *Vincent travels to France in July.*

Éric voyage en Italie en hiver.   *Éric travels to Italy in winter.*

Oral Practice

Ask a question, then answer each question, aloud.

L'anniversaire d'Émilie, c'est mardi ou jeudi?   *Is Émilie's birthday on Tuesday or Thursday?*

L'anniversaire d'Émilie, c'est jeudi.   *Émilie's birthday is on Thursday.*

L'anniversaire de Benoît, c'est dimanche ou lundi?   *Is Benoît's birthday on Sunday or on Monday?*

L'anniversaire de Benoît, c'est dimanche.   *Benoît's birthday is on Sunday.*

L'anniversaire d'Amélie, c'est en septembre ou en octobre?   *Is Amélie's birthday in September or in October?*

L'anniversaire d'Amélie, c'est en octobre.   *Amélie's birthday is in October.*

L'anniversaire de Fabien, c'est en avril ou en mai?   *Is Fabien's birthday in April or in May?*

L'anniversaire de Fabien, c'est en avril.   *Fabien's birthday is in April.*

Written Practice 7

Answer using the following pattern:

Le premier jour de la semaine est _lundi_____.

Le sixième jour de la semaine est _samedi_____.

1. Le quatrième jour de la semaine est _____.
2. Le deuxième jour de la semaine est _____.
3. Le septième jour de la semaine est _____.
4. Le cinquième jour de la semaine est _____.
5. Le troisième jour de la semaine est _____.

French Names

In France, until January 1, 2005, children were required by law to take the surname (last name) of their father, which is no longer the case. This has become article 311–21 of the French Civil code. To ensure the world knows that the baby's double name results from the new law and not from a historic lineage—often involving aristocracy—two hyphens will now be required. So the surname name of a baby called Martin--Dupont becomes "Martin double-dash Dupont." "Double-dash" will not be pronounced in ordinary speech, according to the law's instructions, only in spelling the name. France's most famous single mother—President Chirac's daughter Claude—secured the Chirac name for her son in this way. The gesture to the mothers of France seemed to shake the sacred pillar of patriarchy. However, under the proposed law, once parents have made the choice they have to stick with it. Any subsequent brothers or sisters will have to have the same surname as the first-born child.

Names are indicators of status in France. The reform is important because of France's changing demographics; 45 percent of children are born out of wedlock. In the absence of declared paternity, mothers were previously forced to give their babies their own names. The new law will help remove that stigma.

The law is retroactive only for children under thirteen, and even then only through a formal petition. A husband cannot take the surname of his wife.

Paradoxically, the reform reinforces the spirit of patriarchy, or at least tradition. Aristocratic families that have produced only female offspring no longer will have to watch helplessly as their names die out. In the case of a dispute between mother and father, the father wins.

After pressure from the United Nations, similar measures had already been adopted by Germany (1976), Sweden (1982), Denmark (1983), and Spain (1999).

QUIZ

Using the definite article **le** or **la,** specify the gender of each of the following words.

	château	_le château_
1.	journal	_____
	culture	_____
	tortue	_____
	nationalité	_____
	compliment	_____

Replace the definite article **le, la,** or **les** with the indefinite article **un, une,** or **des.**

	la saison	_une saison_
2.	la voiture	_____
	le sac	_____
	la culture	_____
	les hôtels	_____
	les journaux	_____

Write the appropriate article before the following geographic nouns.

	France	_la France_
3.	Finlande	_____
	Chine	_____

Caroline du Sud   _____

Togo   _____

Colombie   _____

Put the following nouns in the plural form. Watch out for exceptions.

la montre   *les montres*_____

4. le journal   _____

    la maison   _____

    le frère   _____

    la voix   _____

    le chapeau   _____

Put the following nouns in the feminine form.

le danseur   *la danseuse*_____

5. le vendeur   _____

    le directeur   _____

    le mécanicien   _____

    l'acteur   _____

    le Brésilien   _____

Translate the following sentences.

6. Marc's birthday is on Sunday. _____.

7. Call Marc on Monday. _____.

8. Léa's sister is an architect. _____.

9. Léa's office is on the tenth floor. _____.

10. Léa's birthday is on Tuesday. _____.

CHAPTER 3

Asking Questions

In this chapter you will learn:

Subject Pronouns
-er Verb Endings in the Present Tense
Spelling Changes in -er Verbs
Asking Questions
Answering Questions in the Negative
The Negation ni... ni

Subject Pronouns

Below are the subject pronouns in French.

je	*I*	nous	*we*
tu	*you* (singular familiar)	vous	*you* (singular formal and all plurals)

il	*he, it* (masculine)	ils	*they* (masculine plural or mixed masculine and feminine plural)
elle	*she, it* (feminine)	elles	*they* (feminine plural)
on	*one, we, they*		

TWO WAYS TO SAY *YOU*

There are two ways of saying *you* in French. Use **tu** to talk to friends, family members, children, or animals. Use **vous** whenever you are talking to more than one person or when you are addressing a stranger, someone you don't know well, or to maintain a certain degree of distance or respect. Note, however, that the tendency among peers is toward familiarity, so watch the scene around you, stay on your toes, and go with the flow.

THE PRONOUN *ON*

The pronoun **on** takes on different meanings. It may mean *one*, *we*, or *they* depending on how it is used. See the following examples.

Ici, on parle français.	*French is spoken here.*
En Asie, on mange avec des baguettes.	*In Asia, they eat with chopsticks.*
On vend des timbres dans un bureau de tabac.	*One sells stamps in a tobacco shop.*
On dîne au restaurant ce soir? (familiar)	*Shall we eat at the restaurant tonight?*
Toi et moi, on va au cinéma dimanche. (familiar)	*You and me, we're going to the movies on Sunday.*
On est si contents de son succès. (familiar)	*We're so happy he succeeded.*

-er Verb Endings in the Present Tense

Verbs are classified by their infinitive form, such as **manger** (*to eat*) or **écouter** (*to listen*). Most verbs that end in **er** in the infinitive follow the same conjugation. The pattern is easy. You remove the **er** ending to get the root: **parler** → **parl.** Then you add the endings corresponding to the subject pronoun.

The endings for the regular **-er** verbs are: **e, es, e, ons, ez, ent**. The **e, es,** and **ent** endings of the verbs are all silent. The final **s** of **nous, vous, ils,** and **elles** links with verbs beginning with a vowel sound, making a **z** sound. This linking is called a liaison, as we saw in Chapter 1.

Let's conjugate the verb **parler** (*to speak*):

je parl**e**	*I speak*	nous parl**ons**	*we speak*
tu parl**es**	*you speak*	vous parl**ez**	*you speak*
il parl**e**	*he speaks*	ils parl**ent**	*they speak*
elle parl**e**	*she speaks*	elles parl**ent**	*they speak*
on parl**e**	*one/they/we speak*		

Here are some examples:

Parlez-vous une langue étrangère?	*Do you speak a foreign language?*
Parles-tu espagnol?	*Do you speak Spanish?*

THE VERB *HABITER*

Habiter (*to live*) will follow the same pattern as **parler**.

j'habit**e**	*I live*	nous habit**ons**	*we live*
tu habit**es**	*you live*	vous habit**ez**	*you live*
il habit**e**	*he lives*	ils habit**ent**	*they live*
elle habit**e**	*she lives*	elles habit**ent**	*they live*
on habit**e**	*one/they/we live*		

COMMON *-ER* VERBS

Here are some common regular **-er** verbs.

apporter (*to bring*)	vous apportez	*you bring*
chanter (*to sing*)	nous chantons	*we sing*
chercher (*to look for*)	il cherche	*he is looking for*
couper (*to cut*)	je coupe	*I cut*
danser (*to dance*)	elle danse	*she dances*
déjeuner (*to have lunch*)	tu déjeunes	*you are having lunch*
donner (*to give*)	tu donnes	*you give*
garder (*to keep*)	tu gardes	*you keep*

lancer (*to throw*)	je lance	*I throw*
manger (*to eat*)	je mange	*I eat*
mériter (*to deserve*)	elle mérite	*she deserves*
porter (*to carry*)	elle porte	*she wears/carries*
regarder (*to watch*)	ils regardent	*they watch/look at*
sauter (*to jump*)	nous sautons	*we jump*

Oral Practice

Ask the following questions and then answer them, aloud.

Parlez-vous français?	*Do you speak French?*
Oui, je parle français.	*Yes, I speak French.*
Parlez-vous espagnol?	*Do you speak Spanish?*
Oui, je parle espagnol.	*Yes, I speak Spanish.*
Dînez-vous au restaurant ce soir?	*Are you having dinner at the restaurant tonight?*
Oui, je dîne au restaurant ce soir.	*Yes, I am having dinner at the restaurant tonight.*
Chantez-vous bien?	*Do you sing well?*
Oui, je chante bien.	*Yes, I sing well.*
Mangez-vous du fromage?	*Do you eat cheese?*
Oui, je mange du fromage.	*Yes, I eat cheese.*
Aimez-vous l'opéra?	*Do you like opera?*
Oui, j'aime l'opéra.	*Yes, I like opera.*
Regardez-vous la télévision?	*Do you watch television?*
Oui, je regarde la télévision.	*Yes, I watch television.*

Written Practice 1

Match the following verbs with the appropriate subject pronoun.

1. mangez _____ a. ils
2. regardons _____ b. je

3. parles   _____   c. nous

4. chantent   _____   d. vous

5. donne   _____   e. tu

Written Practice 2

Conjugate the following verbs.

1. nous   (parler)   _____

2. je   (garder)   _____

3. elle   (porter)   _____

4. vous   (chanter)   _____

5. on   (donner)   _____

Spelling Changes in *-er* Verbs

Some spelling changes occur with some regular **-er** verbs.

VERBS ENDING IN *-CER*

With verbs ending in **cer**, like **commencer** *(to begin)*, the **c** becomes **ç** before the letter **o.** The cedilla (**ç**) under the **c** is needed to keep the soft pronunciation in these contexts that the **c** has in the infinitive form.

je commence	*I begin*	nous commençons	*we begin*
tu commences	*you begin*	vous commencez	*you begin*
il/elle commence	*he/she begins*	ils/elles commencent	*they begin*

Here are some example sentences:

Je commence un nouveau travail lundi.	*I am starting a new job on Monday.*
Nous commençons la réunion dans dix minutes.	*We are starting the meeting in ten minutes.*

Here are a few examples of other **-cer** verbs:

nous avançons	*we move forward*	nous prononçons	*we pronounce*
nous effaçons	*we erase*	nous remplaçons	*we replace*
nous menaçons	*we threaten*	nous renonçons	*we give up*
nous plaçons	*we place*		

VERBS ENDING IN *-GER*

With verbs ending in **-ger,** like **manger** (*to eat*), the **g** becomes **ge** before the letter **o.**

je mange	*I eat*	nous mangeons	*we eat*
tu manges	*you eat*	vous mangez	*you eat*
il/elle mange	*he/she eats*	ils/elles mangent	*they eat*

Here are some example sentences:

Je mange une pomme.	*I am eating an apple.*
Nous mangeons une tarte aux cerises.	*We are eating a cherry pie.*

Here are a few examples of other **-ger** verbs:

nous changeons	*we change*	nous plongeons	*we dive*
nous déménageons	*we move*	nous protégeons	*we protect*
nous mélangeons	*we mix*	nous voyageons	*we travel*
nous partageons	*we share*		

VERBS ENDING IN *E* + CONSONANT + *-ER*

With some verb endings composed of **e** + consonant + **er**, like **acheter** (*to buy*), some accent changes occur. A grave accent is added in all but the first and the second person plural.

j'achète	*I buy*	nous achetons	*we buy*
tu achètes	*you buy*	vous achetez	*you buy*
il/elle achète	*he/she buys*	ils/elles achètent	*they buy*

Here are a few other verbs following the same pattern:

lever	je lève	*I raise*
enlever	j'enlève	*I remove*
achever	j'achève	*I complete*
mener	je mène	*I lead*
emmener	j'emmène	*I take along, I escort*

With some verbs composed of **é** + consonant + **er,** like **espérer** (*to hope*), changes may also occur. The acute accent on the **e** (**é**) changes to a grave accent (**è**) in all but the first and second persons plural.

j'espère	*I hope*	nous espérons	*we hope*
tu espères	*you hope*	vous espérez	*you hope*
il/elle espère	*he/she hopes*	ils/elles espèrent	*they hope*

Here are a few other verbs following the same pattern:

céder	je cède	*I yield*
gérer	je gère	*I manage*
répéter	je répète	*I repeat*
révéler	je révèle	*I reveal*
exagérer	j'exagère	*I exaggerate*
posséder	je possède	*I own*
considérer	je considère	*I consider*

VERBS ENDING IN *E* + *L* + *-ER*

Some verb endings composed of **e** + l + **er,** like **appeler** (*to call*), take two **l**s in all but the first and second persons plural.

j'appelle	*I call*	nous appelons	*we call*
tu appelles	*you call*	vous appelez	*you call*
il/elle appelle	*he/she calls*	ils/elles appellent	*they call*

Here are a few other verbs following the same pattern:

épeler	j'épelle	*I spell*
ficeler	je ficelle	*I tie*
rappeler	je rappelle	*I remind*
renouveler	je renouvelle	*I renew*

Oral Practice

Ask the following questions and then answer them, aloud.

Commencez-vous lundi ou mardi?	*Are you starting on Monday or Tuesday?*
Nous commençons mardi.	*We're starting on Tuesday.*
Commencez-vous immédiatement?	*Are you starting right away?*
Oui, nous commençons immédiatement.	*Yes, we're starting right away.*
Déménagez-vous samedi?	*Are you moving on Saturday?*
Oui, nous déménageons samedi.	*Yes, we're moving on Saturday.*
Placez-vous des roses sur les tables?	*Are you putting roses on the tables?*
Oui, nous plaçons des roses sur les tables.	*Yes, we are putting roses on the tables.*
Voyagez-vous en Australie?	*Are you traveling to Australia?*
Oui, nous voyageons en Australie.	*Yes, we're traveling to Australia.*
Partagez-vous une chambre d'hôtel?	*Are you sharing a hotel room?*
Oui, nous partageons une chambre d'hôtel.	*Yes, we're sharing a hotel room.*
Achetez-vous des fruits au marché?	*Do you buy fruit at the market?*
Oui, j'achète des fruits au marché.	*Yes, I buy fruit at the market.*
Emmenez-vous Lise au théâtre?	*Are you taking Lise to the theater?*
Oui, j'emmène Lise au théâtre.	*Yes, I am taking Lise to the theater.*
Espérez-vous un changement?	*Are you hoping for a change?*
Oui, j'espère un changement.	*Yes, I am hoping for a change.*
Gérez-vous l'entreprise tout seul?	*Are you managing the firm all alone?*
Oui, je gère l'entreprise tout seul.	*Yes, I am managing the firm all alone.*
Appelez-vous Justine le week-end?	*Do you call Justine on weekends?*
Oui, j'appelle Justine le week-end.	*Yes, I call Justine on weekends.*

Written Practice 3

Conjugate the following verbs.

1. Elle (acheter) des fleurs au marché.   _____

2. Nous (commencer) un nouveau livre.   _____

3. Tu (appeler) Dominique mercredi.   _____

4. Ils (révéler) le secret à la presse.   _____

5. Nous (voyager) en Grèce en avril.   _____

Written Practice 4

Match the left and right columns.

1. Nous déménageons   _____   a. une grande entreprise.

2. Je considère   _____   b. un livre de science-fiction.

3. Il mange   _____   c. la proposition de Paul.

4. Je commence   _____   d. à Lyon.

5. Elle gère   _____   e. une pomme.

Asking Questions

There are three ways of asking questions. You can either do an inversion of the subject and the verb, use the **est-ce que** form, or simply keep the positive form with an upward intonation. Let's start with the inversion, which you saw in Chapters 1 and 2 every time we asked questions.

Aimez-vous le jazz?	*Do you like jazz?*
Étudiez-vous le japonais?	*Are you studying Japanese?*
Commençons-nous maintenant?	*Are we starting now?*
Parles-tu anglais couramment?	*Are you fluent in English?*

If the third person singular of a verb ends with a vowel, a **t** is inserted to facilitate the pronunciation. As is often the case, it's just a matter of aesthetics.

Préfère-t-elle le chapeau jaune ou le bleu?	*Does she prefer the yellow or the blue hat?*
Commence-t-il son nouveau travail en mai ou en juin?	*Is he starting his new job in May or in June?*

A more colloquial way of asking a question is to use the **est-ce que** form in front of the subject and the verb.

Est-ce que vous aimez le vin blanc?	*Do you like white wine?*
Est-ce que tu dînes avec Julien ce soir?	*Are you having dinner with Julien tonight?*
Est-ce que tu emmènes Louis à la plage?	*Are you taking Louis to the beach?*

Est-ce que becomes **est-ce qu'** before a vowel.

Est-ce qu'il aime le tennis?	*Does he like tennis?*
Est-ce qu'elles apportent des gâteaux?	*Are they bringing cakes?*

A third way of asking a question, which is also a colloquial way of doing it, is to keep the structure of subject + verb and to use an upward intonation.

Vous aimez le football?	*Do you like soccer?*
Tu parles portugais?	*Do you speak Portuguese?*
Elle préfère le hip-hop?	*Does she prefer hip-hop?*

Oral Practice

Ask the following questions, using inversion, and then answer, aloud.

Mangez-vous le riz avec des baguettes?	*Do you eat rice with chopsticks?*
Oui, je mange le riz avec des baguettes.	*Yes, I eat rice with chopsticks.*
Cherche-t-il le bonheur?	*Is he looking for happiness?*

Oui, il cherche le bonheur.	*Yes, he is looking for happiness.*
Regardes-tu le match de basket-ball?	*Are you watching the basketball game?*
Oui, je regarde le match de basket-ball.	*Yes, I am watching the basketball game.*
Parlez-vous régulièrement avec M. Fleuriot?	*Do you speak regularly with Mr. Fleuriot?*
Oui, je parle régulièrement avec M. Fleuriot.	*Yes, I speak regularly with Mr. Fleuriot.*
Chantez-vous dans une chorale?	*Do you sing in a choir?*
Oui, je chante dans une chorale.	*Yes, I sing in a choir.*

Written Practice 5

Put the following sentences into the interrogative form, using inversion.

1. Vous aimez les voyages. _____
2. Elle préfère le riz. _____
3. Tu commences en décembre. _____
4. Ils cherchent un appartement. _____
5. Nous regardons le match de base-ball dans le salon.

   _____

Oral Practice

Ask the following questions using the **est-ce que** form, then answer, aloud.

Est-ce qu'elle apporte des hors-d'œuvre?	*Is she bringing hors-d'œuvres?*
Oui, elle apporte des hors-d'œuvre.	*Yes, she is bringing hors d'œuvres.*
Est-ce que vous remplacez Bertrand?	*Are you replacing Bertrand?*
Oui, je remplace Bertrand.	*Yes, I am replacing Bertrand.*
Est-ce qu'il porte des lunettes?	*Does he wear glasses?*
Oui, il porte des lunettes.	*Yes, he wears glasses.*

Est-ce que tu emmènes Laure au club?	*Are you taking Laure to the club?*
Oui, j'emmène Laure au club.	*Yes, I am taking Laure to the club.*
Est-ce que nous dînons chez René?	*Are we having dinner at René's?*
Oui, nous dînons chez René.	*Yes, we are having dinner at René's.*

Written Practice 6

Put the following sentences into the interrogative form, using the **est-ce que** form.

1. J'appelle Samuel. _____
2. Nous remplaçons Jacques et Laurent. _____
3. Tu voyages en Irlande. _____
4. Vous déménagez jeudi. _____
5. Elle prononce le mot correctement. _____

Oral Practice

Ask the following questions using upward intonation, then answer, aloud.

Vous dînez à la brasserie?	*Are you having dinner at the brasserie?*
Oui, nous dînons à la brasserie.	*Yes, we are having dinner at the brasserie.*
Il habite à Bordeaux?	*Does he live in Bordeaux?*
Oui, il habite à Bordeaux.	*Yes, he lives in Bordeaux.*
Vous protégez les intérêts de Rémi?	*Are you protecting Rémi's interests?*
Oui, je protège les intérêts de Rémi.	*Yes, I am protecting Rémi's interests.*
Elle achète le pain ici?	*Does she buy bread here?*
Oui, elle achète le pain ici.	*Yes, she buys bread here.*
Vous gérez l'entreprise avec Claude?	*Are you managing the firm with Claude?*
Oui, je gère l'entreprise avec Claude.	*Yes, I'm managing the firm with Claude.*

Written Practice 7

Put the following sentences into the interrogative form, using upward intonation.

1. Vous cherchez la Place de la Bastille. _____
2. Tu aimes le chocolat. _____
3. Elle habite à Rome. _____
4. Il cherche un nouvel emploi. _____
5. Vous mangez des escargots. _____

QUESTION WORDS

When you want to formulate questions, question words come in handy. Here are a few examples.

combien	*how much*	pourquoi	*why*
comment	*how*	quand	*when*
dans quelle mesure	*to what extent*	que	*what*
où	*where*	qui	*who, whom*

Oral Practice

Ask the following questions and then answer them, aloud.

Combien de personnes invitez-vous?	*How many people are you inviting?*
J'invite dix personnes.	*I'm inviting ten people.*
Comment allez-vous à la plage?	*How are you going to the beach?*
Nous allons à la plage en voiture.	*We're going to the beach by car.*
Qui habite dans la maison bleue?	*Who lives in the blue house?*
Sébastien habite dans la maison bleue.	*Sébastien lives in the blue house.*
Que pensez-vous de ce film?	*What do you think about this film?*
C'est un très bon film.	*It's a very good film.*
Combien coûte la voiture de Zoé?	*How much is Zoé's car?*
La voiture de Zoé coûte cher.	*Zoé's car is expensive.*

Où travaille-t-elle?	*Where does she work?*
Elle travaille à Strasbourg.	*She works in Strasbourg.*
Quand joue-t-il au tennis?	*When does he play tennis?*
Il joue au tennis en été.	*He plays tennis during the summer.*
Pourquoi étudiez-vous le français?	*Why are you studying French?*
J'étudie le français pour le plaisir.	*I'm studying French for fun.*
Quand arrivez-vous?	*When do you arrive?*
J'arrive mercredi.	*I'm arriving on Wednesday.*
Qui chante?	*Who is singing?*
Valérie chante.	*Valérie is singing.*

Written Practice 8

Translate the following sentences, using the inversion form when appropriate.

1. Who speaks French here? _____
2. Where are you traveling in January? (*formal*) _____
3. Why is she moving? _____
4. Where do you live? (*informal*) _____
5. What are you looking for? (*formal*) _____

Answering Questions in the Negative

So far, we have been very positive, answering questions only with **oui**. Let's try to say **non**. To make a sentence negative, you simply place **ne... pas** around the verb. For example:

Parle-t-il hongrois?	*Does he speak Hungarian?*
Non, il ne parle pas hongrois.	*No, he does not speak Hungarian.*
Chante-t-elle en italien?	*Does she sing in Italian?*
Non, elle ne chante pas en italien.	*No, she does not sing in Italian.*

If the **ne** precedes a verb starting with a vowel or a mute **h**, **ne** becomes **n'**.

Aimes-tu les lentilles?	*Do you like lentils?*
Non, je n'aime pas les lentilles.	*No, I do not like lentils.*
Habite-t-elle à Nice?	*Does she live in Nice?*
Non, elle n'habite pas à Nice.	*No, she does not live in Nice.*

Aside from **ne... pas,** there are other negations. Here are a few examples:

Elle ne travaille jamais le dimanche.	*She never works on Sundays.*
Je ne fume plus.	*I don't smoke anymore.*
Vous ne changez rien dans le contrat.	*You are not changing anything in the contract.*
Il ne remplace personne jeudi.	*He is not substituting for anyone on Thursday.*
Il n'a guère d'argent.	*He has hardly any money.*

Oral Practice

Ask the following questions and then answer them, aloud.

Habitez-vous à Nantes?	*Do you live in Nantes?*
Non, je n'habite pas à Nantes.	*No, I do not live in Nantes.*
Aimez-vous la glace au café?	*Do you like coffee ice cream?*
Non, je n'aime pas la glace au café.	*No, I don't like coffee ice cream.*
Mangez-vous quelque chose le matin?	*Do you eat anything in the mornings?*
Non, je ne mange rien le matin.	*No, I don't eat anything in the mornings.*
Chante-t-il dans un club de jazz?	*Does he sing in a jazz club?*
Non, il ne chante pas dans un club de jazz.	*No, he does not sing in a jazz club.*
Travaillez-vous le week-end?	*Do you work on weekends?*
Non, je ne travaille jamais le week-end.	*No, I never work on weekends.*

Habitez-vous toujours à Orléans?	*Do you still live in Orléans?*
Non, je n'habite plus à Orléans.	*No, I no longer live in Orléans.*
Aimez-vous le chocolat chaud?	*Do you like hot chocolate?*
Non, je n'aime pas le chocolat chaud.	*No, I do not like hot chocolate.*
Déménages-tu à Bruxelles?	*Are you moving to Brussels?*
Non, je ne déménage pas à Bruxelles.	*No, I am not moving to Brussels.*

Written Practice 9

Answer the following sentences in the negative form. For questions using **vous**, answer with **je**.

1. Aimez-vous le nouveau film d'Éric Rohmer? _____
2. Habite-t-elle à La Rochelle? _____
3. Cherchez-vous Jacques? _____
4. Apportez-vous quelque chose? _____
5. Voyagez-vous parfois par le train? _____
6. Chantez-vous en allemand? _____
7. Travaillez-vous toujours le samedi? _____
8. Étudiez-vous le chinois? _____
9. Jouez-vous au tennis? _____
10. Écoutez-vous l'émission *2000 ans d'histoire*? _____

The Negation *ni... ni*

The negation **ni... ni** precedes the nouns it negates. Where the definite article **le, la,** or **les** is used in the positive form, the article is used in the negative form as well.

Tu aimes le thé et le café.	*You like tea and coffee.*
Tu n'aimes ni le thé ni le café.	*You like neither tea nor coffee.*
Vous aimez le bois et le marbre.	*You like wood and marble.*
Vous n'aimez ni le bois ni le marbre.	*You like neither wood nor marble.*

When the partitive article, **du, de la, des** (*some*), is introduced in the original sentence, it disappears in the negative form.

Elle mange du pain et du fromage.　*She eats bread and cheese.*

Elle ne mange ni pain ni fromage.　*She eats neither bread nor cheese.*

Ils achètent de la salade et des fruits.　*They buy salad and fruit.*

Ils n'achètent ni salade ni fruits.　*They buy neither salad nor fruit.*

QUIZ

Formulate a question using **tu** and the **est-ce que** form in the present tense.

　　　aimer la Toscane　*Est-ce que tu aimes la Toscane?*

1. jouer au tennis _____

2. parler portugais _____

Change the following verbs from the first person singular to the first person plural of the present tense.

　　　je voyage　　　*nous voyageons*

3. je commence　　　_____

4. j'espère　　　_____

Suggest an activity to your friend, using the familiar **on**.

　　　dîner au restaurant ce soir　*On dîne au restaurant ce soir?*

5. voyager en Inde en février _____

6. écouter le concert dans le parc _____

Answer the following questions first in the affirmative, then in the negative form.

Déjeunez-vous avec Paola?

Oui, je déjeune avec Paola.

Non, je ne déjeune pas avec Paola.

7. Regardez-vous le film de Godard ce soir?

_____

_____

8. Aimez-vous le théâtre moderne?

_____

_____

Translate the following sentences.

9. She does not live in Annecy. _____

10. I do not speak Spanish. _____

CHAPTER 4

To Be or to Have, That Is the Question!

In this chapter you will learn:

The Verb *être*

The verbs **être** and **avoir** are both irregular (**avoir** is covered later in this chapter). They are key verbs that will come in handy in most conversations. So start memorizing their conjugations.

je suis	*I am*	nous sommes	*we are*
tu es	*you are* (familiar)	vous êtes	*you are*
il/elle est	*he/she is*	ils/elles sont	*they are*

Il est français.	*He is French.*

NOTE: *The s of **vous** is pronounced as a z in front of the vowel ê in **êtes.***

Vous êtes anglais?	*Are you English?*

Oral Practice

Ask the following questions and then answer them, aloud.

Vous êtes fatigué?	*Are you tired?*
Non, je ne suis pas fatigué.	*No, I am not tired.*
Elle est australienne?	*Is she Australian?*
Oui, elle est australienne.	*Yes, she is Australian.*
La bibliothèque est ouverte?	*Is the library open?*
Oui, la bibliothèque est ouverte.	*Yes, the library is open.*
Est-il optimiste?	*Is he optimistic?*
Oui, il est optimiste.	*Yes, he is optimistic.*
Êtes-vous contents du résultat?	*Are you happy with the results?*
Oui, nous sommes contents du résultat.	*Yes, we are happy with the results.*
Sont-ils très occupés?	*Are they very busy?*
Non, ils ne sont pas très occupés.	*No, they are not very busy.*
Est-il marié?	*Is he married?*

Non, il n'est pas marié.	*No, he is not married.*
Êtes-vous étudiant?	*Are you a student?*
Oui, je suis étudiant.	*Yes, I am a student.*
Est-il sportif?	*Is he athletic?*
Oui, il est sportif.	*Yes, he is athletic.*
Le projet est réaliste?	*Is the project realistic?*
Oui, le projet est réaliste.	*Yes, the project is realistic.*
Êtes-vous en retard?	*Are you late?*
Oui, nous sommes en retard.	*Yes, we are late.*
La librairie est ouverte aujourd'hui?	*Is the bookstore open today?*
Non, la librairie est fermée aujourd'hui.	*No, the bookstore is closed today.*
C'est cher?	*Is it expensive?*
Non, c'est bon marché.	*No, it's cheap.*
Le bureau est au dixième étage?	*Is the office on the tenth floor?*
Non, le bureau est au neuvième étage.	*No, the office is on the ninth floor.*
Tu es libre jeudi?	*Are you free on Thursday?*
Oui, je suis libre jeudi.	*Yes, I am free on Thursday.*

Written Practice 1

Conjugate the verb **être** in the following sentences.

Nous (être) satisfaits.   <u>sommes</u>

1. Je (être) ravi de faire votre connaissance.   _____
2. Il (être) malade aujourd'hui.   _____
3. Vous (être) irlandais?   _____
4. Tu (ne pas être) libre ce soir?   _____
5. Elles (être) en retard pour le rendez-vous.   _____

The Verb *avoir*

The verb **avoir**, like the verb **être**, has an irregular conjugation you need to learn *by heart*.

j'ai	*I have*	nous avons	*we have*
tu as	*you have*	vous avez	*you have*
il/elle a	*he/she has*	ils/elles ont	*they have*

NOTE: *The* s *of* **nous**, **vous**, **ils**, *and* **elles** *is pronounced as a* z *in front of a vowel.*

Vous avez une voiture?	*Do you have a car?*
Oui, j'ai une voiture.	*Yes, I have a car.*
A-t-elle des amis en France?	*Does she have friends in France?*
Oui, elle a des amis en France.	*Yes, she has friends in France.*

NOTE: *Un*, *une*, *and* *des* *change to* *de* *or* *d'* *in the negative form.*

Est-ce que tu as un vélo?	*Do you have a bicycle?*
Non, je n'ai pas de vélo.	*No, I do not have a bicycle.*
Vous avez des chats?	*Do you have cats?*
Non, je n'ai pas de chat.	*No, I don't have cats.*

The verb **avoir** is used in many common idiomatic expressions. Here are a few examples:

j'ai besoin	*I need*	j'ai l'air	*I seem/I look*
j'ai chaud	*I am hot*	j'ai mal	*I hurt/I have a pain*
j'ai de la chance	*I am lucky*	j'ai peur	*I am afraid*
j'ai envie	*I feel like*	j'ai raison	*I am right*
j'ai faim	*I am hungry*	j'ai soif	*I am thirsty*
j'ai froid	*I am cold*	j'ai tort	*I am wrong*
j'ai honte	*I am ashamed*	j'ai vingt ans	*I am twenty years old*

When referring to the state of one's body, French uses **avoir mal à**. When **avoir mal à** is followed by a verb, however, it means *to have trouble doing something*. Compare:

J'ai mal au dos.	*I have a pain in my back.*
Il a mal au pied gauche.	*His left foot hurts.*
J'ai du mal à comprendre sa réaction.	*I have trouble understanding his reaction.*
Ils ont du mal à s'exprimer.	*They have trouble expressing themselves.*

Oral Practice

Ask the following questions and then answer them, aloud.

Avez-vous un dictionnaire français?	*Do you have a French dictionary?*
Oui, j'ai un dictionnaire français.	*Yes, I have a French dictionary.*
Est-ce qu'elle a un appareil photo numérique?	*Does she have a digital camera?*
Oui, elle a un appareil photo numérique.	*Yes, she has a digital camera.*
As-tu des cousins à Toulon?	*Do you have cousins in Toulon?*
Non, je n'ai pas de cousin à Toulon.	*No, I don't have cousins in Toulon.*
Ont-ils des enfants?	*Do they have children?*
Oui, ils ont deux filles.	*Yes, they have two daughters.*
Avez-vous des lunettes de soleil?	*Do you have sunglasses?*
Oui, j'ai des lunettes de soleil.	*Yes, I have sunglasses.*
Ont-ils un oncle aux États-Unis?	*Do they have an uncle in the United States?*
Oui, ils ont un oncle en Louisiane.	*Yes, they have an uncle in Louisiana.*
Ont-ils un grand jardin?	*Do they have a big garden?*
Oui, ils ont un grand jardin.	*Yes, they have a big garden.*
As-tu de l'huile d'olive pour la salade?	*Do you have olive oil for the salad?*
Oui, j'ai de l'huile d'olive pour la salade.	*Yes, I have olive oil for the salad.*

Written Practice 2

Match the left with the right column.

1. Julie   _____   a. ai

2. je (j')   _____   b. ont

3. vous   _____   c. a

4. M. et Mme Guimet   _____   d. avons

5. nous   _____   e. avez

Oral Practice

Ask the following questions and then answer them, aloud.

Avez-vous froid en hiver?	*Are you cold in the winter?*
Oui, j'ai froid en hiver.	*Yes, I am cold in winter.*
As-tu besoin de quelque chose?	*Do you need anything?*
Non, je n'ai besoin de rien.	*No, I don't need anything.*
Avez-vous faim?	*Are you hungry?*
Non, je n'ai pas faim.	*No, I am not hungry.*
Avez-vous mal à la tête?	*Do you have a headache?*
Non, je n'ai pas mal à la tête.	*No, I don't have a headache.*
Avez-vous chaud dans cette salle?	*Are you hot in this room?*
Non, je n'ai pas chaud.	*No, I am not hot.*
Avez-vous envie de chocolat?	*Do you feel like having chocolate?*
Non, je n'ai pas envie de chocolat.	*No, I don't feel like having chocolate.*
Est-ce qu'il a raison?	*Is he right?*
Oui, il a raison.	*Yes, he is right.*
Quel âge as-tu?	*How old are you?*
J'ai trente ans.	*I am thirty.*

Written Practice 3

Formulate questions according to the model:

faim (tu) _As-tu faim?_ _____

1. soif (vous) _____
2. chaud (elle) _____
3. froid (ils) _____
4. peur (tu) _____
5. raison (il) _____

The Verb *aller*

We saw the regular **-er** verbs in the previous chapter. Now let's study a most useful verb for talking about going places, the irregular verb **aller** (*to go*).

je vais	*I go*	nous allons	*we go*
tu vas	*you go*	vous allez	*you go*
il/elle va	*he/she goes*	ils/elles vont	*they go*

Use the preposition **à** (*to, at, in*) to say where you are going. Watch out for the contractions: **à + le = au, à + les = aux**.

Nous allons au cinéma.	*We are going to the movies.*
Tu vas à la plage?	*Are you going to the beach?*
Elle va aux États-Unis cet été.	*She is going to the United States this summer.*

Aller is used in many idiomatic expressions.

Ça va?	*How are you? How are things going?*
Comment allez-vous?	*How are you?*
Comment vont les enfants?	*How are the children doing?*
Cette robe vous va bien.	*This dress looks good on you.*

Oral Practice

Ask the following questions and then answer them, aloud.

Comment vas-tu?	*How are you?*
Je vais bien.	*I am fine.*
Comment allez-vous?	*How are you?*
Je suis un peu fatigué.	*I am a little tired.*
Tout va bien?	*Is everything OK?*
Oui, tout va bien.	*Yes, everything is OK.*
Tu vas à la bibliothèque ce matin?	*Are you going to the library this morning?*
Non, j'y vais cet après-midi.	*No, I am going there this afternoon.*
Est-ce qu'ils vont chez vous en mai?	*Are they going to your place in May?*
Non, ils vont à Nice en juin.	*No, they are going to Nice in June.*
Est-ce qu'il va à l'hôpital lundi?	*Is he going to the hospital on Monday?*
Oui, il va à l'hôpital lundi.	*Yes, he is going to the hospital on Monday.*

Written Practice 4

Formulate a complete sentence with the elements below.

Bernard/aller/plage   *Bernard va à la plage.* _____

1. vous/aller/librairie/ce matin _____
2. Adèle/aller/Paris/en août _____
3. je/aller/Dublin/avec Flore _____
4. nous/aller/cinéma/ce soir _____
5. tu/aller/plage/dimanche _____

Using *il y a*

Il y a (*there is, there are*) states the existence of people and things. See the following examples:

Il y a un festival de musique celtique ce soir.	*There is a Celtic music festival tonight.*
Y a-t-il une solution?	*Is there a solution?*
Est-ce qu'il y a de l'espoir?	*Is there hope?*
Non, il n'y a pas d'espoir.	*No, there is no hope.*

NOTE: *A* ***t*** *is added for the inversion form and* ***de*** *or* ***d'*** *is used in the negative form.*

Expressions of Quantity

Here are the main expressions of quantity, used as adverbs.

assez de	*enough*	un peu de	*a few, a little*
beaucoup de	*much, many*	plus de	*more*
autant de	*as much, as many*	tant de	*so much, so many*
moins de	*less/fewer*	tellement de	*so much, so many*
peu de	*little, few*	trop de	*too much, too many*

Quantity expressions, in most cases, follow a certain pattern. The definite article (following the **de** that ends the quantity expression) is dropped.

Il a beaucoup d'amis en France.	*He has a lot of friends in France.*
Elle a trop de choses à faire cette semaine.	*She has too many things to do this week.*

Oral Practice

Ask the following questions and then answer them, aloud.

Avez-vous beaucoup de livres français?	*Do you have many French books?*
Oui, j'ai beaucoup de livres français.	*Yes, I have a lot of French books.*
A-t-elle trop de travail?	*Does she have too much work?*
Oui, elle a trop de travail.	*Yes, she has too much work.*
Est-ce que tu as assez de temps?	*Do you have enough time?*
Non, je n'ai pas assez de temps.	*No, I don't have enough time.*
Il y a trop de sel?	*Is there too much salt?*
Oui, il y a trop de sel.	*Yes, there is too much salt.*
Mange-t-il trop de sucre?	*Does he eat too much sugar?*
Oui, il mange trop de sucre.	*Yes, he eats too much sugar.*
Ont-ils tellement de tableaux?	*Do they have so many paintings?*
Oui, ils ont tellement de tableaux!	*Yes, they have so many paintings!*

Written Practice 5

Formulate a sentence with the elements provided.

Élodie/CD/beaucoup   *Élodie a beaucoup de CD.*

1. Anne/chance/peu _____
2. Mélanie/documents/trop _____
3. Vincent/travail/beaucoup _____
4. Valérie/papier/assez _____
5. Bruno/problèmes/tant _____

QUANTITY EXPRESSIONS USING ADJECTIVES

Quantity expressions can take on other forms, using adjectives.

couvert de	*covered with*
décoré de	*decorated with*

entouré de	*surrounded with/by*
plein de	*full of*
rempli de	*full of*

Here are some example sentences:

Le sac est rempli de cadeaux.	*The bag is full of gifts.*
Le magasin est plein de monde.	*The store is full of people.*
La maison est entourée d'arbres.	*The house is surrounded by trees.*
Le chemin est couvert de feuilles.	*The path is covered with leaves.*
La maison est décorée d'objets asiatiques.	*The house is decorated with Asian objects.*

QUANTITY EXPRESSIONS USING NOUNS

Other quantity expressions are formed using nouns.

une assiette de	*a plate of*	une livre de	*a pound of*
une boîte de	*a box of*	un kilo de	*a kilo of*
une bouteille de	*a bottle of*	un mètre de	*a meter of*
un cageot de	*a crate of*	un plat de	*a dish of*
une caisse de	*a case of*	une poignée de	*a handful of*
une demi-livre de	*half a pound of*	un sac de	*a bag of*
une douzaine de	*a dozen of*	une tasse de	*a cup of*
un litre de	*a liter of*	un verre de	*a glass of*

Oral Practice

Ask the following questions and then answer them, aloud.

La maison est entourée d'arbres?	*Is the house surrounded by trees?*
Oui, la maison est entourée d'arbres.	*Yes, the house is surrounded by trees.*
Avez-vous une tasse de thé?	*Do you have a cup of tea?*
Oui, j'ai une tasse de thé.	*Yes, I have a cup of tea.*
Achète-t-elle une douzaine de roses?	*Is she buying a dozen roses?*

Oui, elle achète une douzaine de roses.	*Yes, she is buying a dozen roses.*
Ont-ils envie d'un bol de soupe?	*Do they feel like having a bowl of soup?*
Non, ils n'ont pas envie d'un bol de soupe.	*No, they don't feel like having a bowl of soup.*
Est-ce qu'il y a une bouteille d'eau sur la table?	*Is there a bottle of water on the table?*
Oui, il y a une bouteille d'eau sur la table.	*Yes, there is a bottle of water on the table.*

Written Practice 6

Formulate a sentence with the elements provided.

bol/riz/table   *Il y a un bol de riz sur la table.* _____

1. bouteille/eau/table _____
2. tasse/café/table _____
3. litre/lait/table _____
4. demi-livre/champignons/table _____
5. boîte/sardines/table _____

Demonstrative Adjectives

Sometimes you need to be very specific in identifying things. To do so, you have to use demonstrative adjectives (*this, that, these, those*). Like all adjectives in French, French demonstrative adjectives agree in gender and number with the noun they modify.

Masculine Singular

ce stylo	*this pen*
cet abricot	*this apricot*
cet hôtel	*this hotel*

Note: The singular demonstrative adjective *ce* adds a *t* when a vowel or a mute *h* follows.

Feminine Singular

cette maison   *this house*   cette tasse   *this cup*

Masculine and Feminine Plural

ces plats (*m.*)   *these dishes*
ces montres (*f.*)   *these watches*
ces huîtres (*f.*)   *these oysters*

To make a distinction between two elements, **-ci** and **-là** are added to the noun that follows the demonstrative adjectives.

Préférez-vous cette tasse-ci ou cette tasse-là?	*Do you prefer this cup or that cup?*
Combien coûtent cette sculpture-ci et cette sculpture-là?	*How much are this sculpture and that sculpture?*
Préférez-vous ce romancier-ci ou ce romancier-là?	*Do you prefer this novelist or that one?*

Oral Practice

Ask the following questions and then answer them, aloud.

As-tu ce DVD?	*Do you have this DVD?*
Non, je n'ai pas ce DVD.	*No, I don't have that DVD.*
Vont-ils à cette exposition?	*Are they going to that exhibit?*
Oui, ils vont à cette exposition.	*Yes, they are going to that exhibit.*
Cherche-t-elle ce CD?	*Is she looking for this CD?*
Non, elle ne cherche pas ce CD.	*No, she is not looking for that CD.*
Travaillez-vous à ce nouveau projet?	*Are you working on this new project?*
Oui, nous travaillons à ce nouveau projet.	*Yes, we are working on that new project.*
Que pensez-vous de cet avion?	*What do you think about this plane?*
Cet avion est hyper confortable.	*This plane is most comfortable.*

Cet hôtel est dans le 15ème   *Is this hotel in the 15th arrondissement?*
   arrondissement?

Oui, cet hôtel est dans le 15ème.   *Yes, this hotel is in the 15th.*

Written Practice 7

Match the left and the right columns.

1. homme   _____   a. cette

2. chanteuse   _____   b. cet

3. moutons   _____   c. ce

4. manteau   _____   d. cet

5. anniversaire _____   e. ces

Possessive Adjectives

Possessive adjectives are used to express relationship and ownership. They agree in gender and number with the noun they modify.

Masculine Singular

mon sac	*my bag*	notre sac	*our bag*
ton sac	*your bag*	votre sac	*your bag*
son sac	*his/her bag*	leur sac	*their bag*

Feminine Singular

ma tasse	*my cup*	notre tasse	*our cup*
ta tasse	*your cup*	votre tasse	*your cup*
sa tasse	*his/her cup*	leur tasse	*their cup*

Masculine and Feminine Plural

mes amis	*my friends*	nos amis	*our friends*
tes amis	*your friends*	vos amis	*your friends*
ses amis	*his friends*	leurs amis	*their friends*

NOTE: The masculine form (*mon*, *ton*, *son*) is used before singular feminine nouns beginning with a vowel or a mute *h*.

Mon amie Caroline habite à Lyon.	*My friend Caroline lives in Lyon.*
Ton intuition est remarquable.	*Your intuition is remarkable.*
Son humanité est légendaire.	*Her humaneness is legendary.*

Son, sa, and **ses** can all mean either *his* or *hers*. The context will usually prevent any ambiguity about the owner. Otherwise, the sentence will need to be reformulated.

son vélo	*his/her bike*
sa voiture	*his/her car*
ses documents	*his/her documents*

Another way of expressing possession is to use **à** + a noun or a pronoun.

C'est à qui?	*Whose is it?*
C'est à Sabine?	*Is it Sabine's?*
Non, ce n'est pas à Sabine.	*No, it's not Sabine's.*
C'est à moi.	*It's mine.*

We'll go into this a little further when we study **moi, toi, lui, elle,** etc.

Oral Practice

Ask the following questions and then answer them, aloud.

Aimez-vous sa nouvelle voiture?	*Do you like his/her new car?*
Oui, j'aime sa nouvelle voiture.	*Yes, I like his/her new car.*
Que penses-tu de son projet?	*What do you think about his/her project?*
Son projet est très intéressant.	*His/Her project is very interesting.*
As-tu besoin de mon ordinateur?	*Do you need my computer?*
Oui, j'ai besoin de votre ordinateur.	*Yes, I need your computer.*
Ta sœur est avocate?	*Is your sister a lawyer?*
Non, ma sœur est dentiste.	*No, my sister is a dentist.*

Quel âge a leur fille?   *How old is their daughter?*
Leur fille a quatre ans.   *Their daughter is four.*

Written Practice 8

Match the left and the right columns.

1. chat   _____   a. ma
2. amies   _____   b. mon
3. hôtel   _____   c. ma
4. maison   _____   d. mon
5. belle-sœur   _____   e. mes

The Numbers Fifty and Above

Last time we stopped counting at fifty, right? Let's keep going.

cinquante	*fifty*	soixante	*sixty*
cinquante et un	*fifty-one*	soixante et un	*sixty-one*
cinquante-deux	*fifty-two*	soixante-deux	*sixty-two*
cinquante-trois	*fifty-three*	soixante-trois	*sixty-three*
cinquante-quatre	*fifty-four*	soixante-neuf	*sixty-nine*
cinquante-cinq	*fifty-five*	soixante-dix	*seventy*
cinquante-six	*fifty-six*		
cinquante-sept	*fifty-seven*		
cinquante-huit	*fifty-eight*		
cinquante-neuf	*fifty-nine*		

From seventy-one to seventy-nine, you add the teen numbers:

soixante et onze	*seventy-one*	soixante-seize	*seventy-six*
soixante-douze	*seventy-two*	soixante-dix-sept	*seventy-seven*
soixante-treize	*seventy-three*	soixante-dix-huit	*seventy-eight*
soixante-quatorze	*seventy-four*	soixante-dix-neuf	*seventy-nine*
soixante-quinze	*seventy-five*		

Eighty is really four times twenty. So from eighty to eighty-nine, you'll keep adding to **quatre-vingts.** Note that **quatre-vingts** has an **s.** But once you attach another number to **quatre-vingts**, the **s** will drop.

quatre-vingts	*eighty*	quatre-vingt-dix	*ninety*
quatre-vingt-un	*eighty-one*	quatre-vingt-onze	*ninety-one*
quatre-vingt-deux	*eighty-two*	quatre-vingt-douze	*ninety-two*
quatre-vingt-trois	*eighty-three*	quatre-vingt-treize	*ninety-three*
quatre-vingt-quatre	*eighty-four*	quatre-vingt-quatorze	*ninety-four*
quatre-vingt-cinq	*eighty-five*	quatre-vingt-quinze	*ninety-five*
quatre-vingt-six	*eighty-six*	quatre-vingt-seize	*ninety-six*
quatre-vingt-sept	*eighty-seven*	quatre-vingt-dix-sept	*ninety-seven*
quatre-vingt-huit	*eighty-eight*	quatre-vingt-dix-huit	*ninety-eight*
quatre-vingt-neuf	*eighty-nine*	quatre-vingt-dix-neuf	*ninety-nine*

Now we have reached a hundred! Let's keep going.

cent	*one hundred*	cent deux	*one hundred and two*
cent un	*one hundred and one*	cent trois	*one hundred and three*

Add an **s** to **cent** above one hundred, except when **cent** is followed by another number.

deux cents	*two hundred*	quatre cent vingt	*four hundred and twenty*
trois cents	*three hundred*	mille	*one thousand*
neuf cents	*nine hundred*	deux mille	*two thousand*
deux cent douze	*two hundred and twelve*	dix mille	*ten thousand*

Never add an **s** to **mille**.

un million	*a million*	un milliard	*a billion*

QUIZ

Answer the following questions in the affirmative, using the verb **être** or **avoir**.

1. Êtes-vous canadien?

_____

2. As-tu des animaux domestiques?

_____

3. A-t-elle un appartement dans le treizième arrondissement?

_____

Answer the following questions in the negative form, using **je**. Watch out for the exceptions.

4. Aimez-vous la musique folk? _____

5. Avez-vous un ordinateur? _____

Answer the following questions following the model and using the verb **aller.**

Comment va Paul? _Paul va bien._ _____

6. Comment allez-vous? (*use* **je**) _____

7. Comment va la cousine de Germain? _____

Write in letters the following numbers.

8. 62 _____

77 _____

100 _____

87 _____

315 _____

10 000 _____

Translate the following sentences, using **tu** and the **est-ce que** form when needed.

9. There are a lot of books on the table. _____

10. Are you English? (*masculine*) _____

CHAPTER 5

Describing Things

In this chapter you will learn:

-ir Verbs in the Present Tense

In Chapter 3, we saw the first group of verbs, **-er** verbs. The second group of verbs ends in **ir**. These **-ir** verbs follow two different conjugation patterns.

Type 1: drop the **ir** of the infinitive, add **iss** to the plural forms, then add the appropriate ending.

je finis	*I finish*	nous finissons	*we finish*
tu finis	*you finish*	vous finissez	*you finish*
il/elle finit	*he/she finishes*	ils/elles finissent	*they finish*

Many other verbs have the same conjugation.

j'accomplis	*I accomplish*	nous accomplissons	*we accomplish*
je choisis	*I choose*	nous choisissons	*we choose*
je grandis	*I grow up*	nous grandissons	*we grow up*
je grossis	*I put on weight*	nous grossissons	*we put on weight*
je maigris	*I lose weight*	nous maigrissons	*we lose weight*
j'obéis	*I obey*	nous obéissons	*we obey*
je pâlis	*I turn pale*	nous pâlissons	*we turn pale*
je réfléchis	*I think/reflect*	nous réfléchissons	*we think/reflect*
je remplis	*I fill*	nous remplissons	*we fill*
je réussis	*I succeed*	nous réussissons	*we succeed*
je rougis	*I blush*	nous rougissons	*we blush*
je vieillis	*I grow old*	nous vieillissons	*we grow old*

Type 2: drop the **ir** of the infinitive, then add the appropriate ending.

je pars	*I leave*	nous partons	*we leave*
tu pars	*you leave*	vous partez	*you leave*
il/elle part	*he/she leaves*	ils/elles partent	*they leave*

Two other common verbs that take this conjugation are **courir** (*to run*) and **sortir** (*to go out*).

| je cours | *I run* | nous courons | *we run* |
| je sors | *I go out* | nous sortons | *we go out* |

Many **-ir** verbs have their own idiosyncrasies in the first person. See the following examples.

couvrir (*to cover*)

| je couvre | *I cover* | nous couvrons | *we cover* |

dormir (*to sleep*)

| je dors | *I sleep* | nous dormons | *we sleep* |

mentir (*to lie*)

| je mens | *I lie* | nous mentons | *we lie* |

mourir *(to die)*

| je meurs | *I die* | nous mourons | *we die* |

offrir *(to give/to offer)*

| j'offre | *I offer* | nous offrons | *we offer* |

ouvrir *(to open)*

| j'ouvre | *I open* | nous ouvrons | *we open* |

sentir *(to feel/to smell)*

| je sens | *I feel/I smell* | nous sentons | *we feel/we smell* |

servir *(to serve)*

| je sers | *I serve* | nous servons | *we serve* |

souffrir *(to suffer)*

| je souffre | *I suffer* | nous souffrons | *we suffer* |

Oral Practice

Ask the following questions and then answer them, aloud.

Partez-vous en vacances en juin?	*Are you going on vacation in June?*
Oui, je pars en vacances en juin.	*Yes, I am going on vacation in June.*
Tu remplis le formulaire?	*Are you filling out the form?*
Oui, je remplis le formulaire.	*Yes, I am filling out the form.*
Ça fleurit en mars?	*Does this blossom in March?*
Non, ça fleurit en mai.	*No, it blossoms in May.*
Sors-tu ce soir?	*Are you going out tonight?*
Non, je ne sors pas ce soir.	*No, I am not going out tonight.*
Tu dors?	*Are you sleeping?*
Non, je ne dors pas.	*No, I am not sleeping.*
Courez-vous tous les jours dans le parc?	*Do you run every day in the park?*
Oui, je cours tous les jours dans le parc.	*Yes, I run every day in the park.*

La presse couvre ces événements?   *Is the press covering these events?*

Non, la presse ne couvre pas   *No, the press is not covering these events.*
ces événements.

Written Practice 1

Change the following verbs from the singular to the plural form.

il finit   *ils finissent*

1. tu choisis   _____
2. je sers   _____
3. elle part   _____
4. je remplis   _____
5. tu sors   _____

-re Verbs in the Present Tense

Few third-group verbs ending in **re** are regular. For the regular ones, you remove the **re** ending and add the following endings.

attendre (*to wait*)

j'attends	*I wait*	nous attendons	*we wait*
tu attends	*you wait*	vous attendez	*you wait*
il/elle attend	*he/she waits*	ils/elles attendent	*they wait*

Here are some other verbs that conjugate in the same manner.

entendre (*to hear*)	j'entends	*I hear*
perdre (*to lose*)	je perds	*I lose*
rendre (*to give back*)	je rends	*I give back*
répondre (*to answer*)	je réponds	*I answer*
vendre (*to sell*)	je vends	*I sell*

IRREGULAR -*RE* VERBS

Some fairly common **-re** verbs are irregular. Let's look at **prendre** (*to take*).

je prends	*I take*	nous prenons	*we take*
tu prends	*you take*	vous prenez	*you take*
il/elle prend	*he/she takes*	ils/elles prennent	*they take*

And its variations:

apprendre (*to learn*)	j'apprends	*I learn*
comprendre (*to understand*)	je comprends	*I understand*
surprendre (*to surprise*)	je surprends	*I surprise*

   As we go along, we'll discover verbs with their own minds, ending in **oir** and following no specific rule.

Oral Practice

Ask the following questions and then answer them, aloud.

Tu prends des vitamines?	*Do you take vitamins?*
Oui, je prends des vitamines.	*Yes, I take vitamins.*
Vous entendez ce bruit?	*Can you hear this noise?*
Non, je n'entends rien.	*No, I don't hear anything.*
Comprenez-vous son explication?	*Do you understand his explanation?*
Oui, nous comprenons son explication.	*Yes, we understand his explanation.*
Tu réponds à tous tes courriels?	*Do you answer all your e-mail messages?*
Oui, je réponds à tous mes courriels.	*Yes, I answer all my e-mail messages.*
Apprenez-vous l'arabe?	*Are you learning Arabic?*
Oui, j'apprends l'arabe.	*Yes, I am learning Arabic.*
Attends-tu Frédéric?	*Are you waiting for Frédéric?*
Oui, j'attends Frédéric.	*Yes, I am waiting for Frédéric.*

Written Practice 2

Match the left and the right columns.

1. vendons _____ a. il
2. comprennent _____ b. vous
3. apprend _____ c. nous
4. attendez _____ d. elle
5. perd _____ e. ils

The Imperative Mood

You use the imperative to give orders, to make suggestions, or to give advice. To put a verb into the imperative, you use the **tu**, **nous**, and **vous** forms of the present tense. For the **-er** verbs, the **s** of the **tu** form is dropped.

chante   *sing*
chantons   *let's sing*
chantez   *sing*

Let's look at other verbs.

Finis tes devoirs!   *Finish your homework!*
Prends un parapluie!   *Take an umbrella!*
Choisissez quelque chose!   *Choose something!*
Allons au restaurant!   *Let's go to the restaurant!*

In the negative form, the negation is around the verb.

Ne prends pas cette route.   *Don't take this road.*
Ne perdez pas ce document.   *Don't lose this document!*
Ne va pas à Paris en janvier. *Don't go to Paris in January.*

IRREGULAR IMPERATIVES

Some imperatives are irregular. Let's take a look at **être, avoir,** and **savoir.**

être (*to be*)		avoir (*to have*)		savoir (*to know*)	
sois	*be*	aie	*have*	sache	*know*
soyons	*let's be*	ayons	*let's have*	sachons	*let's know*
soyez	*be*	ayez	*have*	sachez	*know*

The imperative will appear in many idiomatic expressions.

Sois sage!	*Be good!*
Soyez gentil!	*Be nice!*
Allons-y!	*Let's go!*
Faites attention!	*Be careful!*
Voyons, ne soyez pas si pessimiste!	*Come on, don't be so pessimistic!*

The verb **vouloir** (*to want*) only uses the imperative form for **vous.**

Veuillez accepter mes compliments.	*Please accept my compliments.*

Oral Practice

Say aloud the following commands.

Apprenez votre leçon!	*Learn your lesson!*
Sois raisonnable!	*Be reasonable!*
Sachez que c'est inacceptable!	*I'll have you know that it's unacceptable!*
Ne parlez pas si fort!	*Don't speak so loud!*
Soyez à l'heure!	*Be on time!*
Ouvrez la porte!	*Open the door!*
Attendez quelques minutes!	*Wait a few minutes!*
Attends-moi!	*Wait for me!*
Réponds au téléphone!	*Answer the phone!*
Ne cours pas si vite!	*Don't run so fast!*

| N'aie pas peur! | *Don't be afraid!* |
| N'acceptez pas son offre! | *Don't accept his offer!* |

Written Practice 3

Put the following sentences into the imperative form.

1. Tu achètes une demi-livre de beurre. _____

2. Nous allons au théâtre. _____

3. Vous prenez une salade verte. _____

4. Tu es à l'heure. _____

5. Tu as un peu de patience. _____

Qualitative Adjectives

Adjectives agree in gender and number with the noun they modify. One common rule is to add an **e** to the masculine form to make the feminine form.

Mark est américain.	*Mark is American.*
Jennifer est américaine.	*Jennifer is American.*
L'appartement est grand.	*The apartment is big.*
La maison est grande.	*The house is big.*

NOTE: *The final consonant **d** of **grand** is silent, while the **d** of **grande** is pronounced in the feminine.*

If an adjective ends with an **e** in the masculine form, the feminine form remains the same.

Ce train est très rapide.	*This train is very fast.*
Cette voiture est très rapide.	*This car is very fast.*
Cet espace est immense.	*This area is huge.*
Cette région est immense.	*This region is huge.*

Be aware that the feminine of adjectives can be formed in several different ways. Here are a few examples:

Il est italien.	*He is Italian.*
Elle est italienne.	*She is Italian.*
Ashik est indien.	*Ashik is Indian.*
Farida est indienne.	*Farida is Indian.*
Loïc est amoureux.	*Loïc is in love.*
Véronique est amoureuse.	*Véronique is in love.*
Ce conte est mystérieux.	*This tale is mysterious.*
Cette histoire est mystérieuse.	*This story is mysterious.*
Julien est sportif.	*Julien is athletic.*
Amélie est sportive.	*Amélie is athletic.*
Robert est très actif.	*Robert is very active.*
Lucie est très active.	*Lucie is very active.*
C'est un faux document.	*It's a forged document.*
C'est une fausse perle.	*It's an imitation pearl.*

Many adjectives are just plain irregular as shown in these examples:

Le musée est beau.	*The museum is beautiful.*
La maison est belle.	*The house is beautiful.*
Ce projet est fou.	*This project is crazy.*
Cette décision est folle.	*This decision is crazy.*
Son nouveau roman est fantastique.	*His new novel is fantastic.*
Leur nouvelle voiture est grise.	*Their new car is grey.*

POSITION OF ADJECTIVES

As you go along, you'll become acquainted with the irregular feminine form of some adjectives. What is often more difficult is the position of the adjectives. In French, most qualifying adjectives follow the noun.

Dominique aime les films américains.	*Dominique loves American movies.*
Fabien préfère l'art moderne.	*Fabien prefers modern art.*

Some adjectives precede the noun:

C'est un beau spectacle.	*It's a beautiful show.*
Merci pour cette belle soirée.	*Thank you for this beautiful evening.*
C'est un long voyage.	*It's a long journey.*
C'est une longue traversée.	*It's a long crossing.*
C'est un mauvais roman.	*It's a bad novel.*
C'est une mauvaise récolte.	*It's a bad harvest.*
Son nouveau film sort demain.	*His new film will be released tomorrow.*
Sa nouvelle collection est surprenante.	*His new collection is surprising.*
C'est un bon restaurant.	*It's a good restaurant.*
C'est une bonne affaire.	*It's a good deal.*
Il répare ce vieux bateau.	*He is repairing this old boat.*
Cette vieille voiture coûte une fortune.	*This old car costs a fortune.*
Ce jeune musicien a beaucoup de succès.	*This young musician is very successful.*
Cette jeune femme est avocate.	*This young woman is a lawyer.*

Some adjectives change meaning depending on whether they precede or follow the noun. Let's look at a few examples.

son ancien patron	*her former boss*	un meuble ancien	*an antique piece of furniture*
ma chère amie	*my dear friend*	un loyer cher	*an expensive rent*
Notre pauvre Henri!	*Our poor Henri!*	des régions pauvres	*poor areas*
une salle propre	*a clean room*	sa propre affaire	*his own business*
une chemise sale	*a dirty shirt*	une sale situation	*a nasty situation*
un grand homme	*an important man*	une homme grand	*a tall man*
la semaine dernière	*last week*	le dernier mot	*the last word*

ADJECTIVES DESCRIBING COLORS

Adjectives describing colors usually agree in gender and number with the noun they modify.

Elle porte des gants blancs.	*She is wearing white gloves.*
Il a les yeux bleus.	*He has blue eyes.*
Sa robe noire est élégante.	*Her black dress is elegant.*
Tu préfères les cerises rouges ou les blanches?	*Do you prefer red or white cherries?*
Les murs de son salon sont jaunes.	*The walls of her living room are yellow.*
La couverture de son nouveau livre est verte.	*The cover of his new book is green.*
Tu prends le sac noir ou le beige?	*Are you taking the black bag or the beige one?*

Adjectives that are also the names of fruit or plants remain in the masculine singular form.

J'aime ses cheveux châtain.	*I like her light brown hair.*
Ces nappes orange sont magnifiques.	*These orange tablecloths are beautiful.*
Il a les yeux marron.	*His eyes have a chestnut color.*
Ces coussins indigo sont parfaits pour la chambre.	*These indigo cushions are perfect for the bedroom.*

NOTE: *If two adjectives are combined to provide more specificity, both adjectives remain in the masculine singular form.*

Elle aime les tissus bleu clair.	*She likes light blue fabrics.*
Cette veste gris foncé te va bien.	*This dark gray jacket looks good on you.*
Cette peinture vert menthe est ravissante.	*This mint green painting is delightful.*
Achète cette écharpe bleu marine.	*Buy this navy blue scarf.*

Oral Practice

Ask the following questions and then answer them, aloud.

Elle est anglaise?	*Is she English?*
Non, elle est norvégienne.	*No, she is Norwegian.*
Ces vêtements sont sales?	*Are these clothes dirty?*
Non, ces vêtements sont propres.	*No, these clothes are clean.*
Elle est blonde?	*Is she blond?*
Non, elle est rousse.	*No, she has red hair.*
Il porte sa chemise blanche?	*Is he wearing his white shirt?*
Non, il porte une chemise noire.	*No, he is wearing a black shirt.*
C'est une entreprise sérieuse?	*Is it a serious firm?*
Oui, c'est une entreprise sérieuse.	*Yes, it's a serious firm.*
C'est un film amusant?	*Is it a fun movie?*
Non, c'est un film déprimant.	*No, it's a depressing movie.*
C'est un texte court?	*Is it a short text?*
Non, c'est très long.	*No, it's very long.*
Corinne est ambitieuse?	*Is Corinne ambitious?*
Oui, elle est très ambitieuse.	*Yes, she is very ambitious.*
Leur maison est petite?	*Is their house small?*
Non, leur maison est grande.	*No, their house is big.*

Written Practice 4

Circle the appropriate adjective.

1. Les pyramides sont ambitieuses/vieilles/courtes.
2. Son chien est gentil/vert/frais.
3. Le musée du Louvre est brave/dernier/fascinant.
4. Le professeur d'anglais est silencieux/intéressant/final.
5. Sa nouvelle bicyclette est désagréable/folle/noire.

Written Practice 5

Change these sentences from the masculine form to the feminine.

Justin est français. *Justine est française.* _____

1. Justin est gentil. _____
2. Justin est intelligent. _____
3. Justin est généreux. _____
4. Justin est beau. _____
5. Justin est créatif. _____

Making Comparisons

In French, comparisons of adjectives and adverbs can take three forms: **plus... que** (*more . . . than*); **moins... que** (*less . . . than*); and **aussi... que** (*as . . . as*). For example:

Paris est plus grand que Lyon.	*Paris is bigger than Lyon.*
Elle court plus vite que son frère.	*She runs faster than her brother.*
Ton système est moins performant que le sien.	*Your system is less effective than his.*
Bruno travaille moins efficacement que Paul.	*Bruno works less efficiently than Paul.*
Il est aussi sérieux que son collègue.	*He is as serious as his colleague.*

To compare quantities, use the following expressions:

Elle a plus de vêtements que sa copine Chloé.	*She has more clothes than her friend Chloé.*
Ils ont moins d'argent que leurs parents.	*They have less money than their parents.*
J'ai autant de travail que toi.	*I have as much work as you do.*

Some comparatives have irregular forms as shown in these examples:

Ce film-ci est meilleur que ce film-là.	*This film is better than that film.*
Tout va mieux qu'avant.	*Everything is better than it was before.*
La situation économique est pire que jamais.	*The economic situation is worse than ever.*
Cela n'a pas la moindre importance.	*This does not have the slightest importance.*

To express the ideas of *the most, the least, the best, the worst,* etc., one uses the superlative. To form the superlative, simply add the definite article to the comparative form. Note that **de** follows the superlative where *in* is used in English.

C'est le plus grand musée du pays.	*It's the largest museum in the country.*
C'est la plus belle ville du monde.	*It's the most beautiful city in the world.*
C'est son meilleur film.	*It's his best film.*
C'est sa pire décision.	*It's his worst decision.*
C'est le moins cher de tout le quartier.	*It's the least expensive in the whole neighborhood.*

Oral Practice

Repeat aloud the following comparisons.

Je suis plus prudente que lui.	*I am more cautious than he is.*
Cécile est aussi minutieuse qu'Odile.	*Cécile is as meticulous as Odile.*
Le pain de seigle est meilleur que le pain blanc.	*Rye bread is better than white bread.*
Son frère est aussi obstiné qu'elle?	*Is her brother as stubborn as she is?*
Cette salle est moins bruyante que mon bureau.	*This room is less noisy than my office.*
Édouard a autant de chance qu'Antoine?	*Does Édouard have as much luck as Antoine?*
Cet appartement est le plus grand.	*This apartment is the biggest.*

Maud a moins de livres que   *Maud has fewer books than her cousin.*
    sa cousine.

Elle est plus douée que lui?   *Is she more gifted than he is?*

Written Practice 6

Using the words provided, create a full comparison sentence.

André/Odile/ambitieux/+   *André est plus ambitieux qu'Odile.* _____

1. Céleste/Marion/efficace/− _____

2. Agnès/Antoine/amusant/= _____

3. Alexandre/Mélissa/sportif/− _____

4. Laure/José/créatif/+ _____

5. Emmanuel/son frère/doué/= _____

The *Académie Française*

The **Académie Française** (the French Academy) is France's official authority on the usage, vocabulary, and grammar of the French language. The **Académie** grew out of literary salons held in the 1600s. It was formally established as an organization in 1635 by Cardinal Richelieu, the chief minister to King Louis XIII, to maintain standards of literary taste and language. The **Académie** consists of forty members, called **les immortels** (*the immortals*) because **À l'immortalité** appears on the official seal granted by Richelieu. New members are elected by the **Académie** (the original members were appointed). Although most academicians are writers, it is not a requirement for membership. The **Académie** publishes the official dictionary of the French language (*Dictionnaire de l'Académie Française*). The first edition came out in 1694; they are currently still working on the ninth edition. The academy has often been accused of literary conservatism. It endeavors to keep foreign and "loanwords" (for example, *e-mail, workshop*) out of the French language, and while many of France's great writers, such as Corneille, Racine, Voltaire, and Victor Hugo, have been members, it has also snubbed such literary luminaries as Molière, Jean-Jacques Rousseau, Honoré de Balzac, Gustave Flaubert, Stendhal, Émile Zola, and Marcel Proust. Today, the academy includes women and people of other nationalities who write in French. In addition to awarding literary prizes, the French Academy distributes grants and prizes for courage and civic virtue.

QUIZ

Put the verbs in the plural form.

il accomplit *ils accomplissent*

1. tu prends   _____
2. elle finit   _____
3. je pars   _____

Change from the present tense to the imperative mood.

Tu joues au football. *Joue au football!*

4. Vous prenez une semaine de vacances. _____
5. Tu finis le rapport. _____

Change from the masculine to the feminine form.

Il est intelligent. *Elle est intelligente.*

6. Il est espagnol. _____
7. Il est brésilien. _____

Create a comparison sentence using the following elements.

Céline/Paul/amusant/= *Céline est aussi amusante que Paul.*

8. Paolo/Karim/efficace/− _____
9. ce magasin/cette boutique/cher/+ _____
10. ce vieil homme/ce jeune homme/sympathique/= _____

Using the definite article **le** or **la**, specify the gender of the following words.

1. tortue   _____
2. grenouille   _____
3. chocolat   _____
4. courage   _____
5. naissance   _____

Replace the definite **le, la,** or **les** with the indefinite **un, une,** or **des.**

6. la montre   _____
7. la propriété   _____
8. la division   _____
9. l'homme   _____
10. les peintures _____

Write the appropriate definite article before each of the following geographic nouns.

11. Indonésie   _____
12. Maroc   _____
13. Pérou   _____
14. Floride   _____
15. Liban   _____

Put the following nouns in the plural form. Watch out for exceptions.

16. le bijou   _____
17. l'école   _____
18. le nez   _____
19. le cheval   _____
20. le mois   _____

Formulate a question, using **tu** and the **est-ce que** form in the present tense.

21. commander une salade _____

22. acheter des tomates _____

23. habiter à Paris _____

24. remplacer Juliette _____

25. déménager à Toulouse _____

Suggest an activity to your friend, using the informal **on** and complete sentences.

aller au cinema *On va au cinéma?* _____

26. partager un dessert _____

27. acheter des fleurs pour Sonia _____

28. apporter un gâteau à Jean _____

29. appeler Mathieu _____

30. déjeuner sur la terrasse _____

Answer the following questions in the affirmative, using the verb shown (**être** or **avoir**) and complete sentences.

31. Est-ce que tu es content de ton nouveau travail?

_____

32. Est-ce qu'ils ont un dictionnaire français-anglais?

_____

33. Avez-vous des lunettes de soleil?

_____

34. Ce restaurant est cher?

_____

35. Est-ce qu'ils ont peur des résultats?

_____

Answer the following questions, following the model and using the verb **aller** and complete sentences.

Comment allez-vous? _Je vais bien._

36. Comment vont les Dubois? _____

37. Comment va Sylvain? _____

38. Comment vas-tu? _____

39. Comment va ton frère? _____

40. Comment vont tes parents? _____

Change these sentences from the masculine to the feminine form.

41. Il est japonais. _____

42. Il est vietnamien. _____

43. Il est africain. _____

44. Il est capricieux. _____

45. Il est naïf. _____

Translate the following sentences, using **vous** and the inversion form when necessary.

46. Her former boss lives in Paris. _____

47. The quality of this fabric is better. _____

48. How many people live in the blue house? _____

49. Do you like Paris? _____

50. Why is she studying English? _____

PART TWO

SOME ESSENTIAL FRIENDS

CHAPTER 6

Talking About Time and Location

In this chapter you will learn:

Telling Time
Adverbs and Expressions of Time
Adverbs and Expressions of Location
Using depuis
Geographic Names
The French Republic and Government

Telling Time

Quelle heure est-il? This is how you ask and tell time in French.

Quelle heure est-il?	*What time is it?*
Il est quelle heure?	*What time is it? (informal)*

On the hour:

Il est huit heures.	*It is eight o'clock.*
Il est dix heures.	*It is ten o'clock.*
Il est midi.	*It is noon.*
Il est minuit.	*It is midnight.*

On the half or quarter hour:

Il est huit heures et demie.	*It is eight-thirty.*
Il est midi et demi.	*It is half past twelve.*
Il est minuit et demi.	*It is half past twelve.*

NOTE: *Midi and **minuit** are masculine, so **demi** does not take a final e.*

Il est huit heures et quart.	*It is a quarter past eight.*
Il est huit heures moins le quart.	*It is a quarter to eight.*

So let's start over, going around the clock.

Il est une heure.	*It is one o'clock.*
Il est une heure cinq.	*It is five past one.*
Il est une heure dix.	*It is ten past one.*
Il est une heure et quart.	*It is a quarter past one.*
Il est une heure vingt.	*It is twenty past one.*
Il est une heure vingt-cinq.	*It is twenty-five past one.*
Il est une heure et demie.	*It is half past one (one-thirty).*
Il est deux heures moins vingt-cinq.	*It is twenty-five to two.*

Il est deux heures moins vingt.	*It is twenty to two.*
Il est deux heures moins le quart.	*It is a quarter to two.*
Il est deux heures moins dix.	*It is ten to two.*
Il est deux heures moins cinq.	*It is five to two.*
Il est deux heures.	*It is two o'clock.*

To convey the idea of A.M. and P.M., if there is a doubt, you can specify:

Je pars à sept heures du matin.	*I am leaving at 7 A.M.*
Je rentre à quatre heures de l'après-midi.	*I am coming back at 4 P.M.*
On joue aux échecs à neuf heures du soir.	*We're playing chess at 9 P.M.*

Official time, the twenty-four-hour clock, is used for plane and train schedules, meetings, TV programs, etc.

L'avion part à vingt-deux heures.	*The plane leaves at 10 P.M.*
Le match de base-ball commence à dix-neuf heures.	*The baseball game starts at 7 P.M.*
La cérémonie commence à quinze heures.	*The ceremony will start at 3 P.M.*
La réunion est prévue pour seize heures trente.	*The meeting is planned for 4:30 P.M.*

Oral Practice

Ask the following questions and then answer them, aloud.

À quelle heure dînez-vous ce soir?	*What time are you having dinner tonight?*
Nous dînons à huit heures.	*We are having dinner at eight.*
À quelle heure finit le film?	*What time does the film end?*
Le film finit à vingt-deux heures.	*The film ends at 10 P.M.*
À quelle heure pars-tu cet après-midi?	*What time are you leaving this afternoon?*

Je pars à treize heures.	*I am leaving at 1 P.M.*
À quelle heure rentre-t-elle ce soir?	*What time is she coming home tonight?*
Elle rentre vers onze heures.	*She'll be back home around 11 P.M.*
À quelle heure livre-t-on le journal?	*What time is the paper delivered?*
On livre le journal vers six heures du matin.	*The paper is delivered at around 6 A.M.*

Written Practice 1

Write the time in full letters, using the informal way of telling time.

8:10 P.M. *huit heures dix du soir*

1. 11:15 A.M. _____
2. 3:35 P.M. _____
3. 6:45 A.M. _____
4. 3:50 P.M. _____
5. 5:30 A.M. _____

Written Practice 2

Write the time in full letters, using the official time.

6 P.M. *dix-huit heures*

1. 7:30 P.M. _____
2. 3 P.M. _____
3. 11:15 P.M. _____
4. 5:45 P.M. _____
5. 10:15 A.M. _____

Adverbs and Expressions of Time

These expressions are useful when talking about time.

aujourd'hui	*today*
hier	*yesterday*
demain	*tomorrow*
avant-hier	*the day before yesterday*
après-demain	*the day after tomorrow*
la semaine dernière	*last week*
la semaine prochaine	*next week*
dans trois jours	*in three days; three days from today*
dans une quinzaine	*in two weeks*
dans un mois	*in a month*
dans un an	*in a year*
il y a trois jours	*three days ago*
il y a deux semaines	*two weeks ago*
il y a un mois	*a month ago*
il y a un an	*a year ago*

These adverbs will be used when you talk to people directly; for this reason, this is called the direct style. When you relate a story or talk about past and future events, you'll use the **discours indirect** *(indirect speech)*, with the following expressions, which we'll review as soon as we learn the past and the future tenses.

le jour même	*the very day*
la veille	*the day before*
le lendemain	*the day after*
l'avant-veille	*two days before*
le surlendemain	*two days later*
la dernière semaine	*the last week (of a sequence)*
la semaine suivante	*the following week*

Here are other adverbs or expressions of time:

actuellement	*presently*	parfois	*sometimes*
autrefois	*formerly*	quelquefois	*sometimes*
chaque jour	*every day*	rarement	*seldom*
à l'heure actuelle	*at this very moment*	souvent	*often*
d'habitude	*usually*	tard	*late*
ne... jamais	*never*	de temps à autre	*from time to time*
longtemps	*for a long time*	de temps en temps	*from time to time*
maintenant	*now*	tôt	*early*
en ce moment	*at the present time*	toujours	*always, still*
d'ordinaire	*ordinarily*	tous les jours	*every day*

Oral Practice

Ask the following questions and then answer them, aloud.

Pierre arrive demain?	*Is Pierre arriving tomorrow?*
Oui, Pierre arrive demain matin.	*Yes, Pierre is arriving tomorrow morning.*
Tu es libre la semaine prochaine?	*Are you free next week?*
Oui, je suis libre la semaine prochaine.	*Yes, I am free next week.*
Où allez-vous aujourd'hui?	*Where are you going today?*
Nous allons à Versailles.	*We are going to Versailles.*
Vous mangez des pâtes tous les jours?	*Do you eat pasta every day?*
Non, je mange des pâtes un jour sur deux.	*No, I eat pasta every second day.*
Tu rentres tôt ce soir?	*Will you be home early tonight?*
Non, je rentre vers onze heures.	*No, I'll be home around eleven.*
Est-ce qu'il fait souvent des erreurs?	*Does he often make mistakes?*
Non, il fait rarement des erreurs.	*No, he rarely makes mistakes.*
Est-ce qu'ils vont parfois à la piscine?	*Do they sometimes go to the pool?*
Non, ils ne vont jamais à la piscine.	*No, they never go to the pool.*
Tu as beaucoup de travail en ce moment?	*Do you have a lot of work these days?*
Non, en ce moment, c'est très calme.	*No, it is very quiet these days.*

Written Practice 3

Translate the following sentences.

1. Today is the first day of spring. _____
2. He rarely travels. _____
3. She is always on time. _____

4. They are leaving very early. _____

5. Her birthday is next week. _____

Adverbs and Expressions of Location

Here are some words that are helpful when talking about location.

ailleurs	*elsewhere*	dessous	*under*
auprès	*next to, close to*	dessus	*on top*
là-bas	*over there*	devant	*in front of*
à cet endroit	*in this place*	ici	*here*
à côté	*next to, beside*	là	*there*
dedans	*inside*	ça et là	*here and there*
dehors	*outside*	là-haut	*up there*
derrière	*behind*	loin	*far*
partout	*everywhere*	près	*near/close*

Oral Practice

Repeat aloud the following sentences.

Ici, tout est possible.	*Here, everything is possible.*
Les gens d'ici sont très gentils.	*The local people are very nice.*
Balzac est mort ici même.	*Balzac died in this very place.*
Je le vois là, sur la table.	*I see it over there, on the table.*
L'avion est là-haut dans les nuages.	*The plane is up there in the clouds.*
Mets ta valise dessous.	*Put your suicase underneath.*
C'est écrit dessus.	*It's written on it.*
Il désire habiter ailleurs.	*He wants to live elsewhere.*
Vous êtes juste devant.	*You are right in front of it.*
Tu es juste derrière.	*You are right behind it.*
C'est beaucoup trop loin.	*It is much too far.*
Je vois des erreurs ça et là.	*I see mistakes here and there.*

Written Practice 4

Translate the following sentences, using the vous form when necessary.

1. I see mistakes everywhere. _____
2. Tonight, we'll have dinner outdoors. _____
3. They live here but they work elsewhere. _____
4. Put your hat on top of it. _____
5. He lives too far. _____

Using *depuis*

When you want to ask a question regarding how long an action has gone on that began in the past and still continues in the present, you have different possibilities: **depuis, il y a... que, cela (ça) fait... que**.

NOTE: *French uses the present in this context, whereas English uses the past.*

Let's start with **depuis.**

Julie habite à Madrid depuis trois ans.	*Julie has been living in Madrid for three years.*
Murielle joue du piano depuis deux mois.	*Murielle has been playing the piano for two months.*

To ask a question about the duration of an action, use **depuis quand** *(since when)* or **depuis combien de temps** *(how long)*.

Oral Practice

Ask the following questions and then answer them, aloud.

Depuis quand habites-tu à Paris?	*Since when have you lived in Paris?*
J'habite à Paris depuis 2002.	*I have been living in Paris since 2002.*
Depuis combien de temps est-ce qu'elle travaille ici?	*How long has she been working here?*

Elle travaille ici depuis six mois.	*She has been working here for six months.*
Depuis quand est-il malade?	*Since when has he been sick?*
Il est malade depuis mardi.	*He has been sick since Tuesday.*
Depuis combien de temps conduisez-vous?	*How long have you been driving?*
Je conduis depuis cinq ans.	*I have been driving for five years.*
Depuis quand ce magasin est-il ouvert?	*Since when has this store been open?*
Ce magasin est ouvert depuis le premier juillet.	*This store has been open since July first.*
Depuis combien de temps est-ce que tu attends?	*How long have you been waiting?*
J'attends depuis une demi-heure.	*I have been waiting for half an hour.*

NOTE: *There is an exception! In negative sentences, the **passé composé** (which we'll study in the following chapters) is used instead of the present. For example:*

Je ne suis pas allée à Paris depuis trois ans.	*I have not been to Paris for three years.*

Written Practice 5

Write out full sentences according to the model.

Sophie/écouter la radio/une heure *Sophie écoute la radio depuis une heure.*

1. André/apprendre le chinois/quatre ans _____
2. Céline/parler au téléphone/une heure _____
3. tu/regarder la télé/cet après-midi _____
4. ils/aller à l'opéra/leur enfance _____
5. nous/réfléchir à la question/ce matin _____

Written Practice 6

Use complete sentences and change **depuis** or **cela fait... que** into **il y a... que**.

Cela fait une heure que j'attends. _Il y a une heure que j'attends._

1. Elle travaille depuis une demi-heure. _____

2. Cela fait un mois qu'Alex a un nouvel ordinateur. _____

3. Cela fait des semaines qu'elle cherche un emploi. _____

4. Nous sommes en vacances depuis trois jours. _____

5. Agnès étudie la musique depuis des années. _____

Geographic Names

The names of cities are considered to be proper names and most of them do not require definite articles. For example:

J'adore Venise.	*I love Venice.*
Où se trouve Nouméa?	*Where is Nouméa?*

A few cities have a definite article as part of their name: **Le Caire, La Nouvelle-Orléans, Le Havre, La Rochelle, Le Mans.** To express *in* or *to* with a geographical name, the preposition varies. With cities, the preposition **à** is used.

Ils vont à Moscou en juin.	*They are going to Moscow in June.*
Nous habitons à Tokyo.	*We live in Tokyo.*
Ils sont au Caire en ce moment.	*They are presently in Cairo.*
La conférence commence mardi à La Nouvelle-Orléans.	*The lecture is starting on Tuesday in New Orleans.*

To express origin, use the preposition **de** (*from*).

Elle revient de Londres.	*She is coming back from London.*
Ils sont originaires de La Rochelle.	*They are from La Rochelle.*

With countries, states, and provinces, the preposition changes according to gender and number. To refresh your memory, go back to Chapter 2 where you learned the tips for determining gender.

en feminine	**au** masculine
en masculine beginning with a vowel	**aux** plural

Here are some example sentences:

Elle cherche une maison en Italie.	*She is looking for a house in Italy.*
Les Quefellec habitent en Argentine.	*The Quefellecs live in Argentina.*
Actuellement, Hugo travaille au Japon.	*Presently, Hugo is working in Japan.*
Séverine a des amis au Guatemala.	*Séverine has friends in Guatemala.*
Tu vas aux États-Unis cet été?	*Are you going to the United States this summer?*

The continents are feminine. Provinces and states ending in **e** are also feminine, with some exceptions such as **le Mexique, le Cambodge.**

Antoine est en Afrique depuis un mois.	*Antoine has been in Africa for a month.*
Valérie travaille en Asie depuis quelques années.	*Valérie has been working in Asia for some years.*

Oral Practice

Ask the following questions and then answer them, aloud.

Est-ce que Léa est à Oslo?	*Is Léa in Oslo?*
Non, Léa est à Amsterdam.	*No, Léa is in Amsterdam.*
Les Dumas ont une maison à Nice?	*Do the Dumas have a house in Nice?*
Non, les Dumas ont une maison à Biarritz.	*No, the Dumas have a house in Biarritz.*
Allez-vous au Mali cet hiver?	*Are you going to Mali this winter?*

Oui, nous allons au Mali en février.	*Yes, we are going to Mali in February.*
Depuis combien de temps allez-vous au Maroc?	*How long have you been going to Morocco?*
Nous allons au Maroc depuis dix ans.	*We have been going to Morocco for ten years.*
Est-ce que Paolo chantera en Jordanie?	*Will Paolo sing in Jordan?*
Oui, Paolo chantera en Jordanie.	*Yes, Paolo will sing in Jordan.*
Est-ce que tu espères trouver un emploi en Irlande?	*Do you hope to find a job in Ireland?*
Oui, j'espère trouver un emploi en Irlande.	*Yes, I hope to find a job in Ireland.*
Est-ce qu'ils ont une agence au Cambodge?	*Do they have an agency in Cambodia?*
Oui, ils ont une agence au Cambodge et au Laos.	*Yes, they have an agency in Cambodia and in Laos.*
Théo est en Angleterre ou en Écosse?	*Is Théo in England or in Scotland?*
Théo est au Pays de Galles.	*Théo is in Wales.*
Louise voyage avec toi au Vietnam?	*Is Louise traveling with you to Vietnam?*
Non, elle voyage avec moi en Chine.	*No, she is traveling with me to China.*

PROVINCES AND STATES

With French provinces and departments, the preposition may vary. In front of feminine nouns or masculine nouns starting with a vowel, **en** is used. However, in front of masculine nouns, **dans le** often replaces **au.** With names of American states, **en** is used in front of feminine states or states starting with a vowel. For masculine states, the pattern is less fixed, and you may hear **au, dans le,** or **dans l'État de,** depending on the state.

J'espère aller en Normandie cet été.	*I hope to go to Normandy this summer.*
Les meilleurs vins sont en Bourgogne.	*The best wines are in Burgundy.*
Elle a une exposition en Californie.	*She has an exhibition in California.*

| Ils vont toujours dans le Midi. | *They always go to the South of France.* |
| Le festival de cinéma est en Arkansas. | *The film festival is in Arkansas.* |

Oral Practice

Ask the following questions and then answer them, aloud.

Le journaliste est en Bretagne ou en Touraine?	*Is the journalist in Brittany or in Touraine?*
Il est à Saint-Malo, en Bretagne.	*He is in Saint-Malo, in Brittany.*
La maison de campagne de Laure est dans le Languedoc?	*Is Laure's country home is Languedoc?*
Oui, sa maison est dans le Languedoc.	*Yes, her house is in Languedoc.*
Il va à Washington demain?	*Is he going to Washington tomorrow?*
Oui, il a une réunion demain matin à Washington.	*Yes, he has a meeting tomorrow morning in Washington.*
Vous allez dans l'État de Washington en août?	*Are you going to Washington State in August?*
Nous allons d'abord au Montana puis dans l'État de Washington.	*We are first going to Montana, then to the State of Washington.*
Ont-ils un bureau en Allemagne?	*Do they have an office in Germany?*
Oui, ils ont un bureau à Berlin.	*Yes, they have an office in Berlin.*

ISLANDS

Although usage may vary, the preposition **à** (**aux** in the plural) is often used for islands. For example:

La conférence a lieu à Tahiti.	*The conference is taking place in Tahiti.*
Et tes vacances à Hawaii?	*What about your vacation in Hawaii?*
Le festival de musique est à Cuba.	*The music festival is in Cuba.*

Elle rêve d'aller aux Seychelles.	*She dreams of going to the Seychelles islands.*

Some exceptions:

Ce peintre est célèbre en Haïti.	*This painter is famous in Haiti.*
Leur atelier d'écriture a lieu en Guadeloupe.	*Their writing workshop is taking place in Guadeloupe.*

EXPRESSING ORIGIN

Origin is expressed by **de** for continents, feminine countries, provinces, regions, and states. For masculine and plural entities, the definite article is kept.

Ils arrivent de France.	*They are coming from France.*
Elle est originaire de Grèce.	*She comes from Greece.*
Ces fraises viennent de Californie.	*These strawberries come from California.*
Ce vin vient du Chili.	*This wine comes from Chili.*
Ces produits viennent des États-Unis.	*These products come from the United States.*

Written Practice 7

Write full sentences according to the model.

Cheng/aller/Inde/mai *Cheng va en Inde en mai.*

1. Patrice/aller/Afrique/novembre _____
2. Christian/aller/Rome/hiver _____
3. Gérard/aller/Californie/mars _____
4. Géraldine/aller/États-Unis/avril _____
5. Akiko/aller/Portugal/automne _____

The French Republic and Government

The French Republic consists of: (1) metropolitan France, divided into twenty-two regions and subdivided into ninety-six departments; (2) four overseas departments (DOM): Guadeloupe, Martinique, Guyana (French Guiana), and Reunion; and (3) Four overseas territories (TOM): French Polynesia, New Caledonia, Wallis and Futuna, and the French Southern and Antarctic Territories and "Territorial communities" with special status: Mayotte and St-Pierre-et-Miquelon. These last two groups of areas are often referred to collectively as **Les Dom-Tom**.

The President of the French Republic is elected to a five-year term. The president appoints a prime minister and, on the latter's recommendation, appoints the other members of the government. The president presides over the council of ministers, promulgates acts of Parliament, and is commander-in-chief of the Armed Forces. He may dissolve the National Assembly and, in an emergency, exercise special power. The prime minister directs the operation of the government and ensures the implementation of legislation.

The Parliament is formed of two assemblies: (1) the Senate, elected to a nine-year term, with one third renewed every three years; and (2) the National Assembly, whose members (**députés**) are elected to a five-year term. In addition to providing a check on the government, the two assemblies draw up and pass legislation. In case of a disagreement on a law, the National Assembly makes the final decision.

QUIZ

Answer the questions using the informal way of telling time.

À quelle heure commence le film? (8:45 P.M.)
Le film commence à neuf heures moins le quart.

1. À quelle heure pars-tu? (5:30 P.M.) _____
   À quelle heure finit la séance? (1 P.M.) _____
   À quelle heure ouvre ce magasin? (9 A.M.) _____
   À quelle heure est-ce que tu reviens? (4:15 P.M.) _____

Write the time in full letters, using the official time.

8 P.M.   *vingt heures* _____

2. 5:15 P.M.   _____
    1:10 A.M.   _____
    4:55 P.M.   _____
    7:23 A.M.   _____

Answer the questions according to the model.

Allez-vous à Paris la semaine prochaine? (demain)
Non, je vais à Paris demain.

3. Prenez-vous le train à dix-huit heures? (vingt heures)

_____

Commencez-vous le projet cet après-midi? (ce matin)

_____

Partez-vous en vacances aujourd'hui? (après-demain)

_____

Est-ce qu'il déménage dans un mois? (dans une semaine)

_____

Est-ce que tu prends ce médicament chaque jour? (un jour sur deux)

_____

Answer the following questions using complete sentences.

Depuis combien de temps habitez-vous dans cet appartement?
J'habite dans cet appartement depuis dix ans.

4. Depuis combien de temps es-tu dans ce club? (deux ans)

_____

Depuis combien de temps sont-ils mariés? (cinq ans)

_____

Complete the sentences following the model.

Maria/Tokyo/Japon *Maria habite à Tokyo, au Japon.*

5. Frank/La Nouvelle-Orléans/États-Unis _____
   Noémie/Venise/Italie _____
   Ali/Ouagadougou/Burkina Faso _____

Complete the following sentences with the appropriate country.

La Tour Eiffel *La Tour Eiffel est en France* _____.

6. Le palais de Buckingham _____.
   Le château de Versailles _____.
   La tour de Pise _____.
   Le temple d'Angkor Vat _____.
   Le parc national de Yosemite _____.

Translate the following sentences, using the **vous** form and inversion.

7. What time is it? _____
8. Are you taking your vacation in Tunisia? _____
9. Since when have you been living here? _____
10. The meeting starts at noon. _____

CHAPTER 7

Expressing Possibilities, Wishes, and Abilities

In this chapter you will learn:

The Verb devoir

The Verb vouloir

The Verb pouvoir

Irregular -oir *Verbs in the Present Tense*

The Partitive Article

Synonyms

Homonyms

Onomatopoeia

French Etiquette

The Verb *devoir*

The verb **devoir** (*must, to have to*) is a very commonly used verb with various nuances and meanings. The intonation with which it is said will often indicate whether **devoir** implies an obligation or a suggestion. Here is how **devoir** is conjugated:

je dois	*I must*	nous devons	*we must*
tu dois	*you must*	vous devez	*you must*
il/elle doit	*he/she must*	ils/elles doivent	*they must*

There are several different meanings of **devoir.**

DEVOIR AND OBLIGATION

Devoir can be used to express obligation. For example:

Tu dois payer tes impôts avant le quinze avril.	*You must pay your taxes before April fifteenth.*
Elle doit travailler trente-cinq heures par semaine.	*She has to work thirty-five hours a week.*
Il doit s'excuser.	*He has to apologize.*

DEVOIR AND PROBABILITY

Devoir is also used to convey probability. For example:

L'avion doit arriver à vingt-trois heures.	*The plane is supposed to arrive at eleven P.M.*
Elle doit nous rendre visite ce week-end.	*She is supposed to visit us this weekend.*
Ne dois-tu pas l'aider à déménager?	*Aren't you supposed to help him move?*

DEVOIR AND DEBT

In the following examples, you'll see how **devoir** is used to indicate debt:

Florent me doit cent euros.	*Florent owes me a hundred euros.*
Combien est-ce que je vous dois?	*How much do I owe you?*
Vous ne me devez rien.	*You do not owe me anything.*
Il doit la vie au maître nageur.	*He owes his life to the lifeguard.*

DEVOIR AND SUGGESTION AND WARNING

When used in the conditional, which you will learn in a later chapter, **devoir** takes on the meaning of *should*.

Tu devrais être plus prudent.	*You should be more careful.*
Vous devriez ajouter un peu de safran.	*You should add a little bit of saffron.*
Tu ne devrais pas être toujours en retard!	*You should not always be late!*

Oral Practice

Ask the following questions and then answer them, aloud.

Que dois-tu faire cet après-midi?	*What are you supposed to do this afternoon?*
Rien de spécial.	*Nothing special.*
Jusqu'à quelle heure doit-il travailler ce soir?	*Until what time does he have to work tonight?*
Il doit travailler jusqu'à au moins neuf heures.	*He has to work until at least nine o'clock.*
Combien d'argent doit-il à la banque?	*How much money does he owe the bank?*
Il doit une fortune à la banque.	*He owes the bank a fortune.*
Quel jour doit-il arriver?	*What day is he supposed to arrive?*
Il doit arriver mardi.	*He is supposed to arrive on Tuesday.*
À qui doit-elle une explication?	*To whom does she owe an explanation?*

Elle doit une explication à sa collègue.	*She owes her colleague an explanation.*
Pourquoi doivent-ils vendre leur maison?	*Why do they have to sell their house?*
Ils doivent vendre leur maison parce qu'ils ont des dettes.	*They have to sell their house because they have debts.*
Combien de kilos doit-il perdre?	*How many kilos does he have to lose?*
Il doit perdre quinze kilos.	*He has to lose fifteen kilos.*
Je dois te croire?	*Am I supposed to believe you?*
Je t'en prie, tu dois me croire!	*I beg you, you must believe me!*

Written Practice 1

Match the items in the two columns.

1. Il est trop maigre. _____   a. Il doit acheter une maison.
2. Il est en vie. _____   b. Il doit voyager bientôt.
3. Il a de l'argent. _____   c. Il doit grossir.
4. Il a des dettes. _____   d. Il doit cinq cents euros à son ami.
5. Il va peut-être en France. _____   e. Il doit la vie à son médecin.

The Verb *vouloir*

The verb **vouloir** (*to want*) is used to express your wishes and desires. It is also used for a polite request in the conditional form.

je veux	*I want*	nous voulons	*we want*
tu veux	*you want*	vous voulez	*you want*
il/elle veut	*he/she wants*	ils/elles veulent	*they want*

Here are some example sentences:

Il veut du papier.	*He wants some paper.*
Tu veux un jus d'orange?	*Do you want some/a glass of orange juice?*
Je voudrais une chambre plus grande.	*I'd like a larger room.*
Voudriez-vous lui parler?	*Would you like to talk to him?*

When using the adverb **bien** with **vouloir,** the meaning changes. In this case, **bien** weakens the meaning of the verb. Another verb that acts this way with **bien** is the verb **aimer.** Compare the verbs with and without **bien.**

Je veux une réponse!	*I want an answer!*
Je veux une tasse de café!	*I want a cup of coffee!*
Voulez-vous du thé? / Je veux bien.	*Do you want some tea? / Yes, please.*
Tu veux bien accompagner Sara?	*Are you willing to go with Sara?*
Je veux bien le faire.	*I don't mind doing it.*
J'aime Matthieu!	*I love Matthieu!*
J'aime bien Matthieu.	*I like Matthieu.*
J'aime le chocolat!	*I love chocolate!*
J'aime bien les choux-fleurs.	*I like cauliflower.*

The Verb *pouvoir*

Pouvoir (*can, may*), expressing ability and capability, is conjugated like **vouloir.**

je peux	*I can*	nous pouvons	*we can*
tu peux	*you can*	vous pouvez	*you can*
il/elle peut	*she can*	ils/elles peuvent	*they can*

Here are some example sentences:

Je peux vous aider?	*May I help you?*
Il ne peut pas travailler aujourd'hui.	*He can't work today.*
Pouvez-vous appeler Claude?	*Can you call Claude?*

When asking permission in a formal manner, the first person can take a different form.

Puis-je vous aider?	*May I help you?*
Puis-je vous poser une question délicate?	*May I ask you a delicate question?*

Another formal way of asking a question is to use the conditional form of **pouvoir.**

Pourriez-vous me montrer la Tour Eiffel sur le plan?	*Could you show me the Eiffel Tower on the map?*
Pourriez-vous appeler un médecin?	*Could you call a doctor?*
Pourriez-vous nous recommander un bon restaurant?	*Could you recommend a good restaurant?*

Oral Practice

Ask the following questions and then answer them, aloud.

Est-ce que tu peux faire ces exercices?	*Can you do these exercises?*
Oui, je peux faire ces exercices.	*Yes, I can do these exercises.*
Puis-je consulter ces documents?	*May I consult these documents?*
Oui, vous pouvez consulter ces documents.	*Yes, you can consult these documents.*
Elle peut venir ce soir?	*Can she come tonight?*
Non, elle ne peut pas venir ce soir.	*No, she can't come tonight.*
Tu peux marcher plus vite?	*Can you walk faster?*

Non, je ne peux pas marcher plus vite.	*No, I can't walk faster.*
Je peux garder cette casquette?	*May I keep this cap?*
Si tu veux.	*If you want.*
Pourquoi veut-elle vendre son appartement?	*Why does she want to sell her apartment?*
Pour acheter une maison.	*To buy a house.*
Pourrais-je parler à Madame Petit?	*Could I speak to Mrs. Petit?*
Elle est en réunion.	*She is in a meeting.*
Tu veux un verre d'eau?	*Do you want a glass of water?*
Oui, merci.	*Yes, thank you.*
Qu'est-ce qu'elle veut?	*What does she want?*
C'est un mystère.	*It's a mystery.*

Written Practice 2

Conjugate, in the present tense, the verbs in parentheses.

1. Nous (pouvoir) être chez vous avant midi.   _____
2. Tu (vouloir) aller à Paris?   _____
3. Elle (vouloir) ouvrir un magasin.   _____
4. Je (pouvoir) apporter les documents cet après-midi.   _____
5. Ils (ne pas pouvoir) accepter votre proposition.   _____

Irregular *-oir* Verbs in the Present Tense

There are many other verbs ending in **oir,** with no regular conjugation pattern.

apercevoir *(to see/to perceive)*
j'aperçois   *I see*   nous apercevons   *we see*

décevoir *(to disappoint)*
je déçois   *I disappoint*   nous décevons   *we disappoint*

falloir *(to be necessary)*

il faut   *it is necessary*

pleuvoir *(to rain)*

il pleut   *it is raining*

recevoir *(to receive)*

je reçois   *I receive*   nous recevons   *we receive*

savoir *(to know)*

je sais   *I know*   nous savons   *we know*

valoir *(to be worth)*

cela vaut   *it is worth*   nous valons   *we are worth*

voir *(to see)*

je vois   *I see*   nous voyons   *we see*

Oral Practice

Ask the following questions and then answer them, aloud.

Recevez-vous beaucoup de courrier?	*Do you get a lot of mail?*
Oui, je reçois beaucoup de courrier.	*Yes, I get a lot of mail.*
Est-ce qu'il pleut à Paris aujourd'hui?	*Is it raining in Paris today?*
Oui, il pleut à Paris aujourd'hui.	*Yes, it is raining in Paris today.*
Ce vase, ça vaut combien?	*How much is this vase?*
Ça vaut deux cents euros.	*It is two hundred euros.*
Est-ce qu'il faut une réservation?	*Is a reservation necessary?*
Oui, il faut une réservation.	*Yes, a reservation is necessary.*
Vous voyez Charles de temps en temps?	*Do you see Charles from time to time?*
Oui, je vois Charles de temps en temps.	*Yes, I see Charles from time to time.*

Savez-vous parler portugais?   *Can you speak Portuguese?*

Non, je ne sais pas parler   *No, I can't speak Portuguese.*
  portugais.

Written Practice 3

Conjugate the verbs in parentheses.

1. Vous (voir) la Seine de votre chambre.   _____
2. Elle (recevoir) beaucoup de cadeaux.   _____
3. Il (pleuvoir) souvent dans cette région.   _____
4. Ils (apercevoir) un ami dans la rue.   _____
5. Je (savoir) conjuguer les verbes en français.   _____

The Partitive Article

The partitive articles, **du, de la, de l',** and **des** (*some*), designate a part of a whole.
Although they are often omitted in English, they are always used in French.

Elle mange du fromage.   *She eats cheese.*

Tu achètes de la salade.   *You buy salad.*

Ils boivent de l'eau.   *They drink water.*

Nous envoyons des courriels.   *We send e-mails.*

In the negative, the partitive article becomes **pas de.**

Elle ne mange pas de fromage.   *She does not eat cheese.*

Il n'a pas d'amis à Paris.   *He does not have friends in Paris.*

Oral Practice

Ask the following questions and then answer them, aloud.

Avez-vous des chats? *Do you have cats?*

Non, je n'ai pas de chat(s). *No, I don't have cats.*

Buvez-vous du thé? *Do you drink tea?*

Oui, je bois du thé. *Yes, I drink tea.*

Est-ce que vous avez de l'expérience? *Do you have experience?*

Oui, j'ai de l'expérience. *Yes, I have experience.*

Written Practice 4

Formulate questions with the elements below, using the **est-ce que** form.

avoir/chiens (tu) _Est-ce que tu as des chiens?_ _____

1. avoir/patience (il) _____
2. manger/poulet (tu) _____
3. passer/vacances en France (ils) _____
4. prendre/café (vous) _____
5. acheter/eau (tu) _____

Synonyms

Synonyms are different words with similar or identical meanings and are inter-changeable. To better express yourself in French, synonyms will come in handy. They will also allow you to enlarge your vocabulary.

apercevoir	*to see/to perceive*	voir	*to see*
beau	*beautiful*	joli	*pretty*
un appartement	*apartment*	un logement	*housing*
fréquemment	*frequently*	souvent	*often*

It is common in French to use a periphrasis, a longer expression for an idea that could be expressed in a shorter way. For instance, instead of using the name of a language, the name of one of the famous writers in that language is used.

l'allemand	*German*	la langue de Goethe	*Goethe's language*
l'anglais	*English*	la langue de Shakespeare	*Shakespeare's language*
l'espagnol	*Spanish*	la langue de Cervantès	*Cervantes' language*
le français	*French*	la langue de Molière	*Molière's language*
le grec	*Greek*	la langue d'Homère	*Homer's language*
l'italien	*Italian*	la langue de Dante	*Dante's language*

Or instead of using the name of a country, a reference is used.

la Belgique	*Belgium*	le pays plat	*the flat country*
Monaco	*Monaco*	le rocher	*the rock*
la Chine	*China*	le Céleste Empire	*the Celestial Empire*
la Finlande	*Finland*	le pays des mille lacs	*the country with a thousand lakes*

Homonyms

A homonym is a word that has the same pronunciation and spelling as another word, but a different meaning. Being aware of the key homonyms will allow you to avoid misunderstandings in oral comprehension. Here are some examples:

ça	*this*	sa	*his/her*		
car	*bus*	quart	*quarter*		
cent	*hundred*	sans	*without*	sang	*blood*
ces	*these*	ses	*his/her*		
cœur	*heart*	chœur	*choir*		
eau	*water*	haut	*high*	os	*bones*
fin	*end*	faim	*hunger*	feint	*feigned*
foi	*faith*	fois	*time*	foie	*liver*
la	*the*	là	*there*		
mai	*May*	mais	*but*		
mère	mother	mer	*sea*	maire	*mayor*
moi	*me*	mois	*month*		
ou	*or*	où	*where*		
pain	*bread*	pin	*pine*	peint	*painted*

peau	skin	pot	pot/can		
reine	queen	rêne	rein	renne	reindeer
sain	sane	saint	saint	sein	breast
teint	complexion	thym	thyme		
temps	weather	tant	so much		
toi	you	toit	roof		
vin	wine	vingt	twenty	vain	vain

Some words have the same spelling but change gender and meaning.

le livre	book	la livre	pound		
le manche	handle	la manche	sleeve	la Manche	The (English) Channel
le mémoire	thesis	la mémoire	memory		
le moule	mold	la moule	mussel		
le poêle	stove	la poêle	frying pan		
le tour	tour/walk	la tour	tower		
le vase	vase	la vase	slime, mud		
le voile	veil	la voile	sail		

Onomatopoeia

Onomatopoeia, which is the use of interjections whose meaning is clear from their sound, is most useful for attracting someone's attention, for expressing joy or pain, or for reacting to a situation.

Aïe! / Ouille!	Ouch!	Hep!	Hey!
Allô!	Hello!	Hourra!	Hurrah!
Atchoum!	Ah-choo!	Miaou!	Meow!
Au secours!	Help!	Miam-miam!	Yum-yum!
Bing!	Smack!	Ouf!	Whew!
Bof!	Not really!	Patatras!	Crash!
Boum!	Bang!	Peuh!	Pooh!
Bravo!	Bravo!	Plouf!	Splash!
Chic!	Terrific!	Pouah!	Ugh!
Chiche!	I dare you!	Tic-tac!	Tick-tock!
Chut!	Shh!	Toc toc toc!	Knock! Knock!
Hein?	What?	Vlan!	Wham!

Written Practice 5

Match the items in the two columns.

1. Le chat a faim.	_____	a.	Bravo!
2. Ne parlez pas!	_____	b.	Pouah!
3. J'ai mal.	_____	c.	Miaou!
4. Ce n'est pas bon!	_____	d.	Aïe!
5. Félicitations.	_____	e.	Chut!

French Etiquette

The French are very particular about manners and etiquette, and they follow some particular formal rules. A **tu** instead of a **vous,** and you could be potentially upsetting someone. So when you are unsure about what to do, wait and take the lead of the other person. France is still an extremely stratified society with strong competition among the different classes.

To avoid embarrassing moments, it is helpful to remember a few important things: Always shake hands when meeting people and when taking leave. The French handshake is accompanied by a short moment of eye contact. The French have a great respect for privacy, so always announce your visit. Lunch is the best time to conduct business deals. Always apologize for your lack of knowledge of French if that is the case, although most businesspeople speak English. The French love the art of conversation and are entertained by arguments. Intense eye contact is commonplace and frequent and can be intimidating to North Americans. It is important always to address a stranger politely, using **Monsieur** or **Madame**.

QUIZ

Conjugate the verbs in parentheses.

1. Marguerite (devoir) partir avant minuit.   _____
2. Bertrand et Michel (vouloir) visiter la Sicile.   _____
3. Solange et moi, nous (devoir) faire la cuisine ce soir.   _____

4. Est-ce qu'Arnaud (pouvoir) arriver avant sept heures? _____

5. Je (vouloir) voir ce film. _____

6. Match the noun in the left column with its synonym in the right column.

_____ la cerise   a. l'artiste

_____ la tante   b. la peinture

_____ le musicien   c. le marchand

_____ le manteau   d. le fruit

_____ la maison   e. la parente

_____ le cristal   f. la rétrospective

_____ le vendeur   g. le vêtement

_____ le commencement   h. le logement

_____ le tableau   i. le minéral

_____ l'exposition   j. le début

Translate the following sentences, using **vous** and inversion when necessary.

7. Clarisse cannot work today. _____

8. Do you want to go to Nice in November? _____

Translate the following sentences, using the **est-ce que** form when necessary.

9. Knock! Knock! Can we come in? _____

10. The plane is supposed to arrive at 9 A.M. _____

CHAPTER 8

Getting Acquainted

In this chapter you will learn:

The Verb savoir

The Verb connaître

Prefixes

Suffixes

Dans *versus* en

Colors

The Verb *savoir*

Savoir means to know a fact, to know how to do something from memory or study. Here is how it is conjugated:

je sais	*I know*	nous savons	*we know*
tu sais	*you know*	vous savez	*you know*
il/elle sait	*he/she knows*	ils/elles savent	*they know*

Here are some example sentences:

Il sait cette chanson.	*He knows this song (by heart).*
Elle sait tout.	*She knows everything.*

NOTE: *Savoir will sometimes be translated as* can.

Ils savent nager.	*They can swim.*

Savoir is also used before a relative clause or before an infinitive, as previously shown. It often precedes a subordinate clause, as follows.

Je ne sais pas où il est.	*I don't know where he is.*
Il sait qu'elle est occupée.	*He knows she is busy.*

Oral Practice

Ask the following questions and then answer them, aloud.

Est-ce que tu sais jouer au tennis?	*Can you play tennis?*
Oui, je sais jouer au tennis.	*Yes, I can play tennis.*
Savez-vous parler chinois?	*Can you speak Chinese?*
Non, je ne sais pas parler chinois.	*No, I cannot speak Chinese.*
Est-ce qu'il sait danser?	*Can he dance?*
Oui, il sait danser.	*Yes, he can dance.*
Savent-ils pourquoi Jean va déménager?	*Do they know why Jean is moving?*
Non, ils ne savent pas pourquoi Jean déménage.	*No, they don't know why Jean is moving.*

Tu sais combien ça coûte?	*Do you know how much it costs?*
Oui, ça coûte cinquante euros.	*Yes, it costs fifty euros.*
Qu'est-ce que tu veux savoir?	*What do you want to know?*
Je veux tout savoir.	*I want to know everything.*
Elle sait faire la cuisine?	*Can she cook?*
Oui, c'est un vrai cordon bleu.	*Yes, she is a real cordon bleu.*
Le directeur va partir?	*Is the director going to leave?*
C'est difficile à savoir.	*It's hard to know.*
Tu veux ce livre-ci ou ce livre-là?	*Do you want this book or that book?*
Je ne sais pas.	*I don't know.*

Written Practice 1

Conjugate the verbs in parentheses.

1. Tu (savoir) chanter?   _____
2. Elle (savoir) où se trouve la Place des Vosges?   _____
3. Nous (savoir) ce poème de Baudelaire.   _____
4. Ils (savoir) qu'elle est en vacances.   _____
5. Je (savoir) pourquoi il est absent.   _____

The Verb *connaître*

Connaître means *to know, to be acquainted with, to be familiar with*. In a figurative way, it means *to enjoy, to experience*. It is always followed by a direct object. It is never followed by a clause.

je connais	*I know*	nous connaissons	*we know*
tu connais	*you know*	vous connaissez	*you know*
il/elle connaît	*he/she knows*	ils/elles connaissent	*they know*

Here are some example sentences:

Connaissez-vous Gaëtan?	*Do you know Gaëtan?*
Ils connaissent tous les musées de Paris.	*They know all the museums in Paris.*
Son film connaît un grand succès.	*His film is enjoying a great success.*

Oral Practice

Ask the following questions and then answer them, aloud.

Connaissez-vous Quentin Lescot?	*Do you know Quentin Lescot?*
Oui, je connais très bien Quentin.	*Yes, I know Quentin very well.*
Tu connais un bon restaurant dans le quartier?	*Do you know a good restaurant in the area?*
Oui, je connais un très bon restaurant vietnamien.	*Yes, I know a very good Vietnamese restaurant.*
Est-ce que Vivien connaît cette librairie?	*Does Vivien know this bookstore?*
Je ne crois pas.	*I don't think so.*
Connaissez-vous un bon traducteur?	*Do you know a good translator?*
Oui, je connais un des meilleurs traducteurs.	*Yes, I know one of the best translators.*
Est-ce qu'il connaît cette nouvelle technologie?	*Does he know this new technology?*
Oui, il connaît cette nouvelle technologie.	*Yes, he knows this new technology.*
Connaissez-vous Fabrice Henri?	*Do you know Fabrice Henri?*
Je le connais de vue.	*I know him by sight.*
Tu connais cette chanson?	*Do you know this song?*
Non, je ne connais pas cette chanson.	*No, I don't know this song.*
Connaissez-vous cet écrivain?	*Do you know this writer?*
Non, je ne connais pas cet écrivain.	*No, I don't know this writer.*

Written Practice 2

Conjugate the verbs in parentheses.

1. Est-ce que vous (connaître) Venise?   _____
2. Tu (connaître) ce poème?   _____
3. Nous (connaître) une excellente brasserie.   _____
4. Elle (connaître) Roland depuis six mois.   _____
5. Ils (connaître) très bien l'art maya.   _____

Written Practice 3

Connaitre or **savoir**?

1. Est-ce que vous _____ où il habite?
2. Je ne _____ pas les enfants de Marie.
3. Ils _____ le cimetière du Père-Lachaise.
4. Nous ne _____ pas pourquoi le magasin est fermé.
5. Tu _____ jouer au basket-ball?

Prefixes

As we saw in the first chapter, there are many cognates that allow students to easily identify words. Another way to identify words and to figure out their meanings is by looking at prefixes. A prefix precedes a word to modify its meaning or its function. Let's look at a few examples.

a-, an-	*without*	apolitique	*apolitical*
ab-	*away from*	s'abstenir	*to refrain*
anti-	*against*	anticonformiste	*nonconformist*
auto-	*self*	autodestruction	*self-destruction*
co-	*with*	colocataire	*co-tenant*
contre-	*against, opposite*	contre-attaquer	*to counterattack*
dé-	*remove*	débrancher	*unplug*
é-	*remove*	écrémer	*to skim*

entre-	*reciprocity*	s'entraider	*to help one another*
ex-	*out*	exporter	*to export*
ex-	*former*	ex-directeur	*ex-director*
hyper-	*excessive, intensive*	hypersensible	*hypersensitive*
in-, im-, il-, ir-	*negative*	inégal	*unequal*
mini-	*small*	minijupe	*miniskirt*
néo-	*new, recent*	néoclassique	*neoclassical*
para-	*against*	parapluie	*umbrella*
poly-	*many*	polyvalent	*polyvalent, multipurpose*
post-	*after*	postcolonial	*postcolonial*
pré-	*before*	préavis	*advance notice*
pro-	*in favor of*	pro-européen	*pro-European*
re-, ré-	*again, back*	réécrire	*rewrite*
sub-, sous-	*under*	sous-alimenté	*undernourished*
sur-	*above*	surabondant	*overabundant*
trans-	*beyond*	transsibérien	*Trans-Siberian*
vi-, vice-	*substitution*	vicomte	*viscount*

THE PREFIX *DÉ*

Let's look at other common examples with the prefix **dé.**

Il bouche la bouteille.	*He puts a cork on the bottle.*
Il débouche la bouteille.	*He uncorks the bottle.*

Oral Practice

Repeat aloud the following sentences and their opposites.

Elle congèle les petits pois.	*She freezes the peas.*
Elle décongèle les petits pois.	*She defrosts the peas,*
Tu cachettes la lettre.	*You seal the letter.*
Tu décachettes la lettre.	*You unseal the letter.*
Ils connectent le réseau.	*They connect the network.*
Ils déconnectent le réseau.	*They disconnect the network.*
Je couds le bouton.	*I sew the button.*

Je découds le bouton.	*I take the button off.*
Nous chargeons la voiture.	*We load the car.*
Nous déchargeons la voiture.	*We unload the car.*
Vous branchez l'ordinateur.	*You plug in the computer.*
Vous débranchez l'ordinateur.	*You unplug the computer.*

THE PREFIX *RE/RÉ*

And now some examples with the prefix **re/ré.**

Tu fais ta valise.	*You pack your suitcase.*
Tu refais ta valise.	*You repack your suitcase.*

Oral Practice

Repeat aloud the following sentences.

Il écrit la lettre.	*He writes the letter.*
Il réécrit la lettre.	*He rewrites the letter.*
Ils découvrent Victor Hugo.	*They discover Victor Hugo.*
Ils redécouvrent Victor Hugo.	*They rediscover Victor Hugo.*
Elle dit la vérité.	*She tells the truth.*
Elle redit la vérité.	*She tells the truth again.*
Tu bouches la bouteille.	*You put a cork on the bottle.*
Tu rebouches la bouteille.	*You put a cork on the bottle again.*
Il compose un morceau de musique.	*He is composing a piece of music.*
Il recompose un morceau de musique.	*He is recomposing a piece of music.*
Vous vendez votre appartement.	*You are selling your apartment.*
Vous revendez votre appartement.	*You are reselling your apartment.*
Il commence son essai.	*He is starting his essay.*
Il recommence son essai.	*He is starting his essay over.*

Elle voit des films au cinéma.	*She sees movies at the theater.*
Elle revoit des films au cinéma.	*She watches movies for the second time at the theater.*

Written Practice 4

Match the items in the two columns.

1. Il débouche la bouteille. _____   a. Il voit encore ce programme.
2. l'ex-président _____   b. Il ouvre encore le récipient.
3. Il réécrit le contrat. _____   c. Il partage la possession.
4. Il revoit ce film. _____   d. Il n'est plus ici.
5. le copropriétaire _____   e. Il refait le document.

Suffixes

A suffix is a small addition to a word or part of a word that modifies its meaning. In English, for instance, *ish* modifies the meaning of an adjective.

-âtre	*pejorative*	rougeâtre	*reddish*
-able	*relative to possibility*	mangeable	*edible*
-cratie	*relative to power*	démocratie	*democracy*
-ette	*diminutive*	casquette	*small cap*
-graphie	*relative to writing*	calligraphie	*calligraphy*
-lingue	*relative to language*	bilingue	*bilingual*
-logie	*relative to science*	sociologie	*sociology*
-mane	*relative to obsession*	cleptomane	*addicted to theft*
-philie	*relative to love*	anglophilie	*anglophilia*
-phobe	*relative to fear*	acrophobe	*acrophobic*
-scope	*relative to vision*	microscope	*microscope*
-thérapie	*relative to treatment*	physiothérapie	*physical therapy*
-thermie	*relative to heat*	hypothermie	*hypothermia*
-vore	*that feeds itself*	herbivore	*herbivorous*

Oral Practice

Repeat aloud the following sentences.

C'est un vrai balletomane.	*He is a real ballet nut.*
Cet insecte est carnivore.	*This insect is carnivorous.*
Marc est claustrophobe.	*Mark is claustrophobic.*
Ces verres sont incassables.	*These glasses are unbreakable.*
Ils habitent dans une maisonnette au bord du lac.	*They live in a small house by the lake.*
Ce sont des vacances inoubliables.	*This is an unforgettable vacation.*
Estelle vient d'acheter un télescope.	*Estelle has just bought a telescope.*
L'aristocratie vivait dans ce palais.	*The aristocracy lived in this palace.*
Cette peinture bleuâtre est très laide.	*This bluish paint is very ugly.*
Il n'est pas mythomane?	*Doesn't he like to embroider the truth?*
Son histoire est incroyable.	*His story is unbelievable.*
La sociologie étudie les faits sociaux.	*Sociology studies social behaviors.*
Sont-ils francophiles?	*Are they francophile?*
Pourquoi est-il cyclophobe?	*Why is he afraid of bicycles?*
Ses fautes sont inexcusables.	*His mistakes are unforgivable.*

Written Practice 5

Match the items in the two columns.

1. Ce plat n'est pas bon.   _____   a. introuvable
2. Il a peur des chats.   _____   b. toxicomane
3. Il prend des drogues.   _____   c. félinophobe
4. Ce café est horrible.   _____   d. immangeable
5. On le recherche toujours.   _____   e. imbuvable

Dans versus *en*

When expressing time, **en** and **dans** are used differently. **Dans** is used for an action about to begin. **En** indicates the length of time an action has taken, takes, or will take. Compare the example sentences to see the differences.

L'avion part **dans** vingt minutes.	*The plane is leaving in twenty minutes.*
Je pars pour Paris **dans** trois jours.	*I am leaving for Paris in three days.*
Claire a préparé le dîner **en** une heure.	*Claire prepared the dinner in an hour.*
Germain peut traduire une page **en** un quart d'heure.	*Germain can translate a page in a quarter of an hour.*
Sylvain va écrire son roman **en** quelques mois.	*Sylvain will write his novel in a few months.*

Oral Practice

Ask the following questions and then answer them, aloud.

Quand est-ce que René part pour New York?	*When is René leaving for New York?*
René part pour New York dans une semaine.	*René is leaving for New York in a week.*
Combien de temps faut-il à Bernard pour lire un tel manuscrit?	*How long does Bernard need to read such a manuscript?*
Bernard peut lire un tel manuscrit en deux jours.	*Bernard can read a manuscript like that in two days.*
Pouvez-vous faire ce travail en moins d'une semaine?	*Can you do this job in less than a week?*
Oui, je peux faire ce travail en moins d'une semaine.	*Yes, I can do this job in less than a week.*
Quand allez-vous vendre votre maison?	*When are you going to sell your house?*
Je vais vendre ma maison dans six mois.	*I am going to sell my house in six months.*

Il peut réparer cet ordinateur en quelques minutes?	*Can he repair this computer in a few minutes?*
Oui, il peut réparer cet ordinateur en quelques minutes.	*Yes, he can repair this computer in a few minutes.*
Quand vas-tu téléphoner à Sara?	*When are you going to call Sara?*
Je vais téléphoner à Sara dans une heure.	*I am going to call Sara in an hour.*

Written Practice 6

Fill in each blank with either **en** or **dans**.

1. Jeanne quitte Lyon _____ une semaine.
2. Mario va arriver en Martinique le jeudi 15, _____ quatre jours.
3. Elle peut courir un marathon _____ moins de quatre heures.
4. Il fait toujours le ménage _____ deux heures.
5. Appelle-moi _____ cinq minutes.

Colors

To make your descriptions more interesting, you'll need adjectives of color.

blanc	*white*	marron	*brown*
bleu	*blue*	noir	*black*
bleu azur	*sky blue*	orange	*orange*
bleu clair	*light blue*	pourpre	*purple*
bleu foncé	*dark blue*	rose	*pink*
bordeaux	*burgundy*	rouge	*red*
gris	*gray*	vert	*green*
jaune	*yellow*	violet	*violet*

When a color is modified by another color or nuance, both adjectives become invariable, for example:

Elle porte une robe **bleu clair**.	*She is wearing a light blue dress.*

Oral Practice

Repeat the following sentences aloud.

Il adore les films en noir et blanc.	*He loves black and white films.*
Cette couleur est trop foncée.	*This color is too dark.*
Le bleu te va bien.	*Blue suits you well.*
Le jaune ne te va pas.	*Yellow does not suit you.*
Le drapeau français est tricolore.	*The French flag is three-colored.*
Il ne porte que des costumes sombres.	*He only wears dark suits.*
Ce vert tendre est parfait pour elle.	*This soft green is perfect for her.*
Elle aime les tissus unis.	*She likes solid fabrics.*
Il préfère les chemises à carreaux.	*He prefers checked shirts.*
Tu portes une jupe à pois?	*Are you wearing a polka-dot skirt?*
Cette veste à rayures est magnifique.	*This striped jacket is beautiful.*
Il veut ces rideaux vert pomme?	*Does he want these apple-green curtains?*
Sa robe est en soie bleu pâle.	*Her dress is made of pale blue silk.*
Ces chaussures marron foncé sont laides.	*These dark brown shoes are ugly.*

Written Practice 7

Match the items in the two columns.

1. la cerise _____ a. tricolore
2. le ciel _____ b. jaune
3. le maïs _____ c. rouge
4. le drapeau français _____ d. blanche
5. la neige _____ e. bleu

QUIZ

Conjugate the following verbs.

savoir (tu)   *tu sais* _____

1. connaître (ils)   _____
   savoir (je)   _____
   savoir (nous)   _____
   connaître (tu)   _____
   connaître (elle)   _____
   savoir (elles)   _____
   savoir (vous)   _____
   connaître (nous)   _____
   savoir (il)   _____
   connaître (vous)   _____

Connaître or **savoir**?

2. Je _____ qu'elle travaille à Londres.
3. Est-ce que tu _____ cet artiste?
4. Je ne _____ pas qui vous êtes.
5. Tu _____ nager?
6. Vous _____ ma tante Irène?

Translate the following sentences, using **vous** when necessary.

7. I don't know why the bank is closed today. _____
8. You must defrost these vegetables. _____

Translate the following sentences using **tu** and the inversion form when necessary.

9. Does she know Jérôme? _____
10. Are you packing? _____

CHAPTER 9

Talking About the Immediate Future and Past

In this chapter you will learn:

The Immediate Future Tense
The Immediate Past Tense
The Verb tenir
Using the Idiom il s'agit de
The Verb faire

The Immediate Future Tense

To talk about what you are going to do, use the verb **aller** in the present indicative followed by a verb in the infinitive. It can replace the present. And in everyday conversation, it is often a substitute for the real future. Let's first review the verb **aller.**

je vais	*I go*	nous allons	*we go*
tu vas	*you go*	vous allez	*you go*
il/elle va	*he/she goes*	ils/elles vont	*they go*

Compare the French and English of these sentences:

Tu dînes avec Patrick ce soir?	*Are you having dinner with Patrick tonight?*
Tu vas dîner avec Patrick ce soir?	*Are you going to have dinner with Patrick tonight?*
Est-ce que vous prenez des vacances?	*Are you taking a vacation?*
Est-ce que vous allez prendre des vacances?	*Are you going to take a vacation?*

In the negative form, the **ne... pas** is placed around the conjugated verb.

Je ne vais pas aller à Paris en automne.	*I am not going to go to Paris in the fall.*
Nous n'allons pas partir tout de suite.	*We are not going to leave right away.*

Oral Practice

Ask the following questions and then answer them, aloud.

Ils vont travailler en Asie?	*Are they going to work in Asia?*
Oui, ils vont travailler en Asie.	*Yes, they are going to work in Asia.*
Allez-vous dîner au restaurant?	*Are you going to have dinner at the restaurant?*
Non, nous allons dîner chez Charlotte.	*No, we are going to have dinner at Charlotte's.*

Vous allez jouer au tennis en plein air?	*Are you going to play tennis outdoors?*
Oui, nous allons jouer au tennis en plein air.	*Yes, we are going to play tennis outdoors.*
Elles vont passer leurs vacances au Tibet?	*Are they going to spend their vacation in Tibet?*
Oui, elles vont passer leurs vacances au Tibet.	*Yes, they are going to spend their vacation in Tibet.*
Tu vas suivre un cours d'histoire de l'art?	*Are you going to take an art history course?*
Oui, je vais suivre un cours d'histoire de l'art.	*Yes, I am going to take an art history course.*
Pourquoi allez-vous rentrer plus tôt que prévu?	*Why are you going to go home earlier than planned?*
Nous allons rentrer plus tôt car nous sommes fatigués.	*We are going to go home earlier because we are tired.*
Combien de livres vas-tu acheter?	*How many books are you going to buy?*
Je vais acheter trois ou quatre livres.	*I am going to buy three or four books.*
Ils vont partir ce soir?	*Are they going to leave tonight?*
Oui, ils vont partir ce soir.	*Yes, they are going to leave tonight.*

Written Practice 1

Change the sentences from the present to the immediate future.

Il chante à l'Olympia ce soir. <u>*Il va chanter à l'Olympia ce soir.*</u>

1. Nous prenons des photos. _____
2. Tu invites tes amis. _____
3. Ils dansent toute la soirée. _____
4. Vous finissez le roman. _____
5. J'achète ce stylo. _____

Oral Practice

Ask the following questions and then answer them, aloud.

Vous allez visiter le musée d'Orsay ce matin?	*Are you going to visit the Orsay museum this morning?*
Non, nous n'allons pas visiter le musée d'Orsay ce matin.	*No, we are not going to visit the Orsay museum this morning.*
Est-ce que tu vas appeler Anne?	*Are you going to call Anne?*
Non, je ne vais pas appeler Anne.	*No, I am not going to call Anne.*
Va-t-elle accepter ce poste?	*Is she going to accept this position?*
Non, elle ne va pas accepter ce poste.	*No, she is not going to accept this position.*
Ils vont déjeuner avec le directeur?	*Are they going to have lunch with the director?*
Non, ils ne vont pas déjeuner avec le directeur.	*No, they are not going to have lunch with the director.*
Est-ce que tu vas regarder ce film?	*Are you going to watch this film?*
Non, je ne vais pas regarder ce film.	*No, I am not going to watch this film.*
Vous allez ouvrir le magasin plus tôt?	*Are you going to open the store earlier?*
Non, nous n'allons pas ouvrir le magasin plus tôt.	*No, we are not going to open the store earlier.*

Written Practice 2

Change these complete sentences from the positive to the negative form.

Nous allons partir à huit heures. <u>Nous n'allons pas partir à huit heures.</u>

1. Elle va choisir le menu. _____
2. Vous allez prendre le train de dix heures. _____
3. Je vais téléphoner à Laurent. _____
4. Ils vont accepter l'offre. _____
5. Tu vas arriver à l'heure. _____

IMPERSONAL EXPRESSIONS

The immediate future is also used with impersonal expressions. See the following examples:

Il va y avoir beaucoup d'invités à la fête.	*There are going to be a lot of guests at the party.*
Il ne va pas y avoir de discours avant le dîner.	*There is not going to be a speech before dinner.*
Il va être impossible de finir avant midi.	*It is going to be impossible to finish before noon.*
Il va pleuvoir cet après-midi.	*It is going to rain this afternoon.*
Il va faire froid au Vermont.	*It is going to be cold in Vermont.*

The Immediate Past Tense

Just as **aller** combined with the infinitive expresses an action that is going to happen, **venir** (*to come*) in the present tense, plus **de,** combined with a verb in the infinitive, expresses an action that has just taken place. Athough **venir** is in the present in French, it conveys an idea in the past in English. Let's first learn the verb **venir.**

je viens	*I come*	nous venons	*we come*
tu viens	*you come*	vous venez	*you come*
il/elle vient	*he/she comes*	ils/elles viennent	*they come*

Here are some example sentences:

Je viens d'arriver à Rouen.	*I just arrived in Rouen.*
Nous venons d'apprendre la nouvelle.	*We just learned the news.*

Oral Practice

Repeat the following sentences aloud.

Nous venons d'appeler Olivier.	*We just called Olivier.*
Il vient de manger.	*He just ate.*
Elles viennent de rentrer.	*They just came home.*
Tu viens de perdre ta chance.	*You just lost your chance.*
Elle vient de signer le contrat.	*She just signed the contract.*
Nous venons de passer des vacances merveilleuses.	*We just spent a wonderful vacation.*
Elle vient de partir.	*She just left.*
Je viens de manquer mon avion.	*I just missed my plane.*
Je viens de remplacer la cartouche d'encre.	*I just replaced the ink cartridge.*
Il vient de remplir le formulaire.	*He just filled in the form.*
Elle vient de commencer un nouveau travail.	*She just started a new job.*

Written Practice 3

Change these sentences from the immediate future to the immediate past.

Je vais acheter ce dictionnaire. <u>*Je viens d'acheter ce dictionnaire.*</u>

1. Nous allons prendre des vacances. _____
2. Elle va répondre à la lettre. _____
3. Ils vont changer de voiture. _____
4. Je vais parler au directeur. _____
5. Il va envoyer une lettre. _____

The Verb *tenir*

Tenir (*to hold*) is an irregular verb conjugated like **venir**. It is used in many idiomatic expressions.

je tiens	*I hold*	nous tenons	*we hold*
tu tiens	*you hold*	vous tenez	*you hold*
il/elle tient	*he/she holds*	ils/elles tiennent	*they hold*

Here are some example sentences:

Elle tient l'enfant par la main.	*She is holding the child's hand.*
Il ne tient jamais ses promesses.	*He never keeps his promises.*
Le café le tient éveillé.	*Coffee keeps him awake.*
Ils tiennent une auberge en Normandie.	*They run an inn in Normandy.*
Il tient compte de mon avis.	*He takes my opinion into account.*
Toutes ces boîtes ne tiendront pas dans la voiture.	*All these boxes won't fit in the car.*
Il tient à sa moto.	*He is attached to his motorcycle.*
Elle tient à ses amis.	*She is attached to her friends.*
Le patron tient à vous parler.	*The boss insists on talking to you.*
Je tiens à vous rencontrer.	*I am very eager to meet you.*
Le bébé tient de son père.	*The baby looks like his father.*
De qui tient-il?	*Whom does he take after?*
Tiens, tiens, c'est étrange...	*Well, well, this is strange . . .*
Tiens, prends ces trois livres.	*Here, take these three books.*

Written Practice 4

Match the items in the two columns.

1. Il ment. _____
2. Elle est attachée à ses bijoux. _____

a. Elle tient à ces objets précieux.

b. Il ne tient pas compte de ce que vous pensez.

3. Il ressemble à sa grand-mère. _____   c. Elle tient à avoir une discussion.

4. Elle désire vous parler. _____   d. Il ne tient pas ses promesses.

5. Il ignore vos sentiments. _____   e. Il tient d'elle.

Using the Idiom *il s'agit de*

French is full of idioms. **Il s'agit de** (*it is a matter of, it is about*) is another one. See the examples:

De quoi s'agit-il?	*What is it about?*
Il s'agit de garder notre avance.	*It is a matter of maintaining our lead.*
Il ne s'agit pas d'argent.	*It is not a question of money.*
Il s'agit d'amour.	*It is a question of love.*
Il s'agit de vengeance.	*It is about revenge.*
Dans ce roman, il s'agit d'une jeune femme aveugle.	*This novel is about a young blind woman.*
Dans cette nouvelle, il s'agit d'un orphelin.	*This short story is about an orphan.*
Dans ce film, il s'agit de la Grande Guerre.	*This film is about World War I.*

The Verb *faire*

The verb **faire** (*to do, to make*) is one of the key verbs in French. You will find it in many idiomatic expressions. Let's first take a look at its conjugation, which is irregular.

je fais	*I do*	nous faisons	*we do*
tu fais	*you do*	vous faites	*you do*
il/elle fait	*he/she does*	ils/elles font	*they do*

Here are some example sentences:

Qu'est-ce que tu fais?	*What are you doing?*
Je n'ai rien à faire.	*I have nothing to do.*

Faire is used in most expressions relating to the weather.

Quel temps fait-il?	*What's the weather like?*
Il fait frais.	*It is cool.*

Il fait beau.	*It is nice.*	Il fait froid.	*It is cold.*
Il fait chaud.	*It is hot.*	Il fait du soleil.	*It is sunny.*
Il fait doux.	*It is mild.*	Il fait du vent.	*It is windy.*

There are some exceptions:

Il grêle.	*It is hailing.*
Il neige.	*It is snowing.*
Il pleut.	*It is raining.*

Faire is also used in expressions relating to chores, activities, sports, etc.

Il fait la cuisine.	*He is cooking.*
Elle fait la vaisselle.	*She is doing the dishes.*
Je fais une promenade.	*I am taking a walk.*
Nous faisons du tennis.	*We are playing tennis.*

Oral Practice

Ask the following questions, then answer them, aloud.

Est-ce qu'il fait de l'exercice?	*Does he exercise?*
Oui, il fait beaucoup d'exercice.	*Yes, he exercises a lot.*
Depuis combien de temps fais-tu la queue?	*How long have you been standing in line?*

Je fais la queue depuis une demi-heure.	*I have been standing in line for half an hour.*
En général, où fait-il les courses?	*Where does he generally go shopping?*
En général, il fait les courses dans les grands magasins.	*He generally shops in the department stores.*
Tu fais le ménage le samedi?	*Do you clean the house on Saturdays?*
Non, je fais le ménage le dimanche.	*No, I clean the house on Sundays.*
Vous faites une randonnée cet après-midi?	*Are you taking a hike this afternoon?*
Oui, nous faisons une randonnée cet après-midi.	*Yes, we are taking a hike this afternoon.*
Elle fait la grasse matinée le dimanche?	*Does she sleep late on Sundays?*
Oui, elle fait la grasse matinée le dimanche.	*Yes, she sleeps late on Sundays.*
Que fait-elle ces jours-ci?	*What is she doing these days?*
Elle fait un voyage autour du monde.	*She is on a trip around the world.*
Qu'est-ce que vous faites dans la vie?	*What do you do for a living?*
Je suis musicien.	*I am a musician.*

Written Practice 5

Match the items in the two columns.

1. Il aime préparer à manger.	_____	a. faire un voyage
2. Elle aime dormir l'après-midi.	_____	b. faire une randonnée
3. Ils aiment marcher à la montagne.	_____	c. faire les courses
4. Tu aimes explorer des pays.	_____	d. faire la cuisine
5. Vous aimez acheter des choses.	_____	e. faire la sieste

USING *FAIRE* + *INFINITIVE*

The verb **faire** is often followed by an infinitive to express the idea of having something done by someone or of causing something to happen (this is called the *causative form*). Compare these examples:

Il répare l'objet cassé lui-même.	*He repairs the broken object himself.*
Il fait réparer l'objet par un expert.	*He has the broken object repaired by an expert.*
Nous lavons la voiture.	*We wash the car.*
Nous faisons laver la voiture.	*We have the car washed.*
Elle fait une robe pour sa fille.	*She is making a dress for her daughter.*
Elle fait faire une robe pour sa fille.	*She is having a dress made for her daughter.*

Oral Practice

Ask the following questions and then answer them, aloud.

Dessinez-vous les vêtements vous-même?	*Do you draw the clothes yourself?*
Non, je fais dessiner les vêtements par mon associé.	*No, I have the clothes drawn by my assistant.*
Est-ce qu'elle fait la cuisine elle-même?	*Does she do her own cooking?*
Non, elle fait faire la cuisine par son mari.	*No, she has her husband cook for her.*
Tu arroses le jardin toi-même?	*Do you water the garden yourself?*
Non, je le fais arroser par le jardinier.	*No, I have the garden watered by the gardener.*
Elle décore son appartement elle-même?	*Does she decorate her apartment herself?*
Non, elle fait décorer son appartement par un ami.	*No, she has a friend decorate her apartment.*

Est-ce que tu peins les chambres toi-même?	*Are you painting the bedrooms yourself?*
Non, je fais peindre les chambres par René.	*No, I'm having René paint the bedrooms.*

Written Practice 6

Change these sentences to the causative **faire** form.

Je lave ma voiture. *Je fais laver ma voiture.* _____

1. Tu écris l'article. _____
2. Elle fait le ménage. _____
3. Il répare la télévision. _____
4. Vous envoyez le paquet. _____
5. Elles préparent le dîner. _____

MORE EXAMPLES OF USING *FAIRE* + *INFINITIVE*

Here some more examples of **faire** + infinitive as expressing the idea of causing something to happen, in idiomatic expressions that you will want to memorize.

Elle fait bouillir de l'eau.	*She is boiling some water.*
Il fait cuire le gigot d'agneau.	*He is cooking the leg of lamb.*
Le cuisinier fait fondre le beurre.	*The cook is melting the butter.*
Fais mijoter la viande pendant une heure.	*Let the meat simmer for an hour.*
Elle fait frire le poisson.	*She is frying the fish.*
Ses commentaires font réfléchir son adversaire.	*His comments cause his opponent to think.*
Le propriétaire nous fait visiter l'usine.	*The owner shows us around the factory.*
Ils font pousser des tournesols.	*They grow sunflowers.*
Faites entrer Madame Hanska.	*Let Madame Hanska in.*

Cet enfant fait tout tomber. *That child drops everything.*

Nous allons faire venir le médecin. *We are going to send for the doctor.*

Il m'a fait voir son nouveau tableau. *He showed me his new painting.*

QUIZ

Put the following verbs into the immediate future using complete sentences.

Il chante. <u>*Il va chanter.*</u>

1. Elles parlent. _____
   Il danse. _____
   Nous partons. _____
   Vous regardez. _____
   Elle commence. _____

Change these sentences from the affirmative to the negative form.

Je vais acheter cette lampe. <u>*Je ne vais pas acheter cette lampe.*</u>

2. Vous allez envoyer ce document. _____
   Tu vas finir la nouvelle. _____
   Je vais appeler Julie. _____
   Nous allons déménager vendredi. _____
   Elle va sortir ce soir. _____

Change the verbs in these sentences from the immediate future to the immediate past.

Il va partir. <u>*Il vient de partir.*</u>

3. Je vais remplir le réservoir. _____
   Elles vont passer des vacances en Finlande. _____

Elle va répondre à la lettre. _____

Nous allons faire les courses. _____

Il va prendre une décision. _____

Answer the following questions using complete sentences.

Depuis combien de temps faites-vous du ski? (dix ans)

Je fais du ski depuis dix ans. _____

4. Depuis combien de temps fait-il du yoga? (six mois)

_____

Depuis combien de temps fait-elle les courses dans ce magasin? (un an)

_____

Depuis combien de temps font-ils des randonnées? (vingt ans)

_____

Depuis combien de temps fait-il beau dans la région? (deux jours)

_____

Depuis combien de temps fait-il froid sur la Côte d'Azur? (une semaine)

_____

Change the following sentences to the causative **faire** form.

Il nettoie la salle. *Il fait nettoyer la salle.* _____

5. Tu envoies des fleurs. _____

Elle arrose les plantes. _____

Nous écrivons la lettre. _____

Vous préparez les documents. _____

Je fais un gâteau au chocolat. _____

Translate the following sentences, using inversion and the **vous** form when necessary.

6. Are you going to invite Grégoire? _____

7. She has her car washed every week. _____

8. He is boiling some water. _____

9. Is she cooking tonight? _____

10. He just moved. _____

CHAPTER 10

Using Pronominal Verbs

In this chapter you will learn:

The Different Types of Pronominal Verbs
Pronominal Verbs in the Imperative Form
Pronominal Verbs in the Infinitive
Parts of the Body
Disjunctive Pronouns
Intonation in French
The Conjunction donc

The Different Types of Pronominal Verbs

Verbs that are preceded by the pronouns **me, te, se, nous, vous,** and **se** are called *pronominal verbs.* There are four kinds of pronominal verbs: the reflexive, the reciprocal, the subjective, and the passive. Let's start with the reflexive verbs.

REFLEXIVE VERBS

The action of a reflexive verb is, for the most part, reflected back on the subject, the action being done to oneself. The pronouns **me, te,** and **se** drop the **e** before **h** or a vowel.

je m'habille	*dress myself*	nous nous habillons	*we dress ourselves*
tu t'habilles	*you dress yourself*	vous vous habillez	*you dress yourselves*
il/elle s'habille	*he/she dresses him/herself*	ils s'habillent	*they dress themselves*

Here are some examples:

Elle s'habille puis elle prépare le petit déjeuner.

She gets dressed, then she prepares breakfast.

Il se lève à sept heures.

He gets up at seven.

In the negative form, the reflexive pronoun is placed between the **ne** and the verb. For example:

Il ne se lève pas très tôt le dimanche.

He does not get up very early on Sundays.

Nous ne nous couchons pas avant minuit.

We do not go to bed until midnight.

In the interrogative form, there are three ways of asking questions. Here are the first two ways:

Vous vous couchez tôt?

Do you go to bed early?

Est-ce que vous vous couchez tôt?

Do you go to bed early?

When using inversion, the third way of asking a question, the reflexive pronoun remains in front of the verb.

Vous couchez-vous tôt?	*Do you go to bed early?*
Se prépare-t-il rapidement?	*Does he get ready fast?*
Te reposes-tu le samedi?	*Do you rest on Saturdays?*

Oral Practice

Ask the questions and then answer them, aloud.

À quelle heure vous réveillez-vous le matin?	*What time do you wake up in the morning?*
Je me réveille à l'aube.	*I wake up at dawn.*
Est-ce que tu te lèves avant Paul?	*Do you get up before Paul?*
Oui, je me lève avant Paul.	*Yes, I get up before Paul.*
Comment s'appelle ta sœur?	*What is your sister's name?*
Ma sœur s'appelle Mathilde.	*My sister's name is Mathilde.*
Est-ce que vous vous reposez le week-end?	*Do you rest on weekends?*
Oui, nous nous reposons le week-end.	*Yes, we rest on weekends.*
Est-ce qu'elle se promène dans le parc avec ses enfants?	*Does she take walks in the park with her children?*
Oui, elle se promène dans le parc avec ses enfants.	*Yes, she takes walks in the park with her children.*
Est-ce qu'il s'assoit au premier rang?	*Is he sitting in the first row?*
Oui, il s'assoit toujours au premier rang.	*Yes, he always sits in the first row.*
Est-ce que tu t'inquiètes pour l'avenir?	*Are you worried about the future?*
Non, je ne m'inquiète pas pour l'avenir.	*No, I am not worried about the future.*
Se rase-t-il tous les matins?	*Does he shave every morning?*
Oui, il se rase tous les matins.	*Yes, he shaves every morning.*
Elle s'occupe de cette affaire?	*Is she in charge of this business?*

Oui, elle s'occupe de cette affaire.	*Yes, she is in charge of this business.*
Est-ce qu'il va se changer pour la soirée?	*Is he going to change for the party?*
Oui, il va se changer pour la soirée.	*Yes, he is going to change for the party.*
Vous vous amusez en vacances?	*Do you enjoy yourselves on vacation?*
Oui, nous nous amusons en vacances.	*Yes, we enjoy ourselves on vacation.*
Est-ce qu'elle se soigne bien quand elle est malade?	*Does she take good care of herself when she is sick?*
Oui, elle se soigne bien.	*Yes, she takes good care of herself.*
Tu te brosses les dents avant de te coucher?	*Do you brush your teeth before going to bed?*
Oui, je me brosse les dents avant de me coucher.	*Yes, I brush my teeth before going to bed.*

Written Practice 1

Conjugate the verbs in parentheses.

Il (se laver) les cheveux. _Il se lave les cheveux._ _____

1. Elles (se réveiller) à huit heures. _____
2. Nous (se reposer) le dimanche. _____
3. Tu (s'habiller) pour la fête. _____
4. Il (s'appeler) Fabio. _____
5. Vous (s'amuser) à la soirée. _____

RECIPROCAL VERBS

The second type of pronominal verb is called reciprocal. The subjects of the reciprocal verb act on one another. For example:

Elles s'écrivent régulièrement.	*They write to each other on a regular basis.*
Nous nous voyons chaque jeudi.	*We see each other every Thursday.*

Ils se détestent.	*They hate each other.*
On se rappelle demain.	*We'll call each other back tomorrow.*

Oral Practice

Ask the following questions and then answer them, aloud.

Vous parlez-vous souvent?	*Do you often talk to each other?*
Nous nous parlons chaque semaine.	*We talk to each other every week.*
Est-ce qu'ils s'aiment toujours?	*Do they still love each other?*
Oui, ils s'aiment toujours.	*Yes, they still love each other.*
On se retrouve devant le cinéma?	*Shall we meet in front of the theater?*
D'accord, on se retrouve devant le cinéma.	*OK, let's meet in front of the theater.*
Vous vous disputez souvent?	*Do you often argue?*
Oui, nous nous disputons souvent.	*Yes, we often argue.*
On se rappelle demain?	*Shall we call each other back tomorrow?*
Oui, on se rappelle demain.	*Yes, let's call each other back tomorrow.*
Ils se marient cet été?	*Are they getting married this summer?*
Oui, ils se marient en juillet.	*Yes, they are getting married in July.*
Allez-vous vous réconcilier?	*Are you going to reconcile?*
Oui, nous allons nous réconcilier.	*Yes, we are going to reconcile.*

Written Practice 2

Match the items in the two columns.

1. Ils sont amoureux.   _____   a. Ils s'écrivent.
2. Ils font la paix.   _____   b. Ils se téléphonent.
3. Ils sont ennemis.   _____   c. Ils s'aiment.
4. Ils échangent des lettres. _____   d. Ils se réconcilient.
5. Ils parlent ensemble.   _____   e. Ils se détestent.

SUBJECTIVE VERBS

The third type of pronominal verb is called subjective. These verbs are neither reflexive nor reciprocal, they just happen to use the pronominal form. They are very common verbs you will need to memorize. For example:

Il s'aperçoit de son erreur.	*He realizes his mistake.*
Elle se dépêche pour arriver à l'heure.	*She is hurrying up to arrive on time.*
Il s'enfuit parce qu'il a peur.	*He is running away because he is afraid.*
Nous nous rendons compte des répercussions.	*We realize the repercussions.*

Oral Practice

Ask the following questions and then answer them, aloud.

Est-ce qu'il s'aperçoit de ses erreurs?	*Does he realize his mistakes?*
Non, il ne s'aperçoit jamais de ses erreurs.	*No, he never realizes his mistakes.*
Est-ce qu'elle s'en va cet après-midi?	*Is she leaving this afternoon?*
Non, elle s'en va ce soir.	*No, she is leaving tonight.*
Est-ce que tu prends ton temps?	*Are you taking your time?*
Non, je me dépêche!	*No, I am hurrying up!*
Tu te souviens de la date de son anniversaire?	*Do you remember the date of her birthday?*
Non, je ne me souviens pas de la date de son anniversaire.	*No, I don't remember the date of her birthday.*
Pourquoi est-ce que tu te méfies de Jean?	*Why don't you trust Jean?*
Je me méfie de Jean car il est irresponsable.	*I do not trust Jean because he is irresponsible.*
De quoi se plaint-elle?	*What is she complaining about?*
Elle se plaint de tout.	*She complains about everything.*

Written Practice 3

Match the items in the two columns.

1. Pourquoi est-ce qu'elle se dépêche?   _____   a. Elle a peur.
2. Pourquoi est-ce qu'elle s'enfuit?   _____   b. Elle est timide.
3. Pourquoi la maison va-t-elle s'écrouler?   _____   c. Elle n'est pas honnête.
4. Pourquoi se méfie-t-on de Claire?   _____   d. Elle est vieille.
5. Pourquoi est-ce qu'elle se tait?   _____   e. Elle est en retard.

PASSIVE VERBS

The fourth type of pronominal verb is called passive. With the passive pronominal verbs, the subject is not a person or an animal and does not perform the action of the verb but is subjected to it. For example:

Ça ne se fait pas.	*That is just not done.*
Ça ne se dit pas.	*That is not said (you shouldn't say that).*
Les frites se mangent avec les doigts.	*French fries are eaten with your fingers.*
Le vin rouge se boit chambré.	*Red wine is drunk at room temperature.*
Le vin blanc se boit frais.	*White wine is drunk chilled.*
Ces ordinateurs se vendent à la Fnac.	*These computers are sold at Fnac's.*

VERBS THAT ARE REFLEXIVE AND NONREFLEXIVE

Note that, as in English, some verbs can be used both reflexively and nonreflexively. Here are a few examples.

Elle embrasse son fils.	*She gives her son a kiss.*
Ils s'embrassent.	*They are kissing each other.*
Ils aiment les animaux.	*They love animals.*
Ils s'aiment depuis longtemps.	*They have been in love for a long time.*
Nous changeons de chaussures.	*We change shoes.*
Nous nous changeons pour la cérémonie.	*We are changing our clothes for the ceremony.*

La costumière habille l'acteur.	*The wardrobe mistress dresses the actor.*
Le chanteur s'habille pour le concert.	*The singer is getting dressed for the concert.*
Charles lave sa voiture.	*Charles washes his car.*
Martial se lave les cheveux.	*Martial washes his hair.*
Julien sert ses invités.	*Julien serves his guests.*
Julien se sert.	*Julien helps himself.*
Il passe ses vacances en Grèce.	*He spends his vacation in Greece.*
Il se passe de pain.	*He does without bread.*
Elle met une robe bleu azur.	*She puts on a sky-blue dress.*
Elle se met au régime.	*She is going on a diet.*
Lucie attend le train.	*Lucie is waiting for the train.*
Cyrille s'attend à la visite de Lucie.	*Cyrille is expecting Lucie's visit.*

Pronominal Verbs in the Imperative Form

Let's see now how we can put all these pronominal verbs into the imperative form. For the affirmative imperative, use the stressed pronoun **toi, nous,** or **vous** after the verb, connected to the verb with a hyphen.

Lève-toi!	*Get up!*
Baladons-nous dans le parc!	*Let's take a walk in the park!*
Dépêchez-vous!	*Hurry up!*

For the negative imperative of pronominal verbs, use **ne** in front of the pronoun and **pas** after the verb.

Ne te lève pas si tôt!	*Don't get up so early!*
Ne nous réveillons pas avant six heures.	*Let's not wake up before six o'clock.*
Ne vous attendez pas à des miracles!	*Do not expect miracles!*

Pronominal Verbs in the Infinitive

When pronominal verbs are used in the infinitive, the reflexive pronoun is always in the same person and number as the subject, and it precedes the infinitive.

Je vais me promener cet après-midi.	*I am going to take a walk this afternoon.*
Elle va se coucher tard ce soir.	*She is going to go to bed late tonight.*
Ils ont l'intention de se débrouiller tous seuls.	*They intend to manage on their own.*
Tu aimes t'habiller de façon décontractée.	*You like to dress casually.*
Il vient de s'endormir.	*He just fell asleep.*
Nous n'aimons pas nous dire au revoir.	*We do not like to say good-bye.*
Tu n'as pas besoin de te dépêcher.	*You do not need to hurry.*

Parts of the Body

When talking about parts of the body, in most cases, French uses a pronominal verb and the body part takes a definite article, where English uses a nonpronominal verb and a possessive adjective for the body part.

la tête	*head*	les cheveux (*m.*)	*hair*
le crâne	*skull*	la peau	*skin*
le visage	*face*	le front	*forehead*
l'œil (*m.*)	*eye*	les yeux	*eyes*
le sourcil	*eyebrow*	le cil	*eyelash*
le nez	*nose*	la joue	*cheek*
la bouche	*mouth*	les lèvres (*f.*)	*lips*
le menton	*chin*	l'oreille (*f.*)	*ear*
le cou	*neck*	l'épaule (*f.*)	*shoulder*
la gorge	*throat*	la poitrine	*chest/breast*
le torse	*torso*	le dos	*back*
le bras	*arm*	le coude	*elbow*
le poignet	*wrist*	la main	*hand*
le doigt	*finger*	l'ongle (*m.*)	*nail*

la hanche	hip	la taille	waist
la jambe	leg	la cuisse	thigh
le genou	knee	la cheville	ankle
le pied	foot	l'orteil (m.)	toe

Here are some examples:

Je me lave les cheveux.	I wash my hair.
Elle se maquille les yeux.	She puts on eye makeup.
Elle se fait les ongles.	She polishes her nails.
Il se creuse la tête.	He is racking his brains.
Tu te racles la gorge.	You are clearing your throat.
Ne te foule pas la cheville sur le sable!	Don't sprain your ankle in the sand!
Ne te casse pas la jambe dans les Alpes!	Don't break your leg in the Alps!

Disjunctive Pronouns

There are many ways to use disjunctive pronouns, also known as stressed or tonic pronouns. First, let's review the pronouns:

moi	me	nous	us
toi	you	vous	you
lui	him	eux	them
elle	her	elles	them (f.)

THE DISJUNCTIVE PRONOUNS FOR EMPHASIS

The disjunctive pronouns can be used to add extra emphasis to a thought. For example:

Moi, je trouve ce tableau horrible.	Personally, I think this painting is awful.
Toi, tu te plains tout le temps!	You are always complaining!

Lui, il se trompe toujours!	*He is always mistaken!*

THE DISJUNCTIVE PRONOUNS FOR OPINION

The disjunctive pronouns can also be used to solicit an opinion:

Moi, je suis pour! Et toi, qu'est-ce que tu en penses?	*I am all for it. And you, what do you think?*
Eux, ils ne s'ennuient jamais! Et toi?	*They never get bored. What about you?*

THE DISJUNCTIVE PRONOUNS AFTER MOST PREPOSITIONS

You'll often find a disjunctive prounoun used after a preposition. For example:

Il travaille pour eux.	*He is working for them.*
Vous dînez chez elle?	*Are you having dinner at her house?*
Il ne voyage jamais sans moi.	*He never travels without me.*

THE DISJUNCTIVE PRONOUNS AS ONE-WORD RESPONSES

Disjunctive pronouns are also used as one-word questions or answers when there isn't a verb present. See the following examples:

—Qui a faim? —Moi!	*"Who is hungry?" "I am!"*
—Qui est contre la proposition? —Eux!	*"Who is against the proposal?" "They are!"*
—J'aime le thé. —Moi aussi.	*"I like tea." "So do I."*
—Je n'aime pas le café. —Moi non plus.	*"I do not like coffee." "Neither do I."*

THE DISJUNCTIVE PRONOUNS WITH ANOTHER SUBJECT

You'll find disjunctive pronouns as clarification, in conjunction with another subject, as illustrated here:

Elle et ses frères, ils s'entendent parfaitement.	*She and her brothers get along perfectly.*
Roland et moi, nous allons monter une nouvelle entreprise.	*Roland and I are going to start a new business.*

THE DISJUNCTIVE PRONOUNS FOR POSSESSION

Disjunctive pronouns are also used to indicate possession. For example:

—À qui est cet iPod? —C'est à moi.	*"Whose iPod is this?" " It's mine."*
Cette montre n'est pas à moi.	*This watch is not mine.*

THE DISJUNCTIVE PRONOUNS TO STRESS IDENTIFICATION

You'll find disjunctive pronouns used after **c'est/ce sont** in order to stress identification. Disjunctive pronouns are used in French whereas English uses intonation.

C'est lui qui s'occupe de cette affaire.	*He is in charge of this business.*
C'est vous qui allez vous réveiller à l'aube.	*You are going to wake up at dawn.*
Ce ne sont pas eux qui sont coupables.	*They are not guilty.*

THE DISJUNCTIVE PRONOUNS IN COMPARISONS

You can use disjunctive pronouns to make comparisons. For example:

Sabine est plus compétente que lui.	*Sabine is more competent than he is.*
Alice est moins rapide que toi.	*Alice is not as fast as you are.*
Jérôme est aussi efficace qu'eux.	*Jérôme is as competent as they are.*

THE DISJUNCTIVE PRONOUNS REINFORCED BY *MÊME*

You can use disjunctive pronouns with **même** *(self)* to reinforce the pronoun.

Je vais écrire la lettre moi-même.	*I am going to write the letter myself.*
Fais-le toi-même!	*Do it yourself!*
Vous faites vos vêtements vous-même?	*You make your clothes yourself?*

THE DISJUNCTIVE PRONOUNS TO EXPRESS *ONLY* OR *NEITHER*

You will also find the disjunctive pronouns used with **ne... que** *(only)* and **ni... ni** *(neither . . . nor)*. For example:

Il n'admire que toi.	*He only admires you.*
Vous ne respectez ni elle ni lui.	*You respect neither her nor him.*

Oral Practice

Ask the following questions and then answer them, aloud.

Tu es d'accord avec moi?	*Do you agree with me?*
Non, je suis d'accord avec lui.	*No, I agree with him.*
Tu pars en vacances avec elle?	*Are you going on vacation with her?*
Non, je pars en vacances avec vous!	*No, I am going on vacation with you!*
Qu'est-ce que tu préfères, toi?	*What do you prefer?*

Moi, je m'en fiche!	*Personally, I don't care!*
Tu penses qu'elle est plus intelligente que lui?	*Do you think she is smarter than he is?*
Je suis sûre qu'elle est plus intelligente que lui.	*I am sure she is smarter than he is.*
À qui sont ces lunettes de soleil?	*Whose sunglasses are these?*
Elles sont à moi.	*They are mine.*
À qui est ce carnet d'adresses?	*Whose address book is his?*
C'est à lui.	*It's his.*
Vous allez chez eux ce soir?	*Are you going to their place tonight?*
Oui, nous passons la soirée chez eux.	*Yes, we are spending the evening at their place.*
Tu veux jouer avec elle?	*Do you want to play with her?*
Non, je préfère jouer avec toi.	*No, I prefer to play with you.*
Est-ce qu'il travaille toujours pour eux?	*Is he still working for them?*
Non, il travaille pour lui-même.	*No, he is working for himself.*
Selon toi, est-ce qu'il y a encore des problèmes?	*According to you, are there still some problems?*
Selon moi, il n'y a plus de problème.	*According to me, there is no more problem.*

Written Practice 4

Replace the names in parentheses with a disjunctive pronoun.

Elle voyage avec (Pierre). <u>lui</u>

1. Il va faire le tour du monde avec (Benjamin). _____
2. Ce soir, tu dînes avec (Marine)? _____
3. Elle espère travailler avec (Corinne et Gérard). _____
4. Vous déjeunez avec (Léa et Estelle)? _____
5. Il joue au tennis avec (Alain). _____

Written Practice 5

Following the model, replace the subject pronouns in parentheses with a disjunctive pronoun.

      À qui est cette valise? (il)   *C'est à lui.*

1. À qui est ce livre? (je)   _____
2. À qui est ce téléphone cellulaire? (elle)   _____
3. À qui est cette voiture? (nous)   _____
4. À qui est ce dossier? (tu)   _____
5. À qui est ce chien? (ils)   _____

Intonation in French

With the disjunctive pronouns, you have seen that French uses different ways to stress a point. Basically, if you put the French language through an electrocardiogram, you would get small hills whereas English would come out as sharp peaks. This difference in intonation is obvious when you listen to a romantic French song and an American rock 'n' roll hit. Compare these sentences:

Il nous accompagne à l'aéroport.   *He takes us to the airport.*

C'est lui qui nous accompagne   *He takes us to the airport.*
    à l'aéroport.

C'est lui qui is used here as emphasis, meaning it's not someone else who's taking us, it is he.

The Conjunction *donc*

The conjunction **donc** can also be used in many different ways.

DONC FOR STRESS

Donc can be used to stress an interrogation or an exclamation.

Écoute-moi donc!	*Do listen to me!*
Téléphone-lui donc!	*Just call him!*
Pourquoi donc veut-il démissionner!	*Why in the world does he want to resign?*
Allons donc!	*Come on!*
Tais-toi donc!	*Do be quiet!*

DONC TO SHOW SURPRISE

Donc is also used to indicate surprise. For example:

C'était donc un espion?	*So he was a spy?*
Ce n'était donc qu'un mensonge?	*So it was just a lie?*

DONC TO SHOW A CONSEQUENCE

You'll also find **donc** used to show a consequence of an action:

Ils sont d'accord donc tout va bien.	*They agree, so all is well.*
Elle étudie donc elle réussit à tous ses examens.	*She studies, so she passes all her exams.*

QUIZ

Conjugate the following pronominal verbs in the present tense.

(se laver) (nous) *nous nous lavons*

1. (se plaindre) (tu) _____
   (se dépêcher) (vous) _____
   (s'écrire) (ils) _____
   (se souvenir) (je) _____
   (se disputer) (nous) _____

2. Match the pronominal verbs of opposite meaning from each column.

   _____ se coucher   a. s'endormir
   _____ s'habiller   b. se détester
   _____ s'aimer   c. s'ennuyer
   _____ s'amuser   d. se déshabiller
   _____ se réveiller   e. se lever

Answer the following questions following the model.

Pourquoi vous couchez-vous tard ce soir? (avoir un examen demain)
Je me couche tard ce soir car j'ai un examen demain.

3. Pourquoi s'assoit-il dans le fauteuil? (être fatigué)

_____

Pourquoi s'habillent-ils si élégamment? (aller à une soirée)

_____

Pourquoi te lèves-tu si tôt? (avoir une réunion à huit heures)

_____

Pourquoi se lève-t-elle tard le dimanche? (aimer faire la grasse matinée)

_____

Pourquoi vous reposez-vous cet après-midi? (chanter à l'opéra ce soir)

_____

Replace the subject pronoun in parentheses with the disjunctive pronoun.

Elle voyage avec (tu). _Elle voyage avec toi._____

4. Nous allons au cinéma avec (ils). _____

Elle travaille avec (il) depuis longtemps. _____

Ils montent cette affaire avec (tu)? _____

Je préfère travailler chez (je). _____

C'est (il) qui va vous faire visiter l'usine. _____

Translate the following sentences, using **tu** and the **est-ce que** form.

5. "I like coffee." "So do I." _____

6. She is getting dressed for the carnival. _____

7. He is brushing his teeth. _____

8. What time do you get up? _____

9. According to him, there are still many problems. _____

10. He does not agree with me. _____

PART TWO TEST

Answer the questions, using the informal way of telling time.

1. À quelle heure se termine le cours de français? (10:50 P.M.)

   _____

2. À quelle heure dînez-vous ce soir? (7:30 P.M.)

   _____

3. À quelle heure arrive son train? (5:45 P.M.)

   _____

4. À quelle heure ferme ce restaurant? (12 A.M.)

   _____

5. À quelle heure commence la surprise-party? (10 P.M.)

   _____

Answer the questions according to the model.

   Allez-vous à Paris la semaine prochaine? (demain)
   Je vais à Paris demain.

6. Vous allez souvent au cinéma? (jamais)

   _____

7. En général, Édouard arrive tôt? (tard)

   _____

8. Maud téléphone souvent à sa tante? (rarement)

   _____

9. Allez-vous souvent au jardin botanique? (de temps en temps)

   _____

10. Ton anniversaire, c'est demain? (aujourd'hui)

_____

Answer the following questions, using **depuis**.

Depuis combien de temps habitez-vous à Nantes? (six mois)
J'habite à Nantes depuis six mois.

11. Depuis combien de temps est-ce que tu attends une réponse? (dix jours)

_____

12. Depuis combien de temps étudiez-vous la calligraphie? (trois mois)

_____

13. Depuis combien de temps cherchez-vous un bureau? (un mois)

_____

14. Depuis quand avez-vous des animaux domestiques? (mon enfance)

_____

15. Depuis combien de temps est-ce qu'elle travaille à Dijon? (quatre ans)

_____

Complete the sentences following the model.

Maria/Tokyo/Japon *Maria habite à Tokyo, au Japon.*

16. Karim/Le Caire/Égypte _____
17. Anne/Dakar/Sénégal _____
18. Marie/Istanbul/Turquie _____
19. Marc/Hanoi/Vietnam _____
20. Lorraine/Port-au-Prince/Haïti _____

Match the following capitals and countries, then write a full sentence.

Paris/France _Paris est en France._

_____ Rabat a. Côte-d'Ivoire

_____ Le Caire b. Chili

_____ Oulan-Bator c. Égypte

_____ Abidjan d. Maroc

_____ Santiago e. Mongolie

21. Rabat _____ .

22. Le Caire _____ .

23. Oulan-Bator _____ .

24. Abidjan _____ .

25. Santiago _____ .

Fill in the blank spaces with the appropriate country.

La Tour Eiffel est en _France_____ .

26. La Place Rouge est en _____ .

27. Le palais du Potola est au _____ .

28. L'Alhambra est en _____ .

29. Les pyramides sont en _____ .

30. L'Acropole est en _____ .

Savoir or **connaître**?

31. Il _____ cette chanson?

32. Vous _____ combien ça coûte?

33. Il ne _____ pas pourquoi elle est absente ce matin.

34. Est-ce que tu _____ Paris?

35. Est-ce qu'il _____ parler japonais?

Put the following verbs into the immediate future.

36. ils prennent   _____
37. nous choisissons   _____
38. il achète   _____
39. vous finissez   _____
40. elles restent   _____

Replace the subject pronoun in parentheses with the disjunctive pronoun.

Il va voyager avec _toi_? (tu)

41. _____, je suis totalement opposé à cette décision. (je)
42. Tu joues au squash avec _____? (ils)
43. C'est _____ qui as de la chance. (tu)
44. Viens au concert avec _____! (nous)
45. Selon _____, tout va bien. (ils)

Translate the following sentences, using **vous** and the **est-ce que** form when necessary.

46. I don't know why the bank is closed today. _____
47. He is wearing a dark blue suit. _____
48. They have been standing in line for an hour. _____
49. What time do you get up? _____
50. The plane is leaving in five minutes. _____

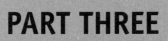

TALKING ABOUT THE PAST

CHAPTER 11

All About Pronouns

In this chapter you will learn:

Direct Object Pronouns
Indirect Object Pronouns
The Pronoun y
The Pronoun en
The Order of the Pronouns

Direct Object Pronouns

In English there are seven direct object pronouns: *me, you, him, her, it, us,* and *them.* There are seven in French as well, but they don't correspond exactly to the seven in English. On the one hand, two forms for the direct object pronoun *you* are used: the informal **te** and the formal and/or plural **vous.** On the other hand, where English distinguishes between a direct object pronoun that replaces a person (*him,* *her,* or *them*) or a thing (*it* or *them*), in French **le, la,** and **les** can all replace both people and things.

Singular		**Plural**	
me	*me*	nous	*us*
te	*you* (familiar)	vous	*you* (plural and/or formal)
le	*him* or *it* (*m.*)	les	*them* (*m.* and *f.*)
la	*her* or *it* (*f.*)		

An object is called direct if it follows the verb immediately, without a preposition. The direct object pronoun replaces the direct object noun. In French, the direct object pronoun must agree in gender and number with the noun it replaces. Unlike in English, the French direct object pronoun precedes the verb. In a sentence with auxiliary or compound verbs, the direct object pronoun precedes the verb to which it directly refers. The direct object pronoun can replace a noun with a definite article or a possessive or demonstrative adjective. The use of pronouns allows speakers to avoid being repetitive, to make communication more efficient, and to link ideas across sentences. For example:

Laurent comprend l'explication.	*Laurent understands the explanation.*
Laurent la comprend.	*Laurent understands it.*
Xavier invite ses amis.	*Xavier invites his friends.*
Xaxier les invite.	*Xavier invites them.*

In a negative sentence, the direct object pronoun also comes immediately before the conjugated verb.

Flore n'aime pas le vert.	*Flore does not like the color green.*
Flore ne l'aime pas.	*Flore does not like it.*
Nous ne posons pas ces questions délicates.	*We don't ask these delicate questions.*
Nous ne les posons pas.	*We don't ask them.*

Oral Practice

Ask the following questions and then answer them, aloud.

Vous invitez Zoé à dîner?	*Are you inviting Zoé for dinner?*
Oui, nous l'invitons.	*Yes, we are inviting her.*
Comprends-tu la décision du patron?	*Do you understand the boss's decision?*
Non, je ne la comprends pas du tout.	*No, I don't understand it at all.*
Tu fais cuire le poulet?	*Are you cooking the chicken?*
Oui, je le fais cuire.	*Yes, I am cooking it.*
Tu m'appelles ce soir?	*Are you calling me tonight?*
Oui, je t'appelle ce soir.	*Yes, I am calling you tonight.*
Je t'inscris sur la liste?	*Shall I put you down on the list?*
D'accord, tu m'inscris sur la liste.	*OK, you put me down on the list.*
Elle cherche toujours ses clés?	*Is she still looking for her keys?*
Oui, elle les cherche toujours.	*Yes, she is still looking for them.*
Vous écoutez les émissions de Radio France?	*Do you listen to the Radio France programs?*
Oui, nous les écoutons fidèlement.	*Yes, we listen to them regularly.*
Elle apprend les poèmes par cœur?	*Does she learn the poems by heart?*
Oui, elle les apprend par cœur.	*Yes, she learns them by heart.*
Est-ce qu'il suit tes conseils?	*Does he follow your advice?*
Non, il ne les suit jamais.	*No, he never follows it.*
Vous annulez le projet?	*Are you canceling the project?*
Oui, nous l'annulons.	*Yes, we are canceling it.*
Vous enseignez le français?	*Do you teach French?*
Oui, je l'enseigne depuis des années.	*Yes, I have been teaching it for years.*

Written Practice 1

Answer the questions in the affirmative, using a direct object pronoun and complete sentences.

Vous aimez les kiwis? *Oui, je les aime.* _____

1. Regardez-vous la télé? _____
2. Cherches-tu le Boulevard Voltaire? _____
3. Apprenez-vous l'italien? _____
4. Finissez-vous votre projet? _____
5. Connaissez-vous Sylvie? _____

USING DIRECT OBJECT PRONOUNS AS A SUBSTITUTE

Note that the direct object pronoun can replace a single word, a group of words, or an entire phrase or clause. For example:

Pascal aime les romans à la guimauve où la fin est toujours heureuse.	*Pascal loves mushy novels where the end is always happy.*
Pascal les aime.	*Pascal loves them.*
Les cadres contestent les change-ments que le patron a mis en place sans les avertir.	*The managerial staff questions the changes the boss has implemented without warning them.*
Les cadres les contestent.	*The managerial staff questions them.*

USING DIRECT OBJECT PRONOUNS WITH INVERSION

In a question using inversion, the direct object pronoun comes immediately before the verb.

Aimez-vous les joueurs de cette équipe?	*Do you like the players on this team?*
Les aimez-vous?	*Do you like them?*

Depuis combien de temps attends-tu la réponse de l'avocat?	*How long have you been waiting for the lawyer's answer?*
Depuis combien de temps l'attends-tu?	*How long have you been waiting for it?*

USING DIRECT OBJECT PRONOUNS WITH INFINITIVES

When an infinitive has a direct object, the direct object pronoun immediately precedes the infinitive.

Allez-vous nettoyer la salle?	*Are you going to clean the room?*
Oui, nous allons la nettoyer.	*Yes, we are going to clean it.*
Ils viennent d'acheter ce terrain?	*Did they just buy this piece of land?*
Oui, ils viennent de l'acheter.	*Yes, they just bought it.*

USING DIRECT OBJECT PRONOUNS IN THE PAST TENSE

In the past tense, the direct object pronoun is placed before the auxiliary verb. The past participle must agree in number and gender with the direct object placed before the verb.

Le syndicat a résolu les problèmes?	*Did the union resolve the problems?*
Oui, le syndicat les a résolus.	*Yes, the union resolved them.*
Qui a pris les photos?	*Who took the pictures?*
C'est moi qui les ai prises.	*I took them.*

USING DIRECT OBJECT PRONOUNS IN THE IMPERATIVE

In the affirmative imperative, the direct object pronoun follows the verb. In the negative imperative, the direct object pronoun remains before the verb. Add a hyphen between the verb and the direct object pronoun in the affirmative imperative.

Traversez le pont!	*Cross the bridge!*
Traversez-le!	*Cross it!*

Apprenez votre grammaire!	*Learn your grammar!*
Apprenez-la!	*Learn it!*
Ne dépensez pas tout votre argent!	*Don't spend all your money!*
Ne le dépensez pas!	*Don't spend it!*
Ne cueillez pas ces fleurs sauvages!	*Don't pick these wildflowers!*
Ne les cueillez pas!	*Don't pick them!*

USING DIRECT OBJECT PRONOUNS WITH *VOICI* AND *VOILÀ*

Direct object pronouns can also be used with **voici** and **voilà** (*here is, here are*).

—Où est Fabrice? —Le voilà!	*"Where is Fabrice?" "Here he comes!"*

—Où sont vos documents?
  —Les voici!
	"Where are your documents?"
	  "Here they are!"

Oral Practice

Ask the following questions and then answer them, aloud.

Avez-vous acheté ces tapis au Maroc?	*Did you buy these rugs in Morocco?*
Oui je les ai achetés au Maroc.	*Yes, I bought them in Morocco.*
Je demande l'addition?	*Shall I ask for the bill?*
Demande-la.	*Ask for it.*
Ils vont vendre leur appartement?	*Are they going to sell their apartment?*
Oui, ils vont le vendre.	*Yes, they are going to sell it.*
Elle a envoyé ce devis au client?	*Did she send this estimate to the client?*
Oui, elle l'a envoyé au client.	*Yes, she sent it to the client.*
Il vient d'acheter cette nouvelle Renault?	*Did he just buy this new Renault?*
Oui, il vient de l'acheter.	*Yes, he just bought it.*
Depuis combien de temps as-tu cet ordinateur?	*How long have you had this computer?*

Je l'ai depuis trois mois.	*I've had it for three months.*
On peut les appeler?	*Can we call them?*
Bien sûr, appelez-les!	*Of course, call them!*
Tu sais qu'il a annulé le rendez-vous?	*Do you know he canceled the appointment?*
Oui, je le sais.	*Yes, I know.*
Tu vas engager Alain Tournier?	*Are you going to hire Alain Tournier?*
Oui, je vais l'engager.	*Yes, I am going to hire him.*

Written Practice 2

Answer the questions in the negative, using a direct object pronoun and complete sentences.

Avez-vous pris l'autoroute? _Non, je ne l'ai pas prise._

1. Tu vas faire les courses? _____
2. Est-ce qu'ils ont réservé les billets? _____
3. Elle a trouvé la solution? _____
4. Vous allez prendre cette route? _____
5. Il a vu l'émission? _____

Indirect Object Pronouns

In English there are seven indirect object pronouns: *me, you, him, her, it, us,* and *them*. As always, French distinguishes between an informal *you* (**te**) and a formal and/or plural *you* (**vous**). The French indirect object pronoun does not, however, distinguish gender; **lui** and **leur** replace both masculine and feminine nouns. In French the indirect object pronoun replaces only animate indirect objects (people, animals). Inanimate ideas and things are replaced with the indirect object pronouns **y** and **en**, which will be discussed later in this chapter. First, let's look at the indirect object pronouns.

Singular		Plural	
me (m')	*me*	nous	*us*
te (t')	*you* (familiar)	vous	*you* (formal or plural)
lui	*him, her* (*m.* and *f.*)	leur	*them* (*m.* and *f.*)

The object is called indirect since the verb is controlled by a preposition. For example: **se souvenir de** (*to remember*), **répondre à** (*to answer*). The indirect object pronoun is placed in front of the conjugated verb; in the compound tenses, it is placed in front of **avoir**. Although the past participle has to agree in gender and number with the direct object pronoun, it does not agree with the indirect object pronoun.

The pronouns **me** and **te** become **m'** and **t'** before vowels and mute **h**. Be aware of the difference between **leur,** the indirect pronoun, and **leur(s),** the possessive adjective.

Elle écrit à son oncle.	*She writes to her uncle.*
Elle lui écrit.	*She writes to him.*
Vous parlez à vos amis.	*You talk to your friends.*
Vous leur parlez.	*You talk to them.*
Vous avez téléphoné à votre nièce.	*You called your niece.*
Vous lui avez téléphoné.	*You called her.*

In the interrogative or negative, the indirect object pronoun comes immediately before the verb.

M'as-tu envoyé les renseignements?	*Did you send me the information?*
Il ne t'a pas encore expliqué les répercussions.	*He has not yet explained the repercussions to you.*

INDIRECT OBJECT PRONOUNS IN THE IMPERATIVE

In the affirmative imperative, the indirect object pronoun follows the verb. In the negative imperative, the indirect object pronoun remains before the verb. Remember to add a hyphen between the verb and the indirect object pronoun in the affirmative imperative, just as you did with the direct object pronoun.

Apporte-lui la déposition d'Elizabeth.	*Bring him Elizabeth's testimony.*
Ne lui prêtez pas un sou.	*Don't lend him a cent.*

PLACEMENT OF INDIRECT OBJECT PRONOUNS

With some verbs, the indirect object pronoun follows the verb and the preposition. There is no rule that you can learn: it's just a matter of memorizing which verbs these are. With these verbs, the indirect object pronoun is replaced by a disjunctive pronoun. See the following examples:

Je pense à Grégoire.	*I am thinking about Grégoire.*
Je pense à lui.	*I am thinking about him.*
Tu songes à Clara.	*You are thinking about Clara.*
Tu songes à elle.	*You are thinking about her.*
Ils parlent des joueurs.	*They are talking about the players.*
Ils parlent d'eux.	*They are talking about them.*
Elle a besoin de ses amis.	*She needs her friends.*
Elle a besoin d'eux.	*She needs them.*
Il a peur de son superviseur.	*He is afraid of his supervisor.*
Il a peur de lui.	*He is afraid of him.*
Il fait attention à ses patients.	*He pays attention to his patients.*
Il fait attention à eux.	*He pays attention to them.*
Ils tiennent à leurs amis.	*They are attached to their friends.*
Ils tiennent à eux.	*They are attached to them.*

INDIRECT OBJECT PRONOUNS WITH REFLEXIVE VERBS

If a reflexive verb is followed by an animate indirect object (a person or animal), the indirect object pronoun is placed after the preposition.

Je me souviens de mon professeur de français.	*I remember my French teacher.*
Je me souviens de lui.	*I remember him.*

Elle s'occupe de son neveu.	*She is taking care of her nephew.*
Elle s'occupe de lui.	*She is taking care of him.*

Oral Practice

Ask the following questions and then answer them, aloud.

Cette île leur appartient?	*Does this island belong to them?*
Oui, cette île leur appartient.	*Yes, this island belongs to them.*
As-tu téléphoné à la secrétaire d'Amélie?	*Did you call Amélie's secretary?*
Non, je ne lui ai pas encore téléphoné.	*No, I have not called her yet.*
Je ne t'ai pas raconté cette histoire?	*Didn't I tell you this story?*
Non, tu ne m'as pas raconté cette histoire.	*No, you did not tell me this story.*
Tu as prêté ton dictionnaire à Raphaël?	*Did you lend your dictionary to Raphaël?*
Oui, je lui ai prêté mon dictionnaire.	*Yes, I lent him my dictionary.*
Est-ce qu'il a parlé au gérant du magasin?	*Did he talk to the store's manager?*
Oui, il lui a parlé.	*Yes, he talked to him.*
Ils ont envoyé le dossier au maire?	*Did they send the file to the mayor?*
Oui, ils lui ont envoyé le dossier.	*Yes, they sent him the file.*
Vous lui avez écrit une lettre de remerciements?	*Did you write her a thank-you letter?*
Oui, je lui ai écrit une lettre de remerciements.	*Yes, I wrote her a thank-you letter.*
Il t'a rendu tes livres?	*Did he give you back your books?*
Oui, il m'a rendu mes livres.	*Yes, he gave me back my books.*
Je lui dis la vérité?	*Shall I tell her the truth?*
Dis-lui la vérité!	*Tell her the truth!*
Je peux lui emprunter sa voiture?	*Can I borrow his car?*
Ne lui emprunte pas sa voiture!	*Don't borrow his car!*

Written Practice 3

Answer the questions in the affirmative, using an indirect object pronoun.

Tu as parlé à Laura? *Oui, je lui ai parlé.*

1. Vous avez répondu à la cliente? _____
2. Il a écrit à ses cousins? _____
3. Tu m'as envoyé le plan de Paris? _____
4. Ils te font des cadeaux? _____
5. Elle raconte des histoires à ses enfants? _____

The Pronoun *y*

Y is an indirect object pronoun that precedes the verb. It usually replaces an inanimate object (thing or idea). The object is indirect because in the noun form, it is preceded by a preposition, usually the preposition **à.**

Il pense à son avenir.	*He is thinking about his future.*
Il y pense.	*He is thinking about it.*
Elle répond aux lettres.	*She answers the letters.*
Elle y répond.	*She answers them.*
Ils s'intéressent au cinéma.	*They are interested in the movies.*
Ils s'y intéressent.	*They are interested in them.*

In the compound tenses, the indirect object pronoun **y** is placed before the auxiliary verb.

NOTE: *The past participle does not agree in gender and number with the indirect object, including* **y.**

Elle a renoncé à son voyage.	*She gave up her trip.*
Elle y a renoncé.	*She gave it up.*
Vous n'avez pas répondu à ma question.	*You did not answer my question.*
Vous n'y avez pas répondu.	*You did not answer it.*

Oral Practice

Ask the following questions and then answer them, aloud.

Elle pense à sa promotion?	*Is she thinking about her promotion?*
Oui, elle y pense.	*Yes, she is thinking about it.*
Tu as goûté au soufflé?	*Did you taste the soufflé?*
Non, je n'y ai pas goûté.	*No, I did not taste it.*
Vous vous êtes habitué au climat?	*Have you gotten used to the climate?*
Oui, je m'y suis habitué.	*Yes, I've gotten used to it.*
Comment peut-on remédier à ce problème?	*How can we solve this problem?*
Je ne sais pas comment on peut y remédier.	*I don't know how we can solve it.*
Je peux toucher à cette sculpture?	*Can I touch this sculpture?*
Oui, bien sûr, vous pouvez y toucher.	*Yes, of course, you can touch it.*
Ils obéissent à ce règlement?	*Do they obey this rule?*
Non, ils n'y obéissent pas.	*No, they don't obey it.*
Tu tiens vraiment à ce vieux vélo tout pourri?	*Are you really attached to this old rotten bicycle?*
Oui, j'y tiens.	*Yes, I am attached to it.*
Il rêve encore à des jours meilleurs?	*Is he still dreaming about better days?*
Oui, il y rêve encore.	*Yes, he is still dreaming about it.*
Je réponds à son invitation?	*Shall I answer his invitation?*
Réponds-y!	*Answer it!*

Written Practice 4

Answer the questions in the affirmative, using the pronoun **y** and complete sentences.

Vous pensez à vos vacances? _J'y pense._ _____

1. Elle a répondu à tes messages? _____
2. Tu t'intéresses au jazz? _____
3. Vous croyez au progrès? _____
4. Il a goûté à la soupe? _____
5. Tu fais attention à la route? _____

The Pronoun *en*

En is an indirect object pronoun that precedes the verb. Like **y**, it usually replaces an inanimate object (thing or idea). The noun that **en** replaces is preceded by the preposition **de**. The pronoun **en** immediately precedes the verb, except in affirmative imperative commands, where it follows the verb, connected with a hyphen.

Elle se souvient de son mauvais caractère.	*She remembers his bad temper.*
Elle s'en souvient.	*She remembers it.*
Il a peur des grosses vagues.	*He is afraid of the big waves.*
Il en a peur.	*He is afraid of them.*
Parlez-en!	*Speak about it!*

In the compound tenses, the indirect object pronoun **y** is placed before the auxiliary verb.

NOTE: *The past participle does not agree in gender and number with the indirect object, including* **en.**

Je me suis approchée de la porte du manoir.	*I came closer to the door of the mansion.*

Je m'en suis approchée.	*I came closer to it.*
Nous avons parlé de nos investissements à Quentin.	*We talked to Quentin about our investments.*
Nous en avons parlé à Quentin.	*We talked to Quentin about them.*

Oral Practice

Ask the following questions and then answer them, aloud.

Vous êtes-vous occupé de leurs réservations?	*Did you take care of their reservations?*
Oui, je m'en suis occupé.	*Yes, I took care of them.*
Est-ce qu'il a parlé de son passé?	*Did he talk about his past?*
Oui, il en a parlé.	*Yes, he talked about it.*
Tu t'es servi de mon iPod?	*Did you use my iPod?*
Oui, je m'en suis servi.	*Yes, I used it.*
Est-ce qu'ils ont envie d'aller au Pérou?	*Do they feel like going to Peru?*
Oui, ils en ont envie.	*Yes, they feel like it.*
Tu peux te passer de pain?	*Can you do without bread?*
Non, je ne peux pas m'en passer.	*No, I can't do without it.*
Elle s'est chargée de tous les détails?	*Did she take care of all the details?*
Oui, elle s'en est chargée.	*Yes, she took care of them.*
Tu t'es débarrassé de tes vieux meubles?	*Did you get rid of your old furniture?*
Oui, je m'en suis enfin débarrassé.	*Yes, I finally got rid of it.*

Written Practice 5

Answer the following questions in the negative, using the pronoun **en** and complete sentences.

Elle a parlé de sa vie? _Elle n'en a pas parlé._ _____

1. Tu te souviens de son nom? _____
2. Elle a l'intention d'acheter ces objets d'art? _____
3. Vous avez peur de sa réaction? _____
4. Il s'est occupé de tes bagages? _____
5. Tu as envie d'aller dans le parc? _____

The Order of the Pronouns

When a direct pronoun and an indirect pronoun appear together in a sentence, the indirect object pronoun comes first unless the direct and indirect pronouns are both in the third person, in which case the direct object pronoun comes first.

Indirect Object	**Direct Object**
me	
te	le, la, l', les
nous	
vous	

Here are some examples:

Tu me décris la situation.	*You describe the situation to me.*
Tu me la décris.	*You describe it to me.*
Elle vous envoie le bail.	*She sends you the lease.*
Elle vous l'envoie.	*She sends it to you.*

If the direct and indirect pronouns are both in the third person, the direct object pronoun comes first.

Direct Object	Indirect Object
le, l'	
la, l'	lui, leur
les	

Here are some example sentences:

Elle montre ses photos à ses amis.	*She shows her pictures to her friends.*
Elle les leur montre.	*She shows them to them.*
Il annonce son départ à son directeur.	*He announces his departure to his director.*
Il le lui annonce.	*He announces it to him.*

In the compound tenses, both object pronouns are placed together before the auxiliary verb, in the order described above. The past participle must agree in number and gender with the direct object placed before the verb.

Elle lui a écrit cette lettre.	*She wrote this letter to him.*
Elle la lui a écrite.	*She wrote it to him.*
Ils lui ont envoyé ces magnifiques photos.	*They sent him these wonderful pictures.*
Ils les lui ont envoyées.	*They sent them to him.*

When **en** is combined with an indirect object pronoun, **en** always follows the other pronoun.

Tu lui prêtes des livres.	*You lend him some books.*
Tu lui en prêtes.	*You lend him some.*
Elle me donne du thé.	*She gives me some tea.*
Elle m'en donne.	*She gives me some.*

Oral Practice

Ask the following questions and then answer them, aloud.

| Tu lui a donné les renseignements? | *Did you give him the information?* |
| Oui, je les lui ai donnés. | *Yes, I gave it to him.* |

Vous me prêtez votre calculette?	*Will you lend me your calculator?*
Je vous la prête, bien sûr.	*I'll lend it to you, of course.*
Est-ce qu'il nous a envoyé son rapport?	*Did he send us his report?*
Non, il ne nous l'a pas envoyé.	*No, he did not send it to us.*
Elle vous a raconté ses aventures?	*Did she tell you about her adventures?*
Oui, elle nous les a racontées.	*Yes, she told them to us.*
Tu lui as laissé le manuel?	*Did you leave the manual for him?*
Oui, je le lui ai laissé.	*Yes, I left it for him.*
Elle t'a posé les mêmes questions?	*Did she ask you the same questions?*
Oui, elle me les a posées.	*Yes, she asked me them.*
Tu lui as emprunté de l'argent?	*Did you borrow money from him?*
Non, je ne lui ai pas emprunté d'argent.	*No, I did not borrow any money from him.*
Il lui a vendu son appareil photo numérique?	*Did he sell her his digital camera?*
Oui, il le lui a vendu.	*Yes, he sold it to her.*
Tu lui as dit ce que tu pensais?	*Did you tell him what you thought?*
Oui, je le lui ai dit.	*Yes, I told him.*
Vous lui avez rendu ses clés?	*Did you return his keys to him?*
Oui, je les lui ai rendues.	*Yes, I returned them to him.*
Il te demande le mot de passe?	*Is he asking you for the password?*
Oui, il me le demande.	*Yes, he is asking me for it.*

Written Practice 6

Answer the following questions in the affirmative using complete sentences.

Elle t'a donné ce livre? <u>Oui, elle me l'a donné.</u>

1. Vous m'envoyez le fichier? _____

2. Tu nous laisse les journaux? _____

3. Ils lui expliquent la situation? _____

4. Elle te donne sa permission? _____

5. Il lui a écrit ces messages? _____

QUIZ

Answer the questions in the affirmative, using a direct object pronoun and complete sentences.

Vous invitez les Sabatier? *Oui, je les invite.* _____

1. Elle préfère les orchidées? _____

Vous contactez Jérôme? _____

Tu m'invites? _____

Il a regardé le match? _____

Elles écoutent la radio? _____

Vous avez engagé cet employé? _____

Answer the questions in the affirmative, using an indirect object pronoun and complete sentences.

Elle a expliqué la situation à Hervé. *Elle lui a expliqué la situation.* _____

2. Vous posez des questions aux étudiants? _____

Tu prêtes tes livres à tes amis? _____

Elle a raconté son voyage à sa mère? _____

Il donne de bons conseils à ses collègues? _____

Vous avez envoyé un guide Michelin à votre cousin? _____

Replace both the direct and the indirect object with a pronoun.

Tu as donné les livres à Marie. *Tu les lui as donnés.* _____

3. Elle a offert ce bracelet à son amie. _____

Ils n'ont pas envoyé les documents à Carole. _____

J'écris ces cartes postales à mes collègues. _____

Vous vendez ces produits à des clients chinois. _____

Elle a raconté cette histoire à ses petits-enfants. _____

Answer the questions in the affirmative, using both a direct and an indirect object pronoun and complete sentences.

Il t'a proposé le poste? *Oui, il me l'a proposé.* _____

4. Elle vous a rendu vos livres? _____

Il t'a parlé de son entreprise? _____

Vous m'avez faxé le devis? _____

Tu nous recommandes ce restaurant? _____

Vous pouvez me décrire l'appartement? _____

Answer the following questions in the affirmative form, using **y** or **en** and complete sentences.

Il pense à son nouveau poste? *Il y pense.* _____

5. Elle s'habitue à son nouveau poste? _____

Ils profitent de leurs vacances? _____

Elle a réfléchi à votre proposition? _____

Tu te souviens de son numéro de téléphone? _____

Vous vous intéressez à cette théorie? _____

Tu as goûté à la bouillabaisse? _____

Translate the following sentences, using **vous** and the **est-ce que** form where needed.

6. Give him these sunglasses! _____

7. Can I borrow it? _____

8. She is interested in it. _____

9. Are you going to buy it? _____

10. They are getting used to it. _____

CHAPTER 12

Talking About the Past with the *passé composé*

In this chapter, you'll learn:

The passé composé

The passé composé *with* avoir

The passé composé *with* être

Using Direct Objects in the passé composé

Pronominal Verbs in the passé composé

Using Adverbs with the passé composé

The *passé composé*

There are several forms that can be used to talk about the past in French. The most common is the **passé composé,** also called **the compound past** or past perfect. It expresses a single action in the past. It has two parts: an auxiliary verb, **avoir** or **être,** and a past participle. Most verbs form their **passé composé** with **avoir.**

The past participle is formed by adding an ending to the verb stem. Regular past participles take the following endings:

- **-er** verbs take **é: chanter** (*to sing*) → **chanté** (*sung*)
- **-ir** verbs take **i: finir** (*to finish*) → **fini** (*finished*)
- **-re** verbs take **u: répondre** (*to answer*) → **répondu** (*answered*)

NOTE: *The passé composé can be translated in different ways in English. Its equivalent depends on the context.*

Il a acheté une nouvelle voiture.
- *He bought a new car.*
- *He has bought a new car.*
- *He did buy a new car.*

As in the present tense, there are three ways to make a question.

Tu as dîné chez Paul?	*You had dinner at Paul's?*
As-tu dîné chez Paul?	*Did you have dinner at Paul's?*
Est-ce que tu as dîné chez Paul?	*Did you have dinner at Paul's?*

In the negative form, the **ne (n')** is placed in front of **avoir** or **être** and the **pas** after **avoir** or **être.**

Elle a parlé à Carole.	*She spoke to Carole.*
Elle n'a pas parlé à Carole.	*She did not speak to Carole.*

The *passé composé* with *avoir*

Let's first review the verb **avoir** and learn the **passé composé** of the **-er** verbs.

j'ai	*I have*	nous avons	*we have*
tu as	*you have*	vous avez	*you have*
il/elle a	*he/she has*	ils/elles ont	*they have*

When **avoir** is used with the **passé composé**, the past participle does not agree in gender and number with the subject of the verb.

THE *PASSÉ COMPOSÉ* WITH *-ER* VERBS

See the following examples of past participles with **-er** verbs:

Il a téléphoné hier soir.	*He called last night.*
Elle a apporté des fleurs.	*She brought flowers.*

Oral Practice

Ask the following questions and then answer them, aloud.

Avez-vous déjeuné dans le jardin?	*Did you have lunch in the garden?*
Oui, nous avons déjeuné dans le jardin.	*Yes, we ate in the garden.*
Est-ce qu'il a voyagé en France?	*Did he travel to France?*
Non, il n'a pas encore voyagé en France.	*No, he has not yet traveled to France.*
Tu as regardé le film à la télé?	*Did you watch the film on TV?*
Oui, j'ai regardé le film à la télé.	*Yes, I watched the film on TV.*
A-t-il préparé sa présentation?	*Has he prepared his presentation?*
Non, il n'a pas encore préparé sa présentation.	*No, he has not prepared his presentation yet.*
Avez-vous écouté ce nouveau CD?	*Have you listened to this new CD?*
Oui, j'ai écouté ce nouveau CD.	*Yes, I have listened to this new CD.*
Vous avez visité le musée Rodin?	*Did you visit the Rodin museum?*

Oui, nous avons visité le musée Rodin.	*Yes, we visited the Rodin museum.*
Tu as étudié le latin?	*Did you study Latin?*
Oui, j'ai étudié le grec et le latin.	*Yes, I studied Greek and Latin.*
Avez-vous renouvelé votre passeport?	*Did you renew your passport?*
Oui, j'ai renouvelé mon passeport.	*Yes, I renewed my passport.*
Elle a commencé son nouveau travail?	*Has she started her new job?*
Non, elle n'a pas encore commencé son nouveau travail.	*No, she has not started her new job yet.*
Il a effacé le tableau?	*Did he erase the blackboard?*
Oui, il a effacé le tableau.	*Yes, he erased the blackboard.*

Written Practice 1

Put the following verbs into the **passé composé**.

Vous étudiez le français. *Vous avez étudié le français.*

1. Il habite à Rome. _____
2. Vous parlez au directeur. _____
3. Tu participes à la conférence. _____
4. Nous jouons au tennis. _____
5. Je prépare un couscous. _____

THE *PASSÉ COMPOSÉ* OF *-IR* AND *-RE* VERBS

Now, let's practice the **-ir** and **-re** verbs conjugated with **avoir**.

J'ai perdu mon portefeuille.	*I lost my wallet.*
Il n'a pas répondu à toutes les questions.	*He did not answer all the questions.*

J'ai attendu une heure.	*I waited an hour.*
Il a senti son parfum.	*He smelled her perfume.*
Je n'ai pas fini mon projet.	*I did not finish my project.*
Ils ont accompli leur mission.	*They have accomplished their mission.*

Oral Practice

Ask the following questions and then answer them, aloud.

Avez-vous choisi un cadeau pour elle?	*Did you choose a present for her?*
Oui, nous avons choisi un joli cadeau.	*Yes, we chose a nice present.*
Tu as vendu ta moto?	*Did you sell your motorbike?*
Oui, j'ai vendu ma moto.	*Yes, I sold my motorbike.*
Il a réussi à son examen?	*Did he pass his exam?*
Non, il a raté son examen.	*No, he failed his exam.*
Où a-t-elle perdu sa bague?	*Where did she lose her ring?*
Elle a perdu sa bague à la plage.	*She lost her ring at the beach.*
Avez-vous rempli le formulaire?	*Did you fill out the form?*
Oui, j'ai rempli le formulaire.	*Yes, I filled out the form.*
Tu as bien dormi?	*Did you sleep well?*
Oui, j'ai très bien dormi.	*Yes, I slept very well.*
Tu as réfléchi à sa proposition?	*Did you think about his proposal?*
Non, je n'ai pas encore réfléchi à sa proposition.	*No, I have not yet thought about his proposal.*
Qu'est-ce que tu as servi?	*What did you serve?*
J'ai servi un canard à l'orange.	*I served duck à l'orange.*
Il a rendu les livres à la bibliothèque?	*Did he return the books to the library?*
Non, il n'a pas rendu les livres à la bibliothèque.	*No, he did not return the books to the library.*

Written Practice 2

Put the following verbs into the passé composé.

Je choisis un fromage. _J'ai choisi un fromage._

1. Elle choisit un restaurant. _____
2. Ils servent les invités. _____
3. Vous répondez au message. _____
4. Elle finit son travail. _____
5. Il perd ses clés. _____

IRREGULAR PAST PARTICIPLES

Many verbs conjugated with **avoir** in the **passé composé** have irregular past participles that you will just have to memorize.

Infinitive		→	Irregular Past Participle	
avoir	*to have*	→	eu	*had*
boire	*to drink*	→	bu	*drunk*
comprendre	*to understand*	→	compris	*understood*
conduire	*to drive*	→	conduit	*driven*
craindre	*to fear*	→	craint	*feared*
devoir	*must*	→	dû	*had to*
dire	*to say*	→	dit	*said*
écrire	*to write*	→	écrit	*written*
être	*to be*	→	été	*been*
faire	*to do, to make*	→	fait	*done, made*
falloir	*to have to*	→	fallu	*had to*
lire	*to read*	→	lu	*read*
mettre	*to put*	→	mis	*put*
offrir	*to offer*	→	offert	*offered*
ouvrir	*to open*	→	ouvert	*open*
peindre	*to paint*	→	peint	*painted*
plaire	*to please*	→	plu	*pleased*
pleuvoir	*to rain*	→	plu	*rained*
pouvoir	*can, to be able to*	→	pu	*could*
prendre	*to take*	→	pris	*taken*

recevoir	to receive	→	reçu	received
rire	to laugh	→	ri	laughed
savoir	to know	→	su	known
suivre	to follow	→	suivi	followed
vivre	to live	→	vécu	lived
voir	to see	→	vu	seen
vouloir	to want	→	voulu	wanted

See the following example sentences:

Elle a bu un verre de lait.	*She drank a glass of milk.*
Il n'a pas pris son vélo.	*He did not take his bike.*
J'ai compris.	*I understood.*
Elle a ouvert le magasin à dix heures.	*She opened the store at ten.*
Il n'a pas écrit à Tante Amélie.	*He did not write to Aunt Amélie.*
Il a plu toute la journée.	*It rained all day long.*
J'ai vu le nouveau film d'Audiard.	*I saw Audiard's new film.*
Dimanche, je n'ai pas fait grand-chose.	*I did not do too much on Sunday.*
Elle a eu une réaction allergique.	*She had an allergic reaction.*
Je lui ai offert un foulard.	*I gave her a scarf.*
J'ai été malade immédiatement.	*I got sick immediately.*
Il a mis son chapeau de paille.	*He put on his straw hat.*
C'est moi qui ai peint le mur en jaune.	*I painted the wall yellow.*
Il n'a rien dit.	*He did not say anything.*
J'ai suivi quelques cours.	*I took a few courses.*
Elle a lu tout le journal.	*She read the whole paper.*
Louis a traduit ce document.	*Louis translated this document.*
J'ai trouvé une place derrière l'église.	*I found a spot behind the church.*
Ils ont reçu votre demande.	*They received your request.*
Le film m'a beaucoup plu.	*I enjoyed the film very much.*
J'ai appris l'espagnol au Mexique.	*I learned Spanish in Mexico.*
C'est René qui a conduit.	*It's René who drove.*
Il n'a pas souffert?	*He didn't suffer?*

Written Practice 3

Put the following verbs into the passé composé.

Tu ouvres les fenêtres. _Tu as ouvert les fenêtres._

1. Tu prends une photo. _____
2. Elle a de la chance. _____
3. Vous mettez un pull. _____
4. Ils reçoivent un document. _____
5. Nous buvons un thé glacé. _____

The *passé composé* with *être*

Some verbs use **être** instead of **avoir** in the **passé composé**: these include the pronominal verbs you studied in Chapter 10, as well as an arbitrary list you need to memorize. The past participles of verbs conjugated with **être** agree in gender and number with the subject. See the following examples:

Il est all**é** en France.	*He went to France.*
Elle est all**ée** en France.	*She went to France.*
Ils sont all**és** en France.	*They went to France.*
Nous sommes arriv**és** à l'heure.	*We arrived on time.*
Il est sort**i** avec ses amis.	*He went out with his friends.*

Oral Practice

Read the following sentences aloud.

Je suis allé chez André.	*I went to André's.*
Nous sommes rentrés à minuit.	*We came home at midnight.*
Ils sont partis en vacances il y a deux jours.	*They went on vacation two days ago.*

Son grand-père est mort en 1980.	*His grandfather died in 1980.*
Je suis monté au dernier étage.	*I went to the top floor.*
Elle est venue toute seule.	*She came alone.*
J'y suis retourné une fois.	*I went back there once.*
Nous y sommes restés quinze jours.	*We stayed there for two weeks.*
Je suis revenu mardi.	*I came back on Tuesday.*
Où est-il né?	*Where was he born?*
Il est né en Espagne.	*He was born in Spain.*
Elle est descendue par l'escalier?	*Did she take the stairs down?*
Je suis passé devant le salon de coiffure ce matin.	*I passed by the hair salon this morning.*
Il est tombé dans un nid de poule.	*He fell into a pothole.*
Elle est tombée follement amoureuse de Vincent.	*She fell madly in love with Vincent.*
Je suis tombé en panne sur l'autoroute.	*I broke down on the highway.*
Il est tombé malade en janvier!	*He got sick in January!*

Written Practice 4

Put the following verbs into the **passé composé**.

Nous retournons à Paris. <u>Nous sommes retournés à Paris.</u>

1. Elle va au théâtre. _____
2. Nous (*m.*) partons à neuf heures. _____
3. J'arrive avant Ludovic. _____
4. Ils viennent avec leurs enfants. _____
5. Il monte au sommet de la montagne. _____

Using Direct Objects in the *passé composé*

Of the verbs that normally use **être** in the **passé composé**, a few take **avoir** and follow the **avoir** agreement when a direct object follows the verb. These verbs are: **descendre**, **monter**, **passer**, **rentrer**, **retourner**, and **sortir**. Note that the meaning of the verb may change depending on whether **être** or **avoir** is used.

Nous sommes rentrés très tard.	*We came home late.*
J'ai rentré les vélos dans le garage.	*I brought the bikes into the garage.*
Ils sont montés au dixième étage.	*They went up to the tenth floor.*
Ils ont monté la valise dans la chambre.	*They took the suitcase up to the room.*
Il est descendu au rez-de-chaussée.	*He went down to the main floor.*
Tu as descendu les bouteilles vides à la cave.	*You took the empty bottles down to the cellar.*
J'ai passé un examen hier.	*I took an exam yesterday.*
Vous êtes passés par Lyon pour aller à Montpellier.	*You went through Lyon to go to Montpellier.*
Ils sont retournés à Tahiti.	*They went back to Tahiti.*
Elle a retourné l'omelette.	*She turned over the omelette.*
Il est sorti à huit heures.	*He went out at eight o'clock.*
Elle a sorti les plantes sur le balcon.	*She took the plants out onto the balcony.*

Oral Practice

Ask the following questions and then answer them, aloud.

Tu as descendu les poubelles?	*Did you take the garbage cans down?*
Oui, j'ai descendu les poubelles.	*Yes, I took the garbage cans down.*
Vous avez sorti la voiture du garage?	*Did you take the car out of the garage?*
Oui, j'ai sorti la voiture.	*Yes, I took the car out.*
À quelle heure a-t-elle sorti son chien?	*What time did she walk the dog?*

Elle a sorti son chien à six heures.	*She walked the dog at six.*
Est-ce qu'il est monté dans sa chambre?	*Did he go up to his room?*
Oui, il est monté dans sa chambre.	*Yes, he went up to his room.*
Il est déjà descendu en bas de la colline?	*Did he already go down the hill?*
Oui, il est déjà descendu en bas de la colline.	*Yes, he already went down the hill.*
Avec qui est-elle sortie hier soir?	*With whom did she go out last night?*
Elle est sortie avec Christophe.	*She went out with Christophe.*
À quelle heure est-elle rentrée?	*What time did she come home?*
Elle est rentrée vers onze heures.	*She came home around eleven.*
A-t-elle monté les boîtes au deuxième étage?	*Did she take the boxes to the second floor?*
Elle a monté les boîtes au deuxième étage.	*She took the boxes up to the second floor.*
Vous êtes passé chez Rémi?	*Did you stop by at Rémi's?*
Oui, nous sommes passés chez Rémi.	*Yes, we stopped by at Rémi's.*
Est-ce qu'il est retourné au magasin?	*Did he go back to the store?*
Non, il n'est pas retourné au magasin.	*No, he did not go back to the store.*
Ils ont passé un mois au bord de la mer?	*Did they spend a month at the seashore?*
Non, ils n'ont passé que trois semaines.	*No, they only spent three weeks.*
Il va pleuvoir. Tu as rentré les chaises?	*It's going to rain. Did you take the chairs in?*
Oui, j'ai rentré les chaises au sous-sol.	*Yes, I took the chairs to the basement.*
Dans quel hôtel sont-ils descendus à Venise?	*What hotel did they stay in in Venice?*
Ils sont descendus au Danieli.	*They stayed at the Danieli.*

Written Practice 5

Put the following verbs into the **passé composé**, choosing **être** or **avoir** according to the meaning.

Je rentre à la maison. *Je suis rentré(e) à la maison.*

1. Elle passe des vacances formidables. _____
2. Tu sors les géraniums sur la terrasse. _____
3. Nous retournons en Turquie. _____
4. Vous montez les valises au premier étage. _____
5. Ils passent devant le casino. _____

Pronominal Verbs in the *passé composé*

Pronominal verbs are always conjugated with **être;** the reflexive pronoun precedes the auxiliary. In most cases, the past participle agrees in gender and number with the subject.

je me suis levé(e)	*I got up*	nous nous sommes levé(e)s	*we got up*
tu t'es levé(e)	*you got up*	vous vous êtes levé(e)(s)	*you got up*
il s'est levé	*he got up*	ils se sont levés	*they got up* (m.)
elle s'est levée	*she got up*	elles se sont levées	*they got up* (f.)

In the negative, the negation is placed around the auxiliary verb. See these examples:

Elle ne s'est pas réveillée à l'heure.	*She did not wake up on time.*
Ils ne se sont pas reposés pendant les vacances.	*They did not rest during their vacation.*

The past participle does not agree when the pronominal verb is followed by a direct object.

Il s'est lavé.	*He washed himself.*
Il s'est lavé les mains.	*He washed his hands.*

Elle s'est coupée.	*She cut herself.*
Elle s'est coupé les cheveux.	*She cut her hair.*
Elle s'est fait une robe.	*She made a dress for herself.*
Elle s'est acheté une nouvelle moto.	*She bought a new motorbike for herself.*
Ils se sont serré la main.	*They shook hands.*

When the reflexive pronoun in a pronominal verb is a direct object, the past participle agrees with it.

Ils se sont embrassés.	*They kissed each other.*
Ils se sont aimés.	*They loved each other.*
Ils se sont quittés.	*They parted.*
Ils ne se sont jamais revus.	*They never saw each other again.*

When the reflexive pronoun in a pronominal verb is an indirect object, the past participle does not agree with it.

Nous nous sommes téléphoné.	*We called each other.*
Elles se sont écrit.	*They wrote to each other.*
Ils se sont parlé à la réunion.	*They talked to each other at the meeting.*
Elles se sont dit bonjour.	*They said hello.*

NOTE: *When **avoir** is the auxiliary, the past participle only agrees with the direct object when it precedes the verb.*

Elle a acheté les roses.	*She bought the roses.*
Elle les a achetées.	*She bought them.*
Il a pris les photos.	*He took the pictures.*
Il les a prises.	*He took them.*

Oral Practice

Ask the following questions and then answer them, aloud.

Est-ce qu'elle s'est habillée pour la soirée?	*Did she get dressed for the party?*
Oui, elle s'est habillée pour la soirée.	*Yes, she got dressed for the party.*
Tu t'es couchée tôt?	*Did you go to bed early?*
Non, je me suis couchée à l'aube.	*No, I went to bed at dawn.*
Vous vous êtes promenés le long de la Seine?	*Did you walk along the Seine?*
Oui, nous nous sommes promenés le long de la Seine.	*Yes, we walked along the Seine.*
Il s'est assis au fond de la salle?	*Did he sit in the back of the room?*
Oui, il s'est assis au fond.	*Yes, he sat in the back.*
Il s'est occupé des enfants?	*Did he take care of the children?*
Oui, il s'est occupé des enfants.	*Yes, he took care of the children.*
Tu t'es réveillé de bonne humeur?	*Did you wake up in a good mood?*
Oui, je me suis réveillé de bonne humeur.	*Yes, I woke up in a good mood.*
Vous vous êtes bien amusés à la soirée?	*Did you have fun at the party?*
Oui, nous nous sommes bien amusés à la soirée.	*Yes, we had a lot of fun at the party.*
Elle s'est inquiétée de votre absence?	*Did she get concerned about your absence?*
Oui, elle s'est inquiétée de notre absence.	*Yes, she got concerned about our absence.*
Ils se sont écrit pendant les vacances?	*Did they write to each other during the vacation?*
Oui, ils se sont écrit quasiment tous les jours.	*Yes, they wrote to each other almost every day.*
Quand vous êtes-vous mariés?	*When did you get married?*
Nous nous sommes mariés en mai.	*We got married in May.*

Elle s'est brossé les dents?	*Did she brush her teeth?*
Oui, elle s'est brossé les dents.	*Yes, she brushed her teeth.*
Ils se sont ennuyés à la réception?	*Did they get bored at the reception?*
Oui, ils se sont ennuyés à la réception.	*Yes, they got bored at the reception.*
Vous vous êtes arrêtés à Nantes?	*Did you stop in Nantes?*
Oui, nous nous sommes arrêtés à Nantes.	*Yes, we stopped in Nantes.*
Pourquoi s'est-il évanoui?	*Why did he faint?*
Il s'est évanoui à cause de la chaleur.	*He fainted because of the heat.*
Est-ce qu'ils se sont disputés?	*Did they have an argument?*
Non, ils ne se sont pas disputés.	*No, they did not have an argument.*
Est-ce que vous vous êtes réconciliés?	*Did you reconcile?*
Oui, nous nous sommes réconciliés.	*Yes, we reconciled.*

Written Practice 6

Put the following verbs into the **passé composé**.

1. Elle se lève tôt. _____
2. Il s'occupe de cette affaire. _____
3. Je me promène dans le parc. _____
4. Elles s'écrivent pendant les vacances. _____
5. Elle se réveille à l'aube. _____

Using Adverbs with the *passé composé*

In the **passé composé**, adverbs of quantity, quality, and frequency are placed between **avoir** or **être** and the past participle. See the following examples.

Il dort beaucoup.	*He sleeps a lot.*
Il a beaucoup dormi.	*He slept a lot.*
Ils mangent trop.	*They eat too much.*
Ils ont trop mangé.	*They ate too much.*
Elle travaille assez.	*She works enough.*
Elle a assez travaillé.	*She worked enough.*
Il écrit très bien les discours.	*He writes speeches very well.*
Il a très bien écrit les discours.	*He wrote the speeches very well.*
Elle s'exprime mal.	*She expresses herself badly.*
Elle s'est mal exprimée.	*She expressed herself badly.*
Il voyage souvent au Brésil.	*He often travels to Brazil.*
Il a souvent voyagé au Brésil.	*He often traveled to Brazil.*
Ils mentent toujours.	*They always lie.*
Ils ont toujours menti.	*They have always lied.*

To express time with the **passé composé, pendant** (*for, during*) is commonly used, although it can be omitted. However, **pour** (*for*) is never used for the past.

Elle a habité trois ans à Paris.	*She lived three years in Paris.*
Elle a habité pendant trois ans à Paris.	*She lived for three years in Paris.*
Ils ont voyagé un mois dans le Midi.	*They traveled for a month in the South of France.*
Ils ont voyagé pendant un mois dans le Midi.	*They traveled for a month in the South of France.*

Written Practice 7

Put the following verbs into the **passé composé**.

1. Elle voyage souvent en France. _____
2. On dîne bien. _____
3. Ils dansent beaucoup. _____

4. Ils écrivent toujours des poèmes. _____

5. Ils ne lisent pas assez. _____

QUIZ

Put the following regular verbs into the **passé composé**.

parler (tu)	*tu as parlé* _____

1. manger (nous) | _____
   regarder (tu) | _____
   téléphoner (ils) | _____
   dîner (vous) | _____
   partager (nous) | _____
   écouter (elles) | _____
   jouer (nous) | _____
   étudier (il) | _____
   visiter (nous) | _____

Put the following verbs into the **passé composé**.

être (il)	*il a été* _____

2. boire (il) | _____
   prendre (elle) | _____
   savoir (je) | _____
   dire (vous) | _____
   pleuvoir (il) | _____
   choisir (vous) | _____
   avoir (je) | _____
   perdre (nous) | _____
   se marier (ils) | _____
   apprendre (nous) | _____

Rewrite the following paragraph putting the verbs in parentheses into the **passé composé**.

3. Pendant les vacances, nous (a. aller) en Bretagne. Nous (b. visiter) la ville
fortifiée de Saint-Malo. Nous (c. se promener) sur les remparts et nous
(d. admirer) les vieilles maisons. Nous (e. nager) dans la mer et nous (f.
reposer) sur la plage. Nous (g. faire) du vélo et nous (h. prendre) beaucoup
de photos. Nous (i. manger) bien et nous (j. s'amuser) bien. Nous (k. dormir)
dans un hôtel au bord de la mer. Nous (l. se lever tard) le matin. Il (m. pleuvoir) seulement un jour. Nous (n. rencontrer) des gens très sympathiques.
Nous (o. revenir) à la maison très contents de nos vacances.

_____

_____

_____

_____

_____

_____

_____

_____

_____

Être or **avoir**?

Elle ___*a sorti*___ les chaises longues dans le jardin. (sortir)

4. Ils _____ en haut de la Tour Eiffel. (monter)

Je (*m.*) _____ avec mes amis hier soir. (sortir)

Ils _____ devant le musée d'Orsay. (passer)

Il _____ le bifteck. (retourner)

Elle _____ l'enfant dans ses bras. (monter)

Nous (*m.*) _____ en Chine. (retourner)

Tu _____ les valises au rez-de-chaussée. (descendre)

Nous _____ une semaine en Martinique. (passer)

Il _____ son chien. (sortir)

Elle _____ par l'escalator. (descendre)

Translate the following sentences, using **vous** and the **est-ce que** form when necessary.

   5. She went to England. _____

   6. Did you understand the explanation? _____

   7. He took care of his sister's children during the summer.

       _____

   8. She fell in love with Laurent. _____

   9. They sold their house. _____

  10. She spent a week in Paris. _____

CHAPTER 13

Talking About the Past with the *imparfait*

In this chapter you will learn:

The *imparfait*

The **imparfait** (*imperfect*) is one of the most complex tenses in French. In Chapter 12, you learned the use of the **passé composé** to talk about an action that took place on a specific occasion in the past. The **imparfait** plays a different role and has many subtle nuances. It is used to describe a state of mind and being in the past as well as continuous or habitual past actions.

To form the imperfect, take the **nous** form of the present tense and remove the **ons** ending, which gives you the stem of the **imparfait**. Then add the **imparfait** endings (**ais, ais, ait, ions, iez, aient**) to this stem. For example:

chanter *(to sing)*
nous chantons → chant-

je chantais	*I sang*	nous chantions	*we sang*
tu chantais	*you sang*	vous chantiez	*you sang*
il/elle chantait	*he/she sang*	ils/elles chantaient	*they sang*

Always remember to use the **nous** form of the verb in the present tense as the basis for the imperfect.

boire *(to drink)*
nous buvons → buv-

je buvais	*I drank*	nous buvions	*we drank*
tu buvais	*you drank*	vous buviez	*you drank*
il/elle buvait	*he/she drank*	ils/elles buvaient	*they drank*

NOTE: *The ais, ait, and aient endings are all pronounced alike.*

Verbs with spelling changes in the present-tense **nous** form, such as **manger** and **commencer,** retain those spelling changes for all the conjugations in the imperfect except for the **nous** and **vous** forms (in other words, for the **je, tu, il, elle, ils,** and **elles** conjugations).

je commençais	*I started*	tu partageais	*you shared*
ils effaçaient	*they erased*	elle prononçait	*she pronounced*
je mangeais	*I ate*	ils voyageaient	*they traveled*

With the **nous** and **vous** forms in the **imparfait,** because the endings begin with a vowel, the extra **e** and the **ç** are not needed.

| nous mangions | *we ate* | vous voyagiez | *you traveled* |

Depending on the context, the **imparfait** can be the equivalent of several different tenses in English.

Il travaillait.
$\left\{\begin{array}{l} \text{\textit{He was working.}} \\ \text{\textit{He used to work.}} \\ \text{\textit{He worked.}} \end{array}\right.$

THE *IMPARFAIT* WITH *ÊTRE*

NOTE: *The verb* être *has an irregular stem in the* **imparfait***.*

j'étais	*I was*	nous étions	*we were*
tu étais	*you were*	vous étiez	*you were*
il/elle était	*he/she was*	ils/elles étaient	*they were*

Using the *imparfait* for Description

The **imparfait** can be used for background and description. It describes a situation that existed in the past, a state of mind or being. For example:

Il faisait beau.	*The weather was nice.*
Il pleuvait.	*It was raining.*
Le métro était bondé.	*The subway was packed.*
Les tableaux étaient merveilleux.	*The paintings were marvelous.*
Ils étaient heureux.	*They were happy.*

Oral Practice

Read the following sentences aloud.

Il pleuvait.	*It was raining.*
Elle avait très faim.	*She was very hungry.*
La librairie était ouverte.	*The bookstore was open.*
Ils étaient très contents.	*They were very happy.*
Il y avait une centaine d'invités.	*There were about a hundred guests.*
Leur projet n'était pas très réaliste.	*Their project was not very realistic.*
La porte de son bureau était fermée.	*His office door was closed.*
L'avion avait une heure de retard.	*The plane was an hour late.*
L'exposition était fascinante.	*The exhibition was fascinating.*
La salle de conférence était climatisée.	*The conference room was air-conditioned.*
Le supermarché était déjà fermé.	*The supermarket was already closed.*
L'ordinateur était éteint.	*The computer was off.*

Written Practice 1

Put the following sentences into the **imparfait**.

Il (avoir) soif. <u>*Il avait soif*</u>   .

1. Je (être) enthousiaste. _____
2. Nous (être) en réunion. _____
3. Il (faire) froid. _____
4. Il (pleuvoir) _____
5. Vous (avoir) peur. _____

COMMON VERBS USED IN THE *IMPARFAIT*

Some verbs are more often used in the **imparfait** than in the **passé composé,** as they express a mental or physical state. Among these verbs are **avoir** (*to have*); **croire** (*to believe*); **espérer** (*to hope*); **être** (*to be*); **paraître** (*to appear*); **penser** (*to think*); **savoir** (*to know*); and **sembler** (*to seem*). However, when these verbs are used in the **passé composé,** they may take on a different meaning. Here are some example sentences:

Il était malade hier.	*He was sick yesterday.*
Il a mangé cet œuf et tout de suite il a été malade.	*He ate that egg and immediately he got sick.*
Je savais qu'elle avait raison.	*I knew she was right.*
Je l'ai écouté et immédiatement j'ai su qu'il était coupable.	*I listened to him and immediately I knew (I recognized) that he was guilty.*

Using the *imparfait* for Habitual Action

Another use of the **imparfait** is for habitual, repetitive action. It describes past events that were repeated in the past. The English *used to* and *would* are translated by the French **imparfait.** Some expressions are indications that you should use the **imparfait:**

souvent	*often*	toujours	*always*
le lundi	*on Mondays*	le dimanche	*on Sundays*
chaque jour	*every day*	chaque semaine	*every week*
chaque mois	*every month*	tous les jours	*every day*
d'ordinaire	*ordinarily*	d'habitude	*usually*

Here are a few example sentences:

Il jouait au basket tous les week-ends.	*He used to play basketball every weekend.*
Nous allions au zoo le jeudi.	*We used to go to the zoo on Thursdays.*
À cette époque, elle travaillait pour Air France.	*At that time, she worked for Air France.*

Quand il était à Paris l'été dernier, il mangeait des croissants tous les matins.	*When he was in Paris last summer, he ate croissants every morning.*

Oral Practice

Read the following sentences aloud.

Je jouais au basket le mercredi.	*I played basketball on Wednesdays.*
On faisait la cuisine à tour de rôle.	*We used to take turns cooking.*
Nous avions deux siamois.	*We used to have two Siamese cats.*
Nous allions au bord de la mer.	*We used to go to the seashore.*
Elle faisait du jogging tous les matins.	*She would jog every morning.*
Je les voyais chaque samedi.	*I used to see them every Saturday.*
Les congés payés n'existaient pas à cette époque.	*At that time, paid vacation did not exist.*
Je faisais les courses à Monoprix.	*I would shop at Monoprix.*
Je mangeais à la cafétéria de la fac ou dans un restaurant marocain.	*I would eat in the college cafeteria or in a Moroccan restaurant.*
Mon plat favori était le tajine d'agneau.	*My favorite dish was lamb tajine.*
Nous avions un petit jardin.	*We used to have a small garden.*
J'avais quatre tortues.	*I had four turtles.*
Il travaillait chez Michelin.	*He used to work at Michelin's.*

Written Practice 2

Put the following sentences into the **imparfait**.

Ils (habiter) à Reims. *Ils habitaient à Reims.*

1. Vous (travailler) le samedi. _____

2. Ils (porter) un uniforme. _____

3. Nous (boire) du cidre. _____

4. Je (faire) du yoga. _____

5. Tu (voir) tes amis le week-end. _____

Using the *imparfait* to Express Interrupted Action

The **imparfait** is also used to describe a continuous action that was going on in the past when another action interrupted it. The interruption is expressed by the **passé composé.** See the following examples:

Fabien dormait quand le téléphone a sonné.	*Fabien was sleeping when the phone rang.*
Ils se promenaient dans le parc quand il a commencé à pleuvoir.	*They were walking in the park when it started to rain.*

When an action had been going on for a period of time before being interrupted, the **imparfait** is used with **depuis.** For example:

Il travaillait depuis des heures quand il a décidé d'aller au cinéma.	*He had been working for hours when he decided to go to the movies.*
Le présentateur parlait depuis quelques secondes quand l'image a disparu.	*The anchorperson had been talking for a few seconds when the image disappeared.*

Oral Practice

Read the following sentences aloud.

Elle rédigeait un rapport quand j'ai appelé.	*She was writing a report when I called.*
Ils jouaient aux échecs quand je suis arrivé.	*They were playing chess when I arrived.*

J'attendais l'autobus depuis vingt minutes quand un taxi est arrivé.	*I had been waiting for a bus for twenty minutes when a cab arrived.*
Louis lisait *Le Monde* quand tu es entré.	*Louis was reading* Le Monde *when you entered.*
J'étudiais l'italien depuis un an quand j'ai décidé d'apprendre le français.	*I had been studying Italian for a year when I decided to learn French.*
Je traversais la rue quand soudain j'ai vu Bernard.	*I was crossing the street when suddenly I saw Bernard.*
Je regardais la télé quand Émilie est arrivée.	*I was watching TV when Émilie arrived.*

Written Practice 3

Put the following sentences into the **imparfait** or **passé composé**. Watch out for a specific versus a continuous action.

Claude (dormir) quand Joël (arriver). _Claude dormait quand Joël est arrivé._

1. Paul (dîner) quand Marie (entrer). _____
2. Vous (se reposer) quand on (frapper) à la porte. _____
3. Tu (se promener) quand tu (voir) un lapin. _____
4. Elle (faire le ménage) quand sa sœur (sonner). _____
5. Nous (regarder) le film quand Julie (poser) une question. _____

THE *IMPARFAIT* WITH *PENDANT*

The **imparfait** is used with **pendant** (*while*) to describe two simultaneous actions in the past.

Je regardais un film pendant qu'il faisait ses devoirs.	*I was watching a film while he was doing his homework.*
Elle se reposait pendant qu'il faisait la cuisine.	*She was resting while he was cooking.*

Using the *imparfait* to Make a Suggestion

With a **si** + **on** construction, the **imparfait** is used to make a suggestion, to invite someone to do something. The informal **on** refers to two or more people and uses the third person singular conjugation.

Si on allait au cinéma?	*What about going to the movies?*
Si on prenait le train?	*What about taking the train?*

Oral Practice

Repeat aloud the following sentences.

Si on allait en France?	*What about going to France?*
Si on achetait cette voiture?	*What about buying this car?*
Si on appelait Maryse?	*What about calling Maryse?*
Si on dînait au restaurant?	*What about having dinner in a restaurant?*
Si on lui offrait ce livre?	*What about giving him this book?*
Si on envoyait une carte postale à Luc?	*What about sending a postcard to Luc?*
Si on déménageait au Brésil?	*What about moving to Brazil?*
Si on jouait au tennis?	*What about playing tennis?*
Si on chantait une chanson?	*What about singing a song?*
Si on attendait encore quelques minutes?	*What about waiting another few minutes?*
Si on vendait ces meubles?	*What about selling this furniture?*
Si on faisait un itinéraire?	*What about making an itinerary?*
Si on invitait les Clément?	*What about inviting the Cléments?*
Si on faisait la sieste?	*What about taking a nap?*
Si on empruntait sa voiture?	*What about borrowing her car?*
Si on lui racontait une histoire?	*What about telling him a story?*
Si on allumait le chauffage?	*What about turning on the heat?*

Written Practice 4

Make a proposition using the elements provided.

      acheter un vélo   *Si on achetait un vélo?* _____

1. aller au parc _____
2. jouer aux échecs _____
3. se lever tôt _____
4. téléphoner à Noémie _____
5. faire une promenade _____

Using the *imparfait* to Express a Wish or Regret

The **imparfait** is also used after **si** to express a wish or a regret. See the following examples:

Si seulement j'avais plus de temps!	*If only I had more time!*
Si seulement je pouvais y aller!	*If only I could go!*
Si seulement il était riche!	*If only he were rich!*
Si seulement elle pouvait dormir!	*If only she could sleep!*

The Immediate Past with the *imparfait*

You studied the immediate past, formed with **venir** + **de** + the infinitive, in Chapter 9. For example:

Je viens de lui téléphoner.	*I just called him.*
Ils viennent de rentrer.	*They just came back.*

To describe an action that *had just happened* at a given time, use **venir** in the **imparfait** + **de** + the infinitive.

Elle venait de partir quand il est arrivé.	*She had just left when he arrived.*
Je venais de finir le rapport quand il a appelé.	*I had just finished the report when he called.*

Oral Practice

Repeat aloud the following sentences.

Ils venaient d'acheter cette maison quand ils ont découvert celle-là.	*They had just bought this house when they discovered that one.*
Elle venait de signer le bail quand elle a appris sa mutation.	*She had just signed the lease when she found out about her transfer.*
Je venais de commencer ce roman quand il m'a dit de lire celui-ci.	*I had just started this novel when he told me to read this one.*
Nous venions d'arriver quand nous avons appris les mauvaises nouvelles.	*We had just arrived when we heard the bad news.*
Le match venait de commencer quand le joueur principal s'est foulé la cheville.	*The game had just started when the key player twisted his ankle.*
Vous veniez de décider de suivre un régime quand elle a apporté un gâteau au chocolat.	*You had just decided to go on a diet when she brought a chocolate cake.*
Nous venions de finir les rénovations quand on a trouvé des fuites.	*We had just finished the renovations when we found some leaks.*
Je venais de refuser une invitation quand un collègue a proposé de me remplacer.	*I had just refused an invitation when a colleague offered to substitute for me.*
Il venait de se marier quand son ancienne petite amie l'a appelé.	*He had just gotten married when his ex-girlfriend called him.*

Written Practice 5

Conjugate the following verbs using **venir de** in the **imparfait**.

commencer (je)   *je venais de commencer*

1. arriver à Paris (il)   _____
2. s'arrêter (je)   _____
3. s'installer (nous)   _____
4. signer le contrat (elle)   _____
5. déménager (vous)   _____

The *imparfait* versus the *passé composé*

The **imparfait** is the tense that engenders the most polemics among French grammarians. Why did Gide or Proust use an **imparfait** here? He probably meant a **passé simple**! And it goes on for hours without any resolution. Almost any time you tell a story, you will have to use different tenses. Pay special attention to the verbs when you read, and remain flexible. The combination of these two tenses, the **imparfait** and the **passé composé**, will remain one of the trickiest items you will have to master in French grammar. Compare and study the following examples.

Je suis allée en Italie en juin.	*I went to Italy in June.*
Dans mon enfance, j'allais en Italie tous les étés.	*When I was young, I used to go to Italy every summer.*
J'ai attendu l'autobus pendant dix minutes.	*I waited ten minutes for the bus.*
J'attendais l'autobus quand il a commencé à pleuvoir.	*I was waiting for the bus when it started to rain.*
Elle s'est promenée dans le parc cet après-midi.	*She took a walk in the park this afternoon.*
Elle se promenait dans le parc quand tout à coup elle a vu un écureuil.	*She was walking in the park when suddenly she saw a squirrel.*

J'ai travaillé dans cette entreprise
pendant dix ans.

I worked in this firm for ten years.

Je travaillais dans cette entreprise
depuis dix ans quand j'ai décidé
de démissionner.

*I had been working in this firm for ten
years when I decided to resign.*

Tu as bien dormi?

Did you sleep well?

Elle dormait quand soudain le
chien s'est mis à aboyer.

*She was sleeping when suddenly the
dog started to bark.*

QUIZ

Put the following verbs into the *imparfait*.

parler (tu)	*tu parlais*

1. savoir (vous)   _____

   penser (je)   _____

   finir (tu)   _____

   être (il)   _____

   dîner (nous)   _____

   vendre (elle)   _____

   boire (vous)   _____

   avoir (nous)   _____

   choisir (tu)   _____

   aller (vous)   _____

Answer the questions with complete sentences, using the **imparfait** of habit, repetition.

s'amuser avec mes copains *Je m'amusais avec mes copains.*

2. lire beaucoup _____

jouer au volley-ball _____

chanter dans une chorale _____

voir beaucoup de films _____

sortir le samedi soir _____

apprendre le chinois _____

se lever tard _____

avoir un correspondant _____

s'habiller de façon décontractée _____

être sportif _____

Put the sentences into the **imparfait**.

Il (aimer) danser. *il aimait danser*

3. Les tableaux de l'exposition (être) magnifiques. _____

Tous les jours, elle (aller) à la piscine. _____

Je (lire) quand le téléphone a sonné. _____

Ils (connaître) bien la région. _____

Il (être) célèbre à vingt ans. _____

Ses parents (avoir) deux chiens. _____

Il (faire) la cuisine lorsque son frère est arrivé. _____

Tu (adorer) regarder les films muets. _____

Elle (finir) un projet quand sa collègue est entrée. _____

Je (ignorer) son état de santé. _____

Change the immediate past from the equivalent of *have just* to *had just* in these sentences, using the **imparfait**.

Vous venez de parler. *Vous veniez de parler.* _____

4. Elle vient de partir. _____

   Ils viennent d'acheter cet appartement. _____

   Je viens de lui laisser un message. _____

   Nous venons d'arriver. _____

   Il vient de gagner le match. _____

   Elle vient de s'installer. _____

   Je viens d'être promu. _____

   Nous venons de prendre une décision. _____

   Elle vient d'apprendre la nouvelle. _____

   Ils viennent de me contacter. _____

Make a suggestion, using **si** + **on** + **imparfait**.

ouvrir la fenêtre *Si on ouvrait la fenêtre?* _____

5. inviter nos voisins _____

   servir un gigot d'agneau _____

   planter des légumes _____

   prendre des photos _____

   se réconcilier _____

Translate the following sentences, using **vous** and the **est-ce que** form.

6. Were you working when I called?

   _____

7. He was watching TV when she walked in.

   _____

Translate the following sentences, using the inversion form where appropriate.

8. I was talking on the phone when the cat jumped on the table.

_____

9. She had just finished the letter when he called.

_____

10. Was the library open?

_____

CHAPTER 14

All About Prepositions

In this chapter you will learn

Prepositions and French Verbs
Verbs Without Prepositions
Verbs Followed by the Preposition à
Verbs Followed by the Preposition de
Verbs That Use Different Prepositions
Common Prepositions

Prepositions and French Verbs

In French, when a conjugated verb is followed by another verb in the same clause, the second verb will be in the infinitive form. When followed by an infinitive, some French verbs take a preposition and others don't. There is no specific rule. You just have to remember whether the verb stands alone without a preposition, or takes **à** or **de**, or takes some other preposition.

Verbs Without Prepositions

Here are some verbs not followed by a preposition in modern French. You may find some exceptions in the literature preceding the twentieth century.

aimer	*to like, to love*	aller	*to go*
avouer	*to admit*	compter	*to intend/to plan*
désirer	*to desire/to wish*	détester	*to hate*
devoir	*must*	écouter	*to listen*
espérer	*to hope*	faire	*to do*
falloir	*must*	laisser	*to let*
oser	*to dare*	paraître	*to appear*
penser	*to think*	pouvoir	*can*
préférer	*to prefer*	prétendre	*to claim*
savoir	*to know*	sentir	*to feel, to think*
sembler	*to seem*	souhaiter	*to wish*
venir	*to come*	voir	*to see*
vouloir	*to want*		

See the following examples:

Il doit aller à la banque.	*He has to go to the bank.*
Ils préfèrent attendre dans le hall de l'hôtel.	*They prefer to wait in the hotel lobby.*

As you probably noticed, the subject of the first verb is the same as that of the second verb; that's why the infinitive form is used. When the subjects are different, a dependent clause introduced by **que** is needed. Compare these sentences:

Il espère aller en Norvège cet été.	*He hopes to go to Norway this summer.*
Il espère que tu iras en Norvège cet été.	*He hopes you'll go to Norway this summer.*

When the infinitive clause is in the negative, the negation stays together and is placed before the infinitive. For example:

Je pense ne pas avoir compris votre explication.	*I think I did not understand your explanation.*
Il préfère ne pas être impliqué dans cette affaire.	*He prefers not to be involved in this business.*

Oral Practice

Read the following sentences aloud.

Nous comptons voyager en Turquie.	*We are planning to travel to Turkey.*
Je préfère arriver le plus vite possible.	*I prefer to arrive as soon as possible.*
Je sais tricoter.	*I know how to knit.*
Je ne souhaite pas les voir.	*I don't wish to see them.*
Il faut s'attendre à des négociations.	*We must expect negotiations.*
Il peut soulever n'importe quoi.	*He can lift anything.*
J'espère déménager avant l'hiver.	*I hope to move before winter.*
Il doit rembourser ses dettes avant le 15 janvier.	*He must pay back his debts before January 15.*
On voudrait bien aller faire un tour en bateau.	*We'd love to go for a boat ride.*
J'aimerais bien devenir membre de votre organisation.	*I'd like to become a member of your organization.*
C'est la pluie contre les volets.	It's the rain against the shutters.

USE OF PREPOSITIONS IN ENGLISH VERSUS FRENCH

In some cases, a French verb does not need a preposition even though its English counterpart requires one, and vice versa. You will notice the confusion when you hear a native speaker of French forgetting the needed preposition in English.

Ils sont entrés.	*They walked in.*
J'attends le métro.	*I am waiting for the subway.*
Nous écoutons la radio.	*We are listening to the radio.*
Elle cherche son parapluie.	*She is looking for her umbrella.*
Il répond **à** la lettre.	*He answers the letter.*
Le directeur permet **à** ses employés de travailler quatre jours par semaine.	*The director allows his employees to work four days a week.*

Written Practice 1

Conjugate the following verbs in the present tense.

       aimer/voyager/il *Il aime voyager.*

1. préférer/rester à la maison (elle) _____
2. savoir/dessiner (nous) _____
3. devoir/partir tôt (ils) _____
4. désirer/aller en Inde (vous) _____
5. espérer/gagner le match (nous) _____

Verbs Followed by the Preposition *à*

Many verbs are followed by the preposition **à** before an infinitive. Again, there is no rule you can follow for this. As in English, you need to learn the verb with its preposition: *to put on, to put up, to put away,* etc.

s'accoutumer à	*to get accustomed to*	faire attention à	*to pay attention to*
aider à	*to help*	s'habituer à	*to get used to*

s'amuser à	*to enjoy*	hésiter à	*to hesitate to*
apprendre à	*to learn, to show how to*	inciter à	*to encourage to*
arriver à	*to manage to*	s'intéresser à	*to get interested in*
aspirer à	*to aspire to*	inviter à	*to invite to*
autoriser à	*to authorize to*	se mettre à	*to start, to begin to*
s'attendre à	*to expect to*	parvenir à	*to manage to*
chercher à	*to try, to attempt to*	préparer à	*to get ready to*
commencer à	*to start to*	renoncer à	*to give up*
consentir à	*to agree, to consent to*	se résigner à	*to resign oneself to*
continuer à	*to continue to, to keep on*	réussir à	*to succeed in*
se décider à	*to make up one's mind to*	songer à	*to think about*
encourager à	*to encourage to*	tenir à	*to insist on, to be eager to*
se faire à	*to get used to*	viser à	*to aim at*

See the following example sentences:

Elle m'aide à ranger mes affaires.   *She is helping me (to) put my things away.*

Il a appris à nager très jeune.   *He learned how to swim at a young age.*

Oral Practice

Ask the following questions and then answer them, aloud.

Elle s'est habituée à vivre en banlieue?   *Has she gotten used to living in the suburbs?*

Oui, elle s'est habituée à vivre en banlieue.   *Yes, she's gotten used to living in the suburbs.*

A-t-il réussi à joindre son ami?   *Did he manage to contact his friend?*

Oui, il a réussi à le joindre.   *Yes, he managed to reach him.*

Ils s'attendent à gagner?   *Do they expect to win?*

Oui, ils s'attendent à gagner.   *Yes, they expect to win.*

À quelle heure commences-tu à travailler?   *What time do you start working?*

Je commence à travailler à huit heures.   *I start working at eight.*

Pourquoi est-ce que le directeur tient à me parler?	*Why does the director insist on talking to me?*
Il tient à te parler du nouveau projet.	*He insists on talking to you about the new project.*
Tu l'as encouragé à apprendre une langue étrangère?	*Did you encourage him to learn a foreign language?*
Oui, je l'ai encouragé à apprendre le portugais.	*Yes, I encouraged him to learn Portuguese.*
Elle aspire à devenir sénateur?	*Is she aspiring to become a senator?*
Je crois qu'elle aspire à devenir présidente.	*I think she is aspiring to become president.*
Fais attention à ne pas la vexer!	*Be careful not to hurt her feelings.*
Bien sûr, je fais attention à ne jamais la vexer.	*Of course, I am careful never to hurt her feelings.*
Tu es arrivé à la persuader?	*Did you manage to persuade her?*
Oui, je suis arrivée à la persuader.	*Yes, I managed to persuade her.*

Verbs Followed by the Preposition *de*

Many verbs are followed by the preposition **de** before an infinitive. As with the verbs followed by **à**, there is no rule to follow.

accepter de	*to accept*	s'excuser de	*to apologize for*
accuser de	*to accuse of*	faire semblant de	*to pretend to*
s'arrêter de	*to stop*	feindre de	*to feign, to pretend to*
avoir besoin de	*to need to*	finir de	*to finish, to end*
avoir envie de	*to feel like*	interdire de	*to forbid to*
avoir l'intention de	*to intend to*	menacer de	*to threaten to*
avoir peur de	*to be afraid of*	mériter de	*to deserve to*
cesser de	*to stop, to cease*	offrir de	*to offer to*
choisir de	*to choose to*	oublier de	*to forget to*
conseiller de	*to advise to*	permettre de	*to allow to, to permit to*
se contenter de	*to be content to*	persuader de	*to persuade to, to convince to*

convaincre de	*to convince to*	se plaindre de	*to complain about*
craindre de	*to fear*	projeter de	*to plan to*
défendre de	*to forbid to*	promettre de	*to promise to*
demander de	*to ask to*	refuser de	*to refuse to*
se dépêcher de	*to hurry to*	regretter de	*to regret*
s'efforcer de	*to try hard to*	remercier de	*to thank for*
empêcher de	*to prevent from*	reprocher de	*to reproach for*
s'empêcher de	*to refrain from*	soupçonner de	*to suspect of*
envisager de	*to contemplate*	se souvenir de	*to remember*
essayer de	*to try to*	tâcher de	*to try*
éviter de	*to avoid*		

See the following example sentences:

J'ai essayé de l'appeler.	*I tried to call him.*
Ils ont accepté d'intervenir.	*They agreed to intervene.*

Oral Practice

Read the following sentences aloud.

Il a promis d'envoyer des médicaments.	*He promised to send some medicine.*
La police nous a empêchés de traverser le pont.	*The police prevented us from crossing the bridge.*
Laura a accepté de participer.	*Laura agreed to participate.*
Nous envisageons de nous installer en France.	*We are thinking about settling in France.*
Je lui ai conseillé d'accepter l'offre.	*I advised him to accept the offer.*
Son voisin l'accuse d'avoir volé ses outils de jardin.	*His neighbor accuses him of having stolen his garden tools.*
L'avocat lui défend de parler à la presse avant jeudi.	*The lawyer is forbidding him to talk to the press until Thursday.*
Il se plaint d'avoir trop de travail.	*He is complaining about having too much work.*

Oh, j'ai complètement oublié de lui demander.	*Oh, I completely forgot to ask her.*
Ils ont vraiment besoin de faire repeindre leur maison.	*They really do need to have their house repainted.*

Written Practice 2

Complete with **à** ou **de**.

1. J'ai oublié _____ fermer la porte à clé.
2. Nous l'avons aidé _____ faire les courses.
3. Elle a refusé _____ nous accompagner.
4. Ils réussissent toujours _____ résoudre les problèmes.
5. Il a peur _____ faire des gaffes.

Verbs That Use Different Prepositions

One thing to keep in mind is that the same verb can be used either without a preposition or with different prepositions, thus changing the meaning. Again, these usages have to be memorized. Let's look at the verb **finir** *(to finish)*, then compare the various uses of other verbs:

Il a fini sa mission?	*Has he finished his mission?*
Est-ce qu'il a fini de payer sa maison?	*Has he finished paying for his house?*
Après des années d'hésitation, il a fini par se marier.	*After years of hesitation, he finally ended up getting married.*
Elle a fini son discours par une citation de Balzac.	*She ended her speech by (with) a quotation of Balzac.*

NOTE: *See how the preposition changes the meaning in the following examples:*

Je lui ai demandé un bureau plus grand.	*I asked him for a larger office.*
Je ne lui ai pas demandé de faire des heures supplémentaires.	*I did not ask him to work overtime.*
Il demande à être entendu au tribunal.	*He is asking to be heard at the court.*
Je crois l'histoire de Gabriel.	*I believe Gabriel's story.*
Elle croit à toutes sortes de phénomènes.	*She believes in all kinds of phenomena.*
Il croit en Dieu.	*He believes in God.*
Croit-elle en toi?	*Does she have confidence in you?*
Nous n'avons pas encore commencé les rénovations.	*We have not yet started the renovations.*
J'ai commencé à jouer du piano à cinq ans.	*I started playing the piano at the age of five.*
Je veux commencer par une salade verte.	*I want to start with a green salad.*
J'ai joué le jeu, comme tu me l'avais conseillé.	*I played the game as you had advised me to do.*
Elle sait très bien jouer au golf.	*She can play golf very well.*
Il joue de la guitare.	*He plays the guitar.*
Elle a parlé à sa mère hier soir.	*She talked to her mother last night.*
Je ne lui en ai pas parlé.	*I did not talk to him about it.*
Je pense à mes vacances.	*I am thinking about my vacation.*
Je pensais à toi.	*I was thinking about you.*
Que pensez-vous de cette pièce?	*What do you think about this play?*
Il tient une bougie.	*He is holding a candle.*
Elle tient sa fille par la main.	*She is holding her daughter's hand.*
Il tient à ses chiens.	*He is attached to his dogs.*
Elle tient à son amie Carole.	*She is attached to her friend Carole.*
Il tient de sa mère.	*He looks like his mother.*
J'ai rêvé de toi.	*I dreamt about you.*

Peut-on rêver à un avenir meilleur?	*Can we dream of better days?*
Elle va me le donner ce soir.	*She is going to give it to me tonight.*
J'ai trouvé un hôtel qui donne sur la Place des Vosges.	*I found a hotel looking out on Place des Vosges.*
Je suis arrivé en retard.	*I arrived late.*
Elle a manqué à sa promesse.	*She failed to keep her word.*
Sa ville natale lui manque.	*She misses her hometown.*
Et il me manque.	*And I miss him.*

Written Practice 3

Complete with the appropriate preposition.

1. Elle a fini le repas _____ une crème brûlée.
2. Odile joue _____ la flûte.
3. Mon bureau donne _____ la Seine.
4. Ils croient _____ la science.
5. Elle manque _____ imagination.

Common Prepositions

Here is a list of commonly used prepositions that will come in handy.

à	*at, in*	hormis	*apart from*
après	*after*	hors	*except, apart from*
avant	*before*	malgré	*in spite of*
avec	*with*	par	*by, through*
chez	*at, with*	parmi	*among*
contre	*against*	pendant	*during*
dans	*in*	pour	*for*
de	*of, from*	sans	*without*
derrière	*behind*	sauf	*except*
dès	*from*	selon	*according to*
devant	*in front of*	sous	*under*
durant	*during*	suivant	*according to*

en	*in, out of*	sur	*on*
entre	*between*	vers	*toward*
envers	*toward*	vu	*considering, given*

Here are some example sentences:

Elle est assise devant moi.	*She is sitting in front of me.*
Il est appuyé contre le mur.	*He is leaning against the wall.*
Selon l'éditeur, ce roman va avoir du succès.	*According to the publisher, this novel will have some success.*
Gare-toi derrière l'église!	*Park behind the church!*

THE PREPOSITION À

Some prepositions will take on different meanings in different contexts. In some instances, the preposition **à** will imply nature, function, or purpose.

un gâteau à la noix de coco	*a coconut cake*
une glace au citron	*a bowl of/an order of lemon ice cream*
une glace à la vanille	*a bowl of/an order of vanilla ice cream*
une machine à coudre	*a sewing machine*
une machine à écrire	*a typewriter*
une machine à laver	*a washing machine*
une machine à sous	*a slot machine*
une machine à tricoter	*a knitting machine*
un métier à tisser	*a loom*
un moulin à café	*a coffee mill*
un moulin à paroles	*a chatterbox*
un moulin à poivre	*a pepper mill*
un moulin à vent	*a windmill*
une mousse au chocolat	*a chocolate mousse*
une tasse à café	*a coffee cup*
une tasse à thé	*a teacup*
un verre à eau	*a water glass*
un verre à liqueur	*a liqueur glass*
un verre à moutarde	*a mustard jar*
un verre à porto	*a port glass*
un verre à vin	*a wineglass*
un verre à whisky	*a whisky glass*

THE PREPOSITION *DE*

While **à** implies function and purpose, **de** implies content or composition.

un bol de soupe	*a bowl of soup*
une boîte de maïs	*a can of corn*
une brassée de fleurs	*an armful of flowers*
une poignée d'amandes	*a handful of almonds*
une tasse de café	*a cup of coffee*
une tasse de thé	*a cup of tea*
un verre d'eau	*a glass of water*
un verre de lait	*a glass of milk*
un verre de limonade	*a glass of lemonade*
un verre de vin	*a glass of wine*

THE PREPOSITION *CHEZ*

Another preposition that can take on different meanings is **chez.** Look at the following example sentences:

Nous avons dîné chez Mathilde.	*We had dinner at Mathilde's.*
Un des restaurants branchés dans le neuvième s'appelle Chez Jean.	*One of the trendy restaurants in the ninth arrondissement is called Chez Jean (Jean's Place).*
On trouve les meilleures confitures chez Hédiard.	*One finds the best jams at Hédiard's.*
Chez Flaubert, tout est perfection.	*With Flaubert, all is perfection.*
Chez les adolescents, les relations sont souvent conflictuelles.	*With teenagers, relationships are often confrontational.*

TRANSLATING *WITH*

Some prepositions present recurrent translation problems. The English preposition *with* is the perfect example.

Il a monté cette entreprise avec son frère.	*He set up this business with his brother.*
La femme aux yeux gris est ma sœur.	*The woman with gray eyes is my sister.*
Le jeune homme à la casquette bleue est le meilleur joueur de l'équipe.	*The young man with the blue cap is the best player in the team.*
La maison aux volets bleus est à vendre.	*The house with blue shutters is for sale.*
Elle l'a regardé d'un air triste.	*She looked at him with a sad look.*
Il a brisé la vitre d'un coup de poing.	*He broke the window with his fist.*
Elle est contente du travail du stagiaire.	*She is pleased with the intern's work.*
Ils sont satisfaits de la décision.	*They are happy with the decision.*

EN VERSUS *DANS*

In Chapter 6, you learned the difference between **en** and **dans** in the context of time. Another nuance with **en** and **dans** is general versus specific. See the following examples:

Marie circule toujours en métro.	*Marie always travels by subway.*
Il lit le journal dans le métro.	*He reads the paper in the subway.*
Ils adorent voyager en avion.	*They love to travel by plane.*
Il faisait très froid dans l'avion.	*It was very cold on the plane.*
Elle habite en Grèce.	*She lives in Greece.*
Dans la Grèce de sa grand-mère, la vie était plus paisible.	*In her grandmother's Greece, life was more peaceful.*

Written Practice 4

Choose the appropriate preposition: **à**, **chez**, **selon**, **sous**, or **vers**.

1. Jacques avance _____ l'entrée du château.
2. Mélanie habite toujours _____ ses parents.
3. _____ le Premier Ministre, la situation économique s'améliore.
4. Il a commandé une glace _____ la fraise.
5. Le chat est _____ le lit.

QUIZ

Conjugate the following verbs in the present tense.

      aimer/nager (vous) _Vous aimez nager._ _____

1. savoir/danser (elle) _____
   préférer/se reposer (nous) _____
   souhaiter/partir (elles) _____
   aller/réussir (ils) _____
   aimer/se promener (vous) _____
   avouer/avoir tort (il) _____
   pouvoir/convaincre (elles) _____
   oser/protester (ils) _____
   devoir/accepter (nous) _____
   désirer/démissionner (vous) _____

Complete with the appropriate preposition.

      Elle apprend _à_ danser.

2. N'oublie pas _____ acheter du pain!
   Nous nous habituons _____ la vie urbaine.
   Tu commences _____ une salade.

La soupe manque _____ poivre?

Elle envisage _____ engager une nouvelle secrétaire.

Il a peur _____ conduire la nuit?

Tu tiens vraiment _____ ces vieilles chaises?

Vous allez l'aider _____ s'installer?

Il m'a parlé _____ ce nouveau film.

Il commence _____ neiger.

Complete the sentence with the appropriate preposition.

3. Laure vient d'acheter une machine _____ tricoter.

Sers-moi un verre _____ vin.

La maison _____ volets verts appartient à M. Valentin.

_____ Balzac, les détails sont exquis.

Il est interdit de se garer _____ un hôpital.

Quel espirit de contradiction! Tu es toujours _____ tout!

Ils sont passés _____ Lyon pour aller à Nice.

Chez Berthillon, les glaces _____ la pistache sont délicieuses.

Ils se sont promenés dans le parc _____ la pluie.

L'homme _____ cheveux gris s'appelle Ludovic.

Translate the following sentences, using **tu** and inversion when necessary.

4. Try to call him! _____

5. I forgot to bring a gift. _____

6. Do you play tennis? _____

7. What are you thinking about? _____

Translate the following sentences, using **vous** form when necessary.

8. They decided to buy a new car. _____

9. Help me write this letter! _____

10. He asked him to invite his sister-in-law. _____

CHAPTER 15

More Past Tenses and Indicating Possession

In this chapter you will learn:

The plus-que-parfait

The passé simple

Possessive Pronouns

Demonstrative Pronouns

The *plus-que-parfait*

The **plus-que-parfait** *(pluperfect)* is used primarily in narration, to report events that had been completed before another past event took place. It is formed with the **imparfait** of **être** or **avoir** and the past participle of the main verb. Let's review the **imparfait** of these two auxiliary verbs.

être *(to be)*

j'étais	*I was*	nous étions	*we were*
tu étais	*you were*	vous étiez	*you were*
il/elle était	*he/she was*	ils/elles étaient	*they were*

avoir *(to have)*

j'avais	*I had*	nous avions	*we had*
tu avais	*you had*	vous aviez	*you had*
il/elle avait	*he/she had*	ils/elles avaient	*they had*

Here are some example sentences:

Sonia était déja partie quand je suis arrivé.	*Sonia had already left when I got there.*
Serge a cru que tu n'avais pas compris la situation.	*Serge thought you had not understood the situation.*

In the **plus-que-parfait,** all the pronominal verbs are conjugated with **être** and agree in gender and number with the subject. See the following examples:

Clément s'est rendu compte qu'il s'était trompé.	*Clément realized he had made a mistake.*
La police a découvert que la jeune fille s'était noyée.	*The police discovered the young woman had drowned.*

Sometimes the **plus-que-parfait** is translated into English as a simple tense. In French, however, if there is any anteriority in a series of actions, the **plus-que-parfait** *must* be used.

Inès a mangé le dessert que le chef avait préparé pour elle.	*Inès has eaten the dessert that the chef (had) prepared for her.*

Oral Practice

Read the following sentences aloud.

Quelqu'un avait déjà loué l'appartement.	*Someone had already rented the apartment.*
Je les ai tous interviewés car mon assistant avait réussi à les joindre tous.	*I interviewed them all, since my assistant had managed to reach them all.*
Elle avait appris la fusion par un journaliste.	*She had found out about the merger through a journalist.*
Il est tombé en panne d'essence car il avait oublié de faire le plein.	*He ran out of gas because he had forgotten to fill up the tank.*
J'allais les inviter mais Alex l'avait déjà fait.	*I was going to invite them, but Alex had already done it.*
Il avait quitté Calais car il ne s'était pas habitué au froid.	*He had left Calais as he had not been able to get used to the cold weather.*
Il était en colère car tout le monde avait oublié son anniversaire.	*He was angry because everyone had forgotten his birthday.*
Il avait plagié tout un chapitre.	*He had plagiarized a whole chapter.*
Ils ont parlé de la station balnéaire où ils s'étaient rencontrés.	*They talked about the resort where they had met.*
Ils ne s'étaient pas revus depuis vingt ans.	*They had not seen each other for twenty years.*
Elle mourait de faim car elle n'avait rien mangé de toute la journée.	*She was starving since she had not eaten the whole day.*

Written Practice 1

Put the following verbs into the **plus-que-parfait**.

perdre (il)   *il avait perdu*_____

1. écouter (vous)   _____
2. s'amuser (ils)   _____
3. partir (elle)   _____

4. dîner (nous) _____

5. finir (tu) _____

USING *DEPUIS* WITH THE *PLUS-QUE-PARFAIT*

In Chapter 6, you learned **depuis** with the present tense. **Depuis** is also used in the past tense when it refers to a continuing action. Note that in these cases, English uses the pluperfect while French uses the **imparfait.** Compare the following examples:

Joséphine habite à Lyon depuis trois ans.	*Joséphine has been living in Lyon for three years.*
Didier roulait depuis des heures quand tout à coup il a aperçu le Mont Blanc.	*Didier had been driving for hours when suddenly he saw Mont Blanc.*

USING *SI* WITH THE *PLUS-QUE-PARFAIT*

The **plus-que-parfait,** when used with **si,** expresses a wish or regret about past events. Note the following examples:

Si seulement je n'avais pas perdu son adresse!	*If only I had not lost his/her address!*
Si seulement il avait fait un peu plus d'efforts!	*If only he had tried a little harder!*

The *passé simple*

The **passé simple** *(simple past),* definitely the most beautiful tense in French, is the equivalent of the **passé composé,** referring to a specific action in the past, and is found in written narration and in formal speeches. When relating events, quality newspapers may use the **passé simple** for refinement and sometimes to convey a sense of drama. If you want to read novels, short stories, and fairy tales, you need to be able to identify the verb forms of the **passé simple.** When reading aloud, you will appreciate the precise, incisive quality of this tense, used by most modern writers who write in French all over the world.

THE PASSÉ SIMPLE WITH *-ER* VERBS

The **passé simple** of regular **-er** verbs, such as **chanter** (*to sing*), is formed by adding the endings **ai, as, a, âmes, âtes,** and **èrent** to the infinitive stem.

chanter → chant-

je chantai	*I sang*	nous chantâmes	*we sang*
tu chantas	*you sang*	vous chantâtes	*you sang*
il/elle chanta	*he/she sang*	ils/elles chantèrent	*they sang*

Since the **passé simple** is mostly used in narration, you will most often encounter it in the third person singular and plural. The usual spelling changes apply to verbs ending in **cer** and **ger,** adding a cedilla or an extra **e.**

Elle commença à parler.	*She started to talk.*
Il ne voyagea jamais en Russie.	*He never traveled to Russia.*

THE *PASSÉ SIMPLE* WITH *-IR* AND *-RE* VERBS

The **passé simple** of regular **-ir** and **-re** verbs, such as **sortir** (*to go out*) and **entendre** (*to hear*), is formed by adding the endings **is, is, it, îmes, îtes,** and **irent** to the infinitive stem.

sortir *(to go out)*

je sortis	*I went out*	nous sortîmes	*we went out*
tu sortis	*you went out*	vous sortîtes	*you went out*
il/elle sortit	*he/she went out*	ils/elles sortirent	*they went out*

entendre *(to hear)*

j'entendis	*I heard*	nous entendîmes	*we heard*
tu entendis	*you heard*	vous entendîtes	*you heard*
il/elle entendit	*he/she heard*	ils/elles entendirent	*they heard*

Être and **avoir** have irregular conjugations in the **passé simple.**

avoir

j'eus	*I had*	nous eûmes	*we had*
tu eus	*you had*	vous eûtes	*you had*
il/elle eut	*he/she had*	ils/elles eurent	*they had*

être

je fus	*I was*	nous fûmes	*we were*
tu fus	*you were*	vous fûtes	*you were*
il/elle fut	*he/she was*	ils/elles furent	*they were*

IRREGULAR VERBS IN THE *PASSÉ SIMPLE*

Other verbs also have an irregular **passé simple.** Sometimes the stem of the **passé simple** is based on the past participle, but this is not a fixed rule. Here are some of the verbs you should start memorizing in the **passé simple.**

boire *(to drink)*

il but	*he drank*	ils burent	*they drank*

conduire *(to drive)*

il conduisit	*he drove*	ils conduisirent	*they drove*

connaître *(to know)*

il connut	*he knew*	ils connurent	*they knew*

convaincre *(to convince)*

il convainquit	*he convinced*	ils convainquirent	*they convinced*

courir *(to run)*

il courut	*he ran*	ils coururent	*they ran*

craindre *(to fear)*

il craignit	*he feared*	ils craignirent	*they feared*

croire *(to believe)*

il crut	*he believed*	ils crurent	*they believed*

devoir *(to have to)*

il dut	*he had to*	ils durent	*they had to*

écrire *(to write)*

il écrivit	*he wrote*	ils écrivirent	*they wrote*

éteindre *(to turn off [a light])*

il éteignit	*he turned off*	ils éteignirent	*they turned off*

faire *(to do)*

il fit	*he did*	ils firent	*they did*

lire *(to read)*

il lut	*he read*	ils lurent	*they read*

mettre

il mit	*he put*	ils mirent	*they put*

mourir *(to die)*

il mourut	*he died*	ils moururent	*they died*

naître *(to be born)*

il naquit	*he was born*	ils naquirent	*they were born*

peindre *(to paint)*

il peignit	*he painted*	ils peignirent	*they painted*

plaire *(to please)*

il plut	*he pleased*	ils plurent	*they pleased*

pleuvoir *(to rain)*

il plut	*it rained*

pouvoir *(to be able to)*

il put	*he could*	ils purent	*they could*

prendre *(to take)*

il prit	*he took*	ils prirent	*they took*

recevoir *(to receive)*

il reçut	*he received*	ils reçurent	*they received*

savoir *(to know)*

il sut	*he knew*	ils surent	*they knew*

tenir *(to hold)*

il tint	*he held*	ils tinrent	*they held*

valoir *(to be worth)*

il valut	*it was worth*	ils valurent	*they were worth*

venir *(to come)*

il vint	*he came*	ils vinrent	*they came*

vivre *(to live)*

il vécut	*he lived*	ils vécurent	*they lived*

Oral Practice

Repeat the following sentences aloud.

Joseph et Étienne Montgolfier inventèrent la montgolfière en 1783.	*Joseph and Étienne Montgolfier invented the hot-air balloon in 1783.*
Napoléon mourut le 5 mai 1821 sur l'île de Sainte-Hélène.	*Napoléon died on May 5th, 1821 on the island of Saint Helena.*
La guerre éclata un dimanche matin.	*The war broke out on a Sunday morning.*
La trêve dura quelques jours.	*The truce lasted a few days.*
Il fit le tour du monde en cent jours.	*He went around the world in a hundred days.*
Jacques-Yves Cousteau fut un des plus grands explorateurs.	*Jacques-Yves Cousteau was one of the greatest explorers.*
Balzac vécut dans l'ancien village de Passy à Paris de 1840 à 1847.	*Balzac lived in the old Passy village in Paris from 1840 to 1847.*
Marguerite Yourcenar fut la première femme élue à l'Académie Française.	*Marguerite Yourcenar was the first woman elected to the French Academy.*

Il but le verre de vin empoisonné et mourut sur-le-champ.

He drank the poisoned glass of wine and died instantly.

Elle le vit et sut tout de suite qu'il était coupable.

She saw him and knew immediately that he was guilty.

Joséphine de Beauharnais, née en Martinique, devint impératrice en 1804.

Joséphine de Beauharnais, born in Martinique, became empress in 1804.

Casanova eut de nombreuses maîtresses.

Casanova had many mistresses.

«Ce fut, Madame, un grand honneur d'avoir connu votre mari.»

"It was, Madame, a great honor to have met your husband."

Jeanne d'Arc naquit en Lorraine en 1412.

Joan of Arc was born in Lorraine in 1412.

Drame sur la Côte d'Azur! «Il tua sa voisine puis se suicida!»

Drama on the Riviera! "He killed his neighbor and then commited suicide!"

Written Practice 2

Put the following verbs into the **passé simple**.

prendre (ils)   *ils prirent*

1. mettre (tu)   _____
2. venir (elles)   _____
3. faire (je)   _____
4. être (elle)   _____
5. boire (il)   _____

Possessive Pronouns

Possessive pronouns replace nouns used with possessive adjectives. They agree in gender and number with the noun they replace, not with the possessor.

For a Masculine Singular Noun		For a Feminine Singular Noun	
le mien	*mine*	la mienne	*mine*
le tien	*yours*	la tienne	*yours*
le sien	*his/hers*	la sienne	*his/hers*
le nôtre	*ours*	la nôtre	*ours*
le vôtre	*yours*	la vôtre	*yours*
le leur	*theirs*	la leur	*theirs*

For a Masculine Plural Noun		For a Feminine Plural Noun	
les miens	*mine*	les miennes	*mine*
les tiens	*yours*	les tiennes	*yours*
les siens	*his/hers*	les siennes	*his/hers*
les nôtres	*ours*	les nôtres	*ours*
les vôtres	*yours*	les vôtres	*yours*
les leurs	*theirs*	les leurs	*theirs*

See the following examples:

J'apporte mes notes et tu apportes les tiennes.	*I bring my notes and you bring yours.*
Tu fais tes valises et il fait les siennes.	*You pack your suitcases and he packs his.*

When the possessive pronoun is preceded by **à** or **de**, the article is contracted, as shown here:

Elle a écrit à ses amis et tu as écrit aux tiens.	*She wrote to her friends and you wrote to yours.*
Ils parlent de leurs problèmes et vous parlez des vôtres.	*They speak about their problems and you speak about yours.*

EXPRESSING POSSESSION WITH *ÊTRE* + *À*

The most common way of expressing possession is by using **être** + **à** + the disjunctive pronoun.

Ce DVD est à moi.	*This DVD is mine.*
Ce sac à dos est à lui.	*This backpack is his.*

If one wishes to stress the ownership or identify items of a similar nature, the possessive pronoun is used.

—C'est la sienne? —Non, c'est la mienne!	*"Is it his?" "No, it is mine!"*
—Tu a pris le sien! —Non, c'est le mien!	*"You took hers!" "No, it is mine!"*

Sometimes when a possessive pronoun is required in English, French requires a possessive adjective instead.

C'est une de mes amies.	*It is a friend of mine.*
C'est un de vos cousins?	*Is it a cousin of yours?*

IDIOMATIC EXPRESSIONS

Possessive pronouns are also used in many idiomatic expressions.

À la tienne!	*Cheers! (informal)*
À la vôtre!	*Cheers! (formal)*
Après une longue absence, il est retourné chez les siens.	*After a long absence, he went back to his own family.*
Cet astronome ne se sent à l'aise que parmi les siens.	*This astronomer feels at ease only among his peers.*
Leur fils a encore fait des siennes!	*Their son has been acting up again!*
Ma voiture a encore fait des siennes ce matin!	*My car has been acting up again this morning!*
Tu vas échouer si tu n'y mets pas du tien!	*You are going to fail if you don't make an effort.*
S'il n'y met pas du sien, on ne pourra jamais s'associer.	*If he does not contribute his share, we'll never be able to become partners.*

Oral Practice

Ask the following questions and then answer them, aloud.

De quelles couleurs sont vos voitures?	*What colors are your cars?*
La mienne est grise. La sienne est bleue.	*Mine is gray. Hers is blue.*
Peux-tu porter sa valise?	*Can you carry his suitcase?*
Je ne peux pas porter la mienne et la sienne.	*I can't carry mine and his.*
Avez-vous composté tous les billets?	*Did you punch all the tickets?*
J'ai composté les leurs et le mien.	*I punched theirs and mine.*
Que pensez-vous de leur matériel?	*What do you think about their equipment?*
Je pense que le nôtre est plus performant.	*I think ours is more effective.*
Tu utilises leurs logiciels?	*Do you use their software?*
Non, car les vôtres sont de meilleure qualité.	*No, because yours are better quality.*
Où avez-vous mis les passeports?	*Where did you put the passports?*
J'ai mis les vôtres et le mien dans le coffre.	*I put yours and mine in the safe.*
Elle a pris ses clés?	*Did she take her keys?*
Oui, elle a pris les siennes mais elle oublié les nôtres.	*Yes, she took hers but she forgot ours.*
Il aime le nouveau chien de Lucille?	*Does he like Lucille's new dog?*
Oui, mais il préfère le mien.	*Yes, but he prefers mine.*
Tu veux m'emprunter des chaises?	*Do you want to borrow some chairs from me?*
Oui, je veux emprunter les tiennes et les siennes.	*Yes, I want to borrow yours and his.*
Tu as emballé tous les cadeaux?	*Did you wrap all the gifts?*
Oui, j'ai emballé les tiens et les miens.	*Yes, I wrapped yours and mine.*
Il va apporter ses CD?	*Is he going to bring his CDs?*

Il va apporter les siens à condition que tu apportes les tiens.	*He is going to bring his provided you bring yours.*
Vous connaissez leurs enfants?	*Do you know their children?*
Oui, ils vont à la même école que les nôtres.	*Yes, they attend the same school as ours.*
Son chat est un chat de gouttière. Et le vôtre?	*His cat is an alley cat. What about yours?*
Le mien est un abyssin.	*Mine is an Abyssinian.*

Written Practice 3

Translate the possessive pronoun in parentheses, using the **vous** form when necessary.

Mon frère est plus grand que <u>le vôtre.</u>_____ (*yours*)

1. Ma maison est plus ensoleillée que _____. (*his*).
2. Votre travail est plus difficile que _____. (*theirs*)
3. Ses enfants sont plus sages que _____. (*mine*)
4. Leur voiture est plus rapide que _____. (*ours*)
5. Tes plantes sont plus belles que _____. (*mine*)

USING POSSESSIVE PRONOUNS WITH *AUSSI* AND *NON PLUS*

The possessive pronoun is also often used with **aussi** and **non plus** to confirm a positive or negative statement.

—Sa présentation était intéressante. —La vôtre aussi.	*"His presentation was interesting."* *"So was yours."*
—Notre guide était passionnant. —Le mien aussi.	*"Our guide was fascinating."* *"So was mine."*

Demonstrative Pronouns

In Chapter 4, you studied the demonstrative adjectives **ce, cet, cette,** and **ces,** used to point out people and things.

ce plat	*this dish*	cette exposition	*this exhibit*
ces gens	*these people*	ces montres	*these watches*

A demonstrative pronoun replaces a demonstrative adjective and a noun or a specific noun. It agrees in gender and number with the noun it replaces. It can refer to people or things.

Singular

celui	*the one (m.)*	celle	*the one (f.)*

Plural

ceux	*the ones (m. or m. and f.)*	celles	*the ones (f.)*

See the following examples:

À qui est ce chapeau ? C'est celui de Laurent?   *Whose hat is this? Is it Laurent's?*

—Il a pris la place d'Amélie ?
—Non, c'est celle de Pierre.   *"He took Amelie's spot?" "No, it's Pierre's."*

COMPOUND DEMONSTRATIVE PRONOUNS

Compound demonstrative pronouns are used to compare elements of the same nature or to reveal a choice between two alternatives. The particles **-ci** and **-là** are added to the demonstrative pronouns.

Singular

celui-ci	*this one (m.)*	celle-ci	*this one (f.)*
celui-là	*that one (m.)*	celle-là	*that one (f.)*

Plural

ceux-ci	*these (ones) (m. or m. and f.)*	celles-ci	*these (ones) (f.)*
ceux-là	*those (ones) (m. or m. and f.)*	celles-là	*those (ones) (f.)*

See the example sentences:

Celui-ci est en laine. Celui-là est en coton.	*This one is wool. That one is cotton.*
Celle-ci est à vendre. Celle-là est vendue.	*This one is for sale. That one is sold.*
Ceux-ci sont en anglais. Ceux-là sont en français.	*These (ones) are in English. Those (ones) are in French.*

Celui-ci and **celui-là** have a derogatory meaning when used to talk about a person who is not present. For example:

—Tu as rencontré son nouvel imprésario? —Oh, celui-là! Ne m'en parle pas!	*"Have you met her new manager?" "Oh, that guy! Don't talk to me about him/it!"*

DEMONSTRATIVE PRONOUNS WITH DEPENDENT CLAUSES

Demonstrative pronouns can be followed by dependent clauses. For example:

Je préfère cette aquarelle à celle qu'il a achetée.	*I prefer this watercolor to the one he bought.*
Celui qui est derrière vous est une reproduction.	*The one behind you is a reproduction.*
Ceux qui sont dans la vitrine sont en solde.	*The ones in the window are on sale.*
Celui avec qui il parle est son ancien patron.	*The man with whom he is talking is his former boss.*
Celle avec qui il danse est sa deuxième femme.	*The woman he is dancing with is his second wife.*

THE DEMONSTRATIVE PRONOUN *CE*

The demonstrative pronoun **ce** is invariable and is often the subject of the verb **être.** It refers to an idea previously introduced; the adjective that follows is always in the

masculine singular even if it refers to a feminine or plural noun. See the example sentences below:

Regarde cette peinture! C'est si beau!	*Look at this painting! It is so beautiful!*
Oh, les desserts qu'il fait! C'est si bon!	*Oh, the desserts he makes! It's (They're) so good!*

CECI, CELA, AND ÇA

The indefinite demonstrative pronouns **ceci** (*this*), **cela** (*that*), and **ça** (*this/that*, familiar) refer to indefinite things or ideas. **Ceci** may initiate a statement and also announce a following sentence. **Cela** may reflect on something already mentioned.

Prenez ceci!	*Take this!*
Ne prenez pas cela!	*Don't take that!*
Ceci va vous intéresser.	*This is going to interest you.*
Ça, c'est génial.	*That's great.*

Oral Practice

Ask the following questions and then answer them, aloud.

Tu va mettre quelle veste?	*What jacket are you going to wear?*
Celle que j'ai achetée dans le Marais.	*The one I bought in the Marais.*
Que penses-tu de son œuvre?	*What do you think about his work?*
C'est génial.	*It's great.*
En quoi sont ces vases?	*What are these vases made of?*
Celui-ci est en argile et celui-là en porcelaine.	*This one is out of clay and that one is porcelain.*
Pourquoi tu n'aimes pas ces prénoms?	*Why don't you like these first names?*
Celui-ci est trop dur. Et celui-là est démodé.	*This one is too harsh and that one is old-fashioned.*

Quels livres est-ce que je peux emprunter?	*What books can I borrow?*
Tu peux emprunter ceux que j'ai déjà lus.	*You can borrow those I have already read.*
Ses livres sont traduits?	*Are his books translated?*
Celui-ci est traduit en anglais et celui-là est traduit en portugais.	*This one is translated into English and that one is translated into Portugese.*
Quel dessert recommandez-vous?	*Which dessert do you recommend?*
Celui-ci aux noisettes.	*This one with hazelnuts.*
Quel est celui qui n'est pas content?	*Which one is the unhappy one?*
Celui qui est assis au dernier rang.	*The man sitting in the back row.*
Je peux écrire sur cette feuille?	*May I write on this piece of paper?*
Non, pas sur celle-là!	*No, not on that one!*
Ces films sont sous-titrés?	*Are these films subtitled?*
Celui-ci est sous-titré mais celui-là est doublé.	*This one is subtitled but that one is dubbed.*
Quels produits vas-tu commander?	*Which products are you going to order?*
Je vais commander ceux qui sont hypoallergéniques.	*I am going to order the ones that are hypoallergenic.*
Tu crois que ça va nous intéresser?	*Do you think that will interest us?*
Je suis sûr que ça va te plaire.	*I am sure you will like it.*
Ça t'étonne?	*Are you surprised?*
Non, ça ne m'étonne pas du tout.	*No, I am not surprised at all.*

Written Practice 4

Replace the demonstrative adjective and the noun with a demonstrative pronoun.

> Ce livre est en français. Ce livre est en espagnol.
> *Celui-ci est en français. Celui-là est en espagnol.*

1. Cette maison est petite. Cette maison est grande.

2. Ces tableaux sont chers. Ces tableaux sont bon marché.

   _____

3. Cet avion est français. Cet avion est anglais.

   _____

4. Cette cravate est en rayonne. Cette cravate est en soie.

   _____

5. Cet homme est mécanicien. Cet homme est électricien.

   _____

QUIZ

Put the following verbs into the **plus-que-parfait**.

choisir (tu)	_tu avais choisi_

1. prendre (vous)   _____
   aller (il)   _____
   se promener (elles) _____
   trouver (nous)   _____
   déjeuner (tu)   _____
   inviter (ils)   _____
   arriver (elle)   _____
   comprendre (je)   _____
   croire (tu)   _____
   recevoir (nous)   _____

Put the first verb into the **passé composé** and the second into the **plus-que-parfait**.

Elle (apprécier) ce que vous (dire) la veille.   *a apprécié*   *aviez dit*

2. Il (recevoir) le paquet que nous (envoyer)   _____   _____
   de Rome.
   Vous (comprendre) ce qu'elle (explique) à   _____   _____
   la dernière réunion.
   Elle (penser) que tu (oublier) le rendez-vous.   _____   _____
   Je (se rendre compte) qu'ils (se tromper).   _____   _____
   Ils (obtenir) ce qu'ils (demander).   _____   _____
   On (apprendre) que les entreprises (fusionner). _____   _____

Put the following verbs into the **passé simple**.

courir (il)   *il courut*_____

3. voyager (elle)   _____
   faire (je)   _____
   mettre (il)   _____
   parler (nous)   _____
   sortir (ils)   _____
   manger (tu)   _____
   entendre (je)   _____
   vivre (il)   _____
   être (elle)   _____
   danser (nous)   _____

Put the first verb into the **imparfait** and the second into the **passé simple**.

Elle (lire) quand on (frapper) à la porte.   *lisait*   *frappa*

4. Ils (dîner) quand ils (entendre) un grand bruit.   _____   _____
   Elle (conduire) quand il (se mettre) à pleuvoir.   _____   _____
   Nous (discuter) de politique quand ils (arriver).   _____   _____

Je (dormir) quand le téléphone (sonner). _____ _____
Elle (écrire) quand le chat (sauter) sur son bureau. _____ _____

Replace the boldfaced possessive adjective and noun with a possessive pronoun.

Mon bureau est en bois. *Le mien est en bois.* _____

5. **Son lycée** est près de chez lui. _____
Leur ordinateur est tout neuf. _____
Ta cuisine est très agréable. _____
Ma guitare est dans le salon. _____
Sa vie est trépidante. _____
Nos amis sont en vacances. _____
Votre appartement est confortable. _____
Notre hôtel donne sur la Seine. _____
Leurs chaussures sont en cuir. _____
Mes photos sont en couleur. _____

Replace the demonstrative adjective and the noun with a demonstrative pronoun.

Cette veste est en lin. Cette veste est en cuir.
Celle-ci est en lin. Celle-là est en cuir. _____

6. Ce journal est de gauche. Ce journal est de droite.

_____

Ces machines sont vieilles. Ces machines sont neuves.

_____

Cette voiture est japonaise. Cette voiture est coréenne.

_____

Cet appartement est sombre. Cet appartement est ensoleillé.

_____

Ces verres sont fragiles. Ces verres sont incassables.

_____

Cet artiste est inconnu. Cet artiste est célèbre.

_____

Translate the following sentences, using **vous** and the **est-ce que** form.

    7. Is your apartment bigger than his? _____

    8. Do you like this one or that one? (*m.*) _____

    9. I had not understood the problem. _____

  10. "Is it yours?" "Yes, it is mine." _____

PART THREE TEST

Answer the questions in the affirmative, using a direct object pronoun.

Vous invitez les Sabatier? *Oui, je les invite.*

1. Vous avez engagé cet employé? _____
2. Tu entends les oiseaux? _____
3. Elles ont accepté l'invitation? _____
4. Tu as vu le dernier film d'Audiard? _____
5. Il a annulé la soirée? _____

Answer the questions in the affirmative, using an indirect object pronoun.

Elle a parlé à Hervé? *Oui, elle lui a parlé.*

6. Tu vas offrir ces fleurs à Émilie? _____
7. Il rend souvent visite à ses grands-parents? _____
8. Tu transmets mes amitiés à ta femme? _____
9. Il a présenté ses excuses à Amélie? _____
10. Tu as téléphoné à l'agent de voyages? _____

Answer the following questions in the affirmative form, using **y** or **en**.

Il pense à son nouveau poste? *Oui, il y pense.*

11. Vous avez envie de faire un voyage en France? _____
12. Vous pensez à votre prochain livre? _____
13. Elle s'occupe de cette affaire? _____
14. Il a fait attention à tous les détails? _____
15. As-tu l'intention d'aller à Paris? _____

Put the following regular verbs into the **passé composé**.

16. apprendre (il) _____
17. lire (elle) _____

18. croire (je) _____
19. finir (nous) _____
20. dire (tu) _____

Put the verbs in the following sentences into the **passé composé**, choosing between **être** and **avoir**.

21. Ils _____ les bicyclettes du garage. (sortir)
22. Nous (*m.*) _____ devant le musée Picasso. (passer)
23. Elle _____ les plantes sur le balcon. (sortir)
24. Tu _____ les crêpes. (retourner)
25. Je _____ les chaises de jardin. (rentrer)

Put the following verbs into the **imparfait**.

26. regarder la télévision (nous) _____
27. prendre des photos (tu) _____
28. être photographe (elle) _____
29. dîner dans ce restaurant (ils) _____
30. avoir un chien (vous) _____

Describe an event that had just happened, using the **imparfait**.

lire le journal (je) *Je venais de lire le journal.* _____

31. faire un voyage en Asie (nous) _____
32. apprendre l'espagnol (vous) _____
33. dîner sur la terrasse (elles) _____
34. arroser le jardin (tu) _____
35. suivre des cours de danse (il) _____

Complete with the appropriate preposition.

36. Nous apprenons _____ chanter.
37. Il manque _____ imagination.
38. Ils ont peur _____ perdre le match.
39. Aide-moi _____ faire les valises.
40. Parlez-nous _____ votre voyage.

Put the following verbs into the **plus-que-parfait**.

41. apprendre (nous) _____
42. devoir (ils) _____
43. boire (il) _____
44. dire (elles) _____
45. se demander (je) _____

Translate the following sentences, using **vous** and the **est-ce que** form where appropriate.

46. You had not understood the problem. _____
47. What are they thinking about? _____
48. They decided to buy a new house. _____
49. What about reading this Indian novel? _____
50. Chloé left at midnight. _____

PART FOUR

ALL IS SUBJECTIVE

CHAPTER 16

Using the Infinitive, Present Participle, Gerund, and Passive Voice

In this chapter you will learn:

The Present Infinitive

While in English the infinitive is often replaced by a present participle, in French, the infinitive has a wide spectrum of uses. Since a verb in the infinitive mode is by definition not conjugated, the negation does not surround the verb but precedes the verb. For example:

Je lui ai dit de ne pas être en retard.	*I told him not to be late.*
Il lui a promis de ne jamais révéler la vérité.	*He promised him never to reveal the truth.*
Nous lui avons demandé de ne plus mettre de prospectus dans notre boîte aux lettres.	*We asked him not to put junk mail in our mailbox any more.*

THE INFINITIVE AS A SUBJECT OF A VERB

The infinitive can be used as the subject of a verb. For example:

Escalader des montagnes, c'est sa passion.	*Climbing mountains is her passion.*
Voyager par le train est commode.	*Traveling by train is convenient.*

THE INFINITIVE FOR GENERAL INSTRUCTIONS

The infinitive is used for general instructions, prescriptions, public notices, and proverbs where the imperative is often used in English.

Conserver à l'abri de la lumière.	*Store away from light.*
Ne pas laisser à la portée des enfants.	*Keep out of the reach of children.*
Éteindre votre téléphone cellulaire.	*Turn off your cell phone.*

The infinitive is most important for recipes in professional cookbooks. For example:

Ajouter une cuillérée d'huile.	*Add a spoonful of oil.*
Mélanger les ingrédients.	*Mix the ingredients.*

Verser doucement dans la casserole.   *Pour slowly into the pan.*

Remuer avec une spatule en bois.   *Stir with a wooden spatula.*

THE INFINITIVE IN INTERROGATIVES

The infinitive is used in the interrogative infinitive.

Que faire?   *What is there to do?*

Pourquoi se plaindre?   *Why complain?*

THE INFINITIVE AFTER VERBS OF PERCEPTION

The infinitive is used after verbs of perception where the present participle is used in English. See the following examples:

Elle entend l'enfant pleurer.   *She hears the child crying.*

Nous écoutons la soprane chanter.   *We listen to the soprano singing.*

Vous avez vu le sans-abri traverser   *You saw the homeless person crossing*
la rue.   *the street.*

THE INFINITIVE AFTER THE VERBS *FAIRE* AND *LAISSER*

The infinitive is used after the verbs **faire** (*to do*) and **laisser** (*to let, allow*).

Elle a fait venir le médecin.   *She sent for the doctor.*

Il nous a fait entrer dans la salle   *He showed us into the waiting room.*
d'attente.

Je l'ai laissé y aller seul.   *I allowed him to go there alone.*

Laisse-nous partir.   *Let us go.*

You learned the causative form **faire faire** in Chapter 9. Let's review with the following examples:

Ils ont fait construire une maison au bord du lac.	*They had a house built by the lake.*
Elle se fera faire une robe en taffetas pour le mariage de son fils.	*She'll have a taffeta dress made for her son's wedding.*

THE INFINITIVE AFTER CERTAIN VERBS

As you saw in Chapter 14, some verbs are followed directly by the infinitive.

Elle n'osera pas soulever le sujet.	*She won't dare bring up the topic.*
Il voudrait être reconnu en tant qu'artiste.	*He would like to be acknowledged as an artist.*

THE INFINITIVE AFTER EXPRESSIONS OF TIME AND POSITION

The infinitive is used after expressions of spending time. The preposition **à** precedes the infinitive. For example:

Vous passez votre vie à travailler.	*You spend your life working.*
Elle passe ses après-midi à jouer au tennis.	*She spends her afternoons playing tennis.*

The infinitive, again preceded by **à**, is also used after expressions of position.

Je suis assise à feuilleter un magazine.	*I am sitting leafing through a magazine.*
Il est appuyé contre le mur à bavarder avec son voisin.	*He is leaning against the wall chatting with his neighbor.*

Oral Practice

Repeat the following sentences aloud.

Ne rien jeter par la fenêtre.	*Don't throw anything out of the window.*
Il est allongé sur le canapé à lire des bandes dessinées.	*He is lying on the sofa reading comic strips.*
Elles sont adossées à la clôture à contempler les étoiles.	*They are leaning back against the fence contemplating the stars.*
Nous avons fait réparer notre appareil photo numérique.	*We had our digital camera fixed.*
Ne pas marcher sur la pelouse.	*Do not walk on the lawn.*
Ils passent leur vie à danser le tango.	*They spend their lives dancing the tango.*
Il a gaspillé sa vie à ne rien faire.	*He wasted his life doing nothing.*
Elle est accroupie dans le jardin à planter des légumes.	*She is squatting in the garden planting vegetables.*
Nous avons décidé de ne jamais remettre les pieds dans ce magasin.	*We have decided never to set foot in this store again.*
J'entends le chat miauler.	*I hear the cat meowing.*
Vous passez vos vacances à vous reposer.	*You spend your vacation resting.*
Ajouter une pincée de sel.	*Add a pinch of salt.*
Prendre deux fois par jour.	*Take twice a day*
Que dire?	*What is there to say?*

Written Practice 1

Make full sentences following the model below. Watch out for the possessive adjectives.

rêver (elle) _Elle passe sa vie à rêver._ _____

1. dormir (il) _____
2. jouer de la guitare (je) _____
3. visiter les musées (ils) _____
4. faire des courses (vous) _____
5. inventer des histoires (tu) _____

The Past Infinitive

The past infinitive is used to indicate anteriority. It is formed with the infinitive of **être** or **avoir** and the past participle of the main verb. See the following examples.

Carmen s'excuse d'avoir oublié le rendez-vous.	_Carmen apologizes for having forgotten the appointment._
Il m'a remercié de l'avoir aidé à trouver un emploi.	_He thanked me for having helped him find a job._
Il ne s'est jamais pardonné d'être arrivé en retard au mariage de son frère.	_He has never forgiven himself for having been late to his brother's wedding._
Laurence s'est excusée d'être retournée à Venise sans lui.	_Laurence apologized for having returned to Venice without him._

THE PRESENT AND PAST INFINITIVE WITH PREPOSITIONS

When introducing an action with the preposition **avant,** the present infinitive is used preceded by the preposition **de.** In this case, the subjects of the main clause and of the infinitive clause are the same.

Laure enregistre l'émission avant de sortir.	*Laure records the show before going out.*
Les comédiens ont le trac avant d'entrer en scène.	*The actors are nervous before going on stage.*

When introducing a past action with the preposition **après**, the past infinitive is used. For example:

Céline est rentrée chez elle après avoir assisté à la répétition générale.	*Céline went home after attending the dress rehearsal.*
Julien a écouté sa boîte vocale après être rentré de vacances.	*Julien listened to his voice mail after he got back from vacation.*

Oral Practice

Read the following sentences aloud.

Il va vous appeler après être rentré à la maison.	*He'll call you after having gone back home.*
Il prend une douche après avoir déjeuné.	*He takes a shower after having breakfast.*
Les enfants se lavent les mains avant de manger et après avoir mangé.	*The children wash their hands before and after eating.*
Nous avons lu le guide après être arrivé(e)s à Paris.	*We read the guide after we arrived in Paris.*
Elle veut parler à Henri après avoir consulté un avocat.	*She wants to talk to Henri after consulting with her lawyer.*
Je vais prendre des vacances après avoir achevé mon roman.	*I'll take a vacation after I finish my novel.*
Je lis les critiques après avoir lu le livre.	*I read the reviews after reading the book.*
Il fait la cuisine après avoir passé l'aspirateur.	*He cooks after vacuuming.*

Written Practice 2

Replace **avant de** with **après** in the following sentences.

Il téléphone avant de rencontrer son client. *Il téléphone après avoir rencontré son client.*

1. Elle fait son jogging avant d'aller au supermarché. _____
2. Tu écoutes de la musique avant d'écrire la lettre. _____
3. Nous faisons une promenade avant de dîner. _____
4. Je lis le journal avant d'emmener les enfants à l'école. _____
5. Vous appelez Xavier avant d'inviter Quentin. _____

The Present Participle

The **participe présent** (*present participle*) is formed by dropping the **ons** ending from the present-tense **nous** form and adding **ant.** See the following examples.

faire (*to do*)

nous faisons	*we do*	faisant	*doing*

finir (*to finish*)

nous finissons	*we finish*	finissant	*finishing*

manger (*to eat*)

nous mangeons	*we eat*	mangeant	*eating*

parler (*to speak*)

nous parlons	*we speak*	parlant	*speaking*

voir (*to see*)

nous voyons	*we see*	voyant	*seeing*

The following list includes some exceptions:

avoir	*to have*	ayant	*having*
être	*to be*	étant	*being*
savoir	*to know*	sachant	*knowing*

THE PRESENT PARTICIPLE AS A NOUN

The present participle can be used as a noun. When used as a noun, the present participle changes gender and number depending on the meaning. For example:

un gagnant	*a winner (m.)*	une gagnante	*a winner (f.)*
un perdant	*a loser (m.)*	une perdante	*a loser (f.)*

THE PRESENT PARTICIPLE AS AN ADJECTIVE

The present participle can also be used as an adjective. When used as an adjective, the present participle agrees with the noun it modifies. For example:

une histoire émouvante	*a moving story*
une ville fascinante	*a fascinating city*
des films amusants	*funny films*

THE PRESENT PARTICIPLE AS A VERB

Finally, the present participle can also be used as a verb. When used as a verb, the present participle is invariable.

Je l'ai vu sortant du cybercafé.	*I saw him as he was leaving the Internet café.*
Étant à l'étranger, M. Pariseau ne pourra pas répondre à votre demande avant lundi.	*Since he is abroad, Mr. Pariseau won't be able to answer your request until Monday.*
Ne sachant pas quoi faire, elle a appelé son avocat.	*Not knowing what to do, she called her lawyer.*

The Gerund

When the present participle is introduced by **en**, it is referred to as **le gérondif** *(gerund)*. The gerund describes the relationship between two actions. It can express simultaneity, manner, condition, or causality. Look at the following examples.

Je lis le journal en écoutant la radio.	*I read the newspaper while listening to the radio.*
Il s'est cassé la jambe en faisant du ski.	*He broke his leg skiing.*
En refusant sa proposition, vous perdriez de nombreux clients.	*If you refused his proposal, you would lose many clients.*
C'est en forgeant qu'on devient forgeron.	*Practice makes perfect.*
Sa famille a perdu sa fortune en spéculant à la Bourse.	*His family lost its fortune speculating on the stock market.*

When **tout** precedes the gerund, it underscores a contradiction between two actions. For example:

Tout en pleurant, l'enfant riait.	*Even while crying, the child was laughing.*
Tout en écoutant la conférence de l'ambassadeur, il faisait des dessins.	*While he was listening to the ambassador's talk, he was also drawing.*

Oral Practice

Repeat the following sentences aloud.

Ils ont vu les champs de tournesols en passant.	*They saw the sunflower fields while driving by.*
Il est tombé de l'échelle en cueillant des cerises.	*He fell from the ladder while picking cherries.*
En allant à Amsterdam, il s'est arrêté à Bruxelles.	*On his way to Amsterdam, he stopped in Brussels.*
Étant toujours en retard, elle s'est fait renvoyer.	*Since she was always late, she got fired.*
C'est en répétant ces phrases que vous vous perfectionnerez en français.	*It's by repeating these sentences that you'll improve your French.*

Il écrit son rapport tout en parlant au téléphone avec ses copains.	*He is writing his report while talking on the phone with his friends.*
Ils ont cherché un taxi en arrivant à Rouen.	*They looked for a cab upon arriving in Rouen.*
Son témoignage était très émouvant.	*Her testimony was very moving.*
Sachant la vérité, il a préféré se taire.	*Knowing the truth, he chose to remain silent.*
Ayant vu le film l'an passé, j'ai décidé de ne pas le revoir.	*Having seen the film last year, I decided not to see it again.*
Ils se sont enrichis en investissant judicieusement.	*They got rich by investing wisely.*
Je l'ai aperçue en traversant la rue.	*I saw her while crossing the street.*

Written Practice 3

Make complete sentences using the present tense and the gerund.

      prendre une douche/chanter (il) <u>*Il prend une douche en chantant.*</u>

1. écouter de la musique/travailler (nous) _____
2. faire de l'exercice/regarder la télé (elle) _____
3. écrire/parler (ils) _____
4. faire le ménage/écouter la radio (il) _____
5. raconter une histoire/conduire (vous) _____

The Passive Voice

A sentence can be either in the active or in the passive voice. In the active voice, the subject performs the action, while in the passive voice, the subject is acted upon. Compare the following examples.

Le roi construit le château.	*The king builds the castle.*
Le château est construit par le roi.	*The castle is being built by the king.*

The passive voice is formed with **être** in the tense required plus the past participle of the main verb.

il est découvert	*he is discovered*	il était découvert	*he was discovered*
il a été découvert	*he has been discovered*	il sera découvert	*he will be discovered*

The passive voice is used to emphasize the subject.

La découverte de ce site archéologique a été faite récemment.	*The discovery of this archeological site was made recently.*
La décision du jury n'a pas encore été revélée.	*The decision of the jury has not yet been revealed.*

The passive voice is also used to avoid specifying the agent of the action.

Aucun rapport n'a été envoyé.	*No report was sent.*
Leur négligence a été remarquée.	*Their negligence has been noticed.*

Although the passive voice is usually followed by the preposition **par**, it can also be followed by the preposition **de. De** indicates a less active role than is indicated by **par**. Compare:

La reine est suivie **de** son entourage.	*The queen is followed by her entourage.*
La reine est suivie **par** les espions du roi.	*The queen is being followed by the king's spies.*
Le manoir est entouré **d'**arbres.	*The mansion is surrounded with trees.*
Le manoir est entouré **par** des soldats.	*The mansion is surrounded by soldiers.*

The passive voice is much less common in French than in English. Although it is important to learn the passive voice, it is even more important to learn the cases where the passive voice cannot be used in French or is better avoided, for example, using **on** in the third-person singular.

Ici, **on parle** français.	*French is spoken here.*
On vous **demande** au téléphone.	*You are wanted on the phone.*

The passive voice can also be replaced by the active voice, using the following reflexive verbs: **se laisser, se faire, se voir, s'entendre.** Note that the past participle of the conjugated verb does not agree with the subject.

Ils ne se sont pas laissé facilement convaincre.	*They were not easily convinced.*
Elle s'est fait faire une robe.	*She had a dress made.*

As you learned in Chapter 10, one type of pronominal verb is called the passive pronominal verb. Let's review.

Ce nouveau produit se vend en pharmacie.	*This new product is being sold in drugstores.*
Ça ne se fait pas.	*That is not done.*

Oral Practice

Repeat the following sentences aloud.

La pelouse est couverte de neige.	*The lawn is covered with snow.*
Le toit a été recouvert de chaume.	*The roof has been covered with thatch.*
Ce verbe est suivi du subjonctif.	*This verb is followed by the subjunctive.*
Ce verbe est suivi de la préposition de.	*This verb is followed by the preposition de.*
Il est suivi par la police depuis des mois.	*The police have been following him for months.*
Son téléphone a été mis sur écoute.	*His phone has been wiretapped.*
Il s'est fait prendre en flagrant délit.	*He got caught in the act.*
Ce remède a été découvert au début du vingtième siècle.	*This remedy was discovered at the beginning of the twentieth century.*
Le choix a été fait anonymement.	*The choice was made anonymously.*
Cette forteresse a été détruite en 1450.	*This fortress was destroyed in 1450.*
La décision du comité sera annoncée à midi.	*The committee's decision will be announced at noon.*

Le marais a été drainé.	*The swamp has been drained.*
Il s'est vu contraint de démissionner.	*He found himself forced to resign.*
Elle s'est fait conduire au palais par le chauffeur.	*She had herself driven to the palace by her driver.*
Ça ne se dit pas en public.	*That is not to be said in public.*

Written Practice 4

Change from the active voice to the passive voice. Watch for tenses and agreement.

On a construit la maison. *La maison a été construite.*

1. On a fermé la porte. _____
2. On écrit la lettre. _____
3. On a résolu le problème. _____
4. On a engagé un employé. _____
5. On prend une décision. _____

QUIZ

Make full sentences following the model below. Watch out for the possessive adjectives.

être assis/lire le journal (ils) *Ils sont assis à lire le journal.*

1. passer son temps/travailler (vous) _____
   être allongé/regarder le film (elle) _____
   être debout/chanter (il) _____
   passer ses vacances/visiter les musées (ils) _____
   être accroupi/jardiner (il) _____

Replace **avant de** with **après** in the following sentences.

> Il appelle son ami avant de trouver un emploi.
> *Il appelle son ami après avoir trouvé un emploi.*

2. Elle enregistre de la musique avant de partir en vacances.

   _____

   Tu as écrit l'article avant d'aller à Paris.

   _____

   Vous avez lu le livre avant de voir le film.

   _____

Put the verbs in parentheses into the gerund.

> Il a rencontré Rémi en *allant*_____ à la poste. (aller)

3. J'ai vu un lapin en _____ les Jardins du Luxembourg. (traverser)
4. Tout en _____ la réponse, il faisait semblant de l'ignorer. (savoir)
5. Ce n'est pas en _____ si pessimiste que vous allez réussir. (être)

Translate the following sentences using the appropriate form of the passive voice or a substitute.

6. The decision has been made. _____
7. The bridge has been built by the king of Morocco. _____
8. English is spoken here. _____

Translate the following sentences using the infinitive.

9. Traveling is fun. _____
10. Why do this? _____

CHAPTER 17

Making Suggestions and Hypotheses

In this chapter you will learn:

The Simple Future

You have already learned the immediate future, in Chapter 9. French also has a simple future tense. As in English, the future tense is used to describe events that will take place in the future. To form the simple future of most verbs, use the infinitive as the stem and add the endings **ai, as, a, ons, ez,** and **ont.** For **-re** verbs, drop the **e** from the infinitive first.

NOTE: *The simple future endings resemble the present tense of the verb **avoir**.*

Let's take, as examples, one **-er** verb, one **-ir** verb, and one **-re** verb.

regarder *(to watch)*

je regarderai	*I'll watch*	nous regarderons	*we'll watch*
tu regarderas	*you'll watch*	vous regarderez	*you'll watch*
il/elle regardera	*he/she'll watch*	ils/elles regarderont	*they'll watch*

sortir *(to go out)*

je sortirai	*I'll go out*	nous sortirons	*we'll go out*
tu sortiras	*you'll go out*	vous sortirez	*you'll go out*
il/elle sortira	*he/she'll go out*	ils/elles sortiront	*they'll go out*

attendre *(to wait)*

j'attendrai	*I'll wait*	nous attendrons	*we'll wait*
tu attendras	*you'll wait*	vous attendrez	*you'll wait*
il/elle attendra	*he/she'll wait*	ils/elles attendront	*they'll wait*

The simple future endings are the same for all verbs; however, some verbs have irregular stems.

j'irai	*I'll go*	je pourrai	*I'll be able to*
j'apercevrai	*I'll notice*	je recevrai	*I'll receive*
j'aurai	*I'll have*	je saurai	*I'll know*
je courrai	*I'll run*	je serai	*I'll be*
je devrai	*I'll have to*	je tiendrai	*I'll hold*
j'enverrai	*I'll send*	il vaudra	*it will be worth*
il faudra	*one will have to*	je verrai	*I'll see*
je ferai	*I'll do*	je viendrai	*I'll come*
je mourrai	*I'll die*	je voudrai	*I'll want*
il pleuvra	*it'll rain*		

Slight spelling modifications occur with some verbs.

acheter (*to buy*)   j'achèterai
appeler (*to call*)   j'appellerai
jeter (*to throw*)   je jetterai
nettoyer (*to clean*)   je nettoierai

NOTE: *Many verbs that are irregular in the present tense are regular in the simple future. Here are a few examples:*

je boirai   *I'll drink*   je lirai   *I'll read*
je conduirai   *I'll drive*   je mettrai   *I'll put*
j'écrirai   *I'll write*   je prendrai   *I'll take*

Oral Practice

Read the following sentences aloud.

Il viendra en France en mars.	*He'll come to France in March.*
Elle prendra le train.	*She'll take the train.*
Je pourrai me reposer quelques jours.	*I'll be able to rest for a few days.*
Est-ce qu'ils feront une escale à Tahiti?	*Will they stop in Tahiti?*
Ils feront une escale à Tahiti et une en Nouvelle-Calédonie.	*They'll make one stop in Tahiti and one in New Caledonia.*
Je pense qu'ils seront tous là.	*I think they'll all be there.*
Elle habitera quelques mois chez sa tante.	*She'll live at her aunt's for a few months.*
Elle fera un stage de deux mois.	*She'll do an internship for two months.*
Je vous tiendrai au courant.	*I'll keep you informed.*
Je l'appellerai à mon arrivée.	*I'll call her as soon as I arrive.*
Je passerai après-demain.	*I'll stop by the day after tomorrow.*
Il devra d'abord s'inscrire.	*He'll have to sign up first.*

Written Practice 1

Put the following sentences into the future tense.

Je parle à Claude. *Je parlerai à Claude.*

1. Nous allons en Chine. _____
2. Tu arrives à l'heure. _____
3. Elle pose des questions. _____
4. Vous avez de la chance. _____
5. Ils dînent chez Hervé. _____

USES OF THE SIMPLE FUTURE

The simple future is used after certain conjunctions when expressing a future action where in English, the present tense would be used.

Marielle ira à Paris quand elle pourra.	*Marielle will go to Paris when she can.*
Lorsqu'il aura dix-huit ans, Ludovic votera.	*When he is eighteen, Ludovic will vote.*
Nous commencerons la réunion dès que tout le monde sera là.	*We'll start the meeting as soon as everybody gets here.*

The simple future is also used in combination with a **si** clause in the present tense. For example:

Nous irons au vernissage si c'est possible.	*We'll go to the show opening if it's possible.*
S'il pleut demain, nous irons au cinéma.	*If it rains tomorrow, we'll go to the movies.*
Je ferai une tarte aux pommes s'ils ont faim.	*I'll make an apple tart if they are hungry.*

In a narration, the simple future can be used to express a future idea from the standpoint of the past, as shown in the following examples.

La plus belle voix de Milan et elle ne connaîtra jamais la célébrité.	*The most beautiful voice in Milano, and she would never become famous.*
Un des plus grands pianistes de son époque et il mourra seul et sans un sou.	*One of the greatest pianists of his time, and he was to die alone and without a penny.*

Oral Practice

Ask the following questions and then answer them, aloud.

Vous serez là?	*Will you be there?*
Nous serons là quand vous arriverez.	*We'll be there when you arrive.*
Quand partira-t-elle?	*When will she leave?*
Elle partira dès qu'elle aura son visa.	*She'll leave as soon as she gets her visa.*
Combien de temps resterez-vous à la campagne?	*How long will you stay in the country?*
Nous resterons à la campagne tant qu'il fera beau.	*We'll stay in the country as long as the weather is nice.*
Quand prendra-t-il la décision?	*When will he decide?*
Il prendra la décision lorsqu'il aura plus d'information.	*He'll decide when he has more information.*
Elle va bientôt prendre sa retraite?	*Is she going to retire soon?*
Pas du tout! Elle travaillera tant qu'elle vivra!	*Not at all! She's going to work as long as she lives.*
Quand me préviendrez-vous?	*When will you let me know?*
Je vous préviendrai dès que je saurai la date.	*I'll let you know as soon as I know the date.*
Où iront-ils quand ils seront en Italie?	*Where will they go when they are in Italy?*
Ils commenceront par Venise.	*They'll start with Venice.*
Qu'est-ce qu'il fera quand il sera grand?	*What is he going to do when he grows up?*
Quand il sera grand, il sera pilote.	*When he grows up, he's going to be a pilot.*

Written Practice 2

Put both verbs in parentheses into the **futur simple**.

Il (venir) quand il (pouvoir).   *viendra*   *pourra*

1. Elle (suivre) des cours d'italien
   quand elle (avoir) le temps.   _____   _____
2. Nous (aller) au Canada aussitôt que
   nous (pouvoir).   _____   _____
3. Ils (téléphoner) dès qu'ils (arriver).   _____   _____
4. Tu (contacter) Pierre quand tu (être)
   à Paris.   _____   _____
5. Il (voir) la Joconde quand il (visiter)
   le Louvre.   _____   _____

The Future Perfect

The **futur antérieur** *(future perfect)* describes a future action that will take place and be completed before another future action. It is formed with the future tense of **être** or **avoir** and the past participle of the main verb. Agreement rules are the same as for the **passé composé**. Although the corresponding construction is rarely used in English, the future perfect is fairly common in French. Let's look at some example conjugations:

arriver *(to arrive)*

je serai arrivé(e)	*I'll have arrived*	nous serons arrivé(e)s	*we'll have arrived*
tu seras arrivé(e)	*you'll have arrived*	vous serez arrivé(e)(s)	*you'll have arrived*
il/elle sera arrivé(e)	*he'll have arrived*	ils/elles seront arrivé(e)s	*they'll have arrived*

finir *(to finish)*

j'aurai fini	*I'll have finished*	nous aurons fini	*we'll have finished*
tu auras fini	*you'll have finished*	vous aurez fini	*you'll have finished*
il/elle aura fini	*he/she will have finished*	ils/elles auront fini	*they'll have finished*

Here are some example sentences:

Elle aura passé toute sa vie à écrire. *She'll have spent her whole life writing.*

D'ici 2050, la planète aura changé. *By 2050, the planet will have changed.*

THE SIMPLE FUTURE VERSUS THE FUTURE PERFECT

Sometimes you have a choice between the **futur simple** and the **futur antérieur.** When both clauses use the simple future, the implication is that both actions take place simultaneously. If you want to mark one as coming before the other, use the **futur antérieur.** Compare:

Vous m'appellerez dès que vous atterrirez à Roissy. *Call me as soon as you land in Roissy.*

Vous m'appellerez dès que vous serez arrivé à l'aéroport. *Call me as soon as you arrive at the airport.*

The **futur antérieur** can also express the probability of a past action.

Il aura encore perdu son portefeuille! *He probably lost his wallet again!*

Elle aura raté l'avion. *She probably missed the plane.*

The **futur antérieur** is also used after **si**, implying a completed action.

Il se demande s'il aura terminé à temps. *He wonders whether he'll be finished on time.*

Je me demande s'ils auront signé le contrat. *I wonder whether they've signed the contract.*

Oral Practice

Ask the following questions and then answer them, aloud.

Quand étudierez-vous l'allemand? *When will you study German?*

J'étudierai l'allemand quand j'aurai maîtrisé le français. *I'll study German when I have mastered French.*

Est-ce qu'il va démissionner?	*Is he going to resign?*
Il démissionnera dès qu'il aura trouvé un autre emploi.	*He'll resign as soon as he finds another job.*
Elle n'a pas encore acheté de voiture?	*She has not yet bought a car?*
Elle achètera une voiture quand elle aura décroché un poste.	*She'll buy a car when she gets herself a job.*
On s'en va bientôt?	*Are we going soon?*
On s'en ira dès que j'aurai réglé la note.	*We'll go as soon I settle the bill.*
Dépêche-toi! On sort dans cinq minutes!	*Hurry up! We are leaving in five minutes!*
Je sortirai une fois que j'aurai rangé mes affaires.	*I'll go out as soon as I have my things put away.*
Carole n'est pas encore arrivée?	*Carole has not arrived yet?*
Elle aura manqué le train de quinze heures.	*She probably missed the three o'clock train.*
Vous lui avez envoyé sa commande?	*Did you send him his order?*
Je ne lui enverrai pas sa commande tant qu'il ne m'aura pas payé.	*I won't send him his order until he pays me (Lit. as long as he has not paid me).*
Vous pouvez nous aider?	*Can you help us?*
Je vous aiderai aussitôt que j'aurai pris mon petit déjeuner.	*I'll help you as soon as I finish breakfast.*

Written Practice 3

Put the first verb into the **futur simple** and the second verb into the **futur antérieur**.

Il (se coucher) quand il (défaire)   <u>se couchera</u>   <u>aura défait</u>
ses valises.

1. Vous (faire) le tour du monde quand   _____   _____
   vous (gagner) à la loterie.
2. Le public (applaudir) le ténor quand il   _____   _____
   (terminer) sa chanson.

3. Elle (se sentir) mieux dès qu'ils _____ _____
   (atterrir) à Tahiti.
4. Nous (regarder) la télé aussitôt que les _____ _____
   enfants (dîner).
5. Il (envoyer) un chèque quand vous _____ _____
   (finir) le travail.

The Present Conditional

The **conditionnel présent** *(present conditional)* has many uses we'll explore in this chapter. It is formed by adding the endings of the imperfect to the future stem of a verb. (Remember: for **-re** verbs, drop the **e** from the infinitive.) As you saw earlier in this chapter, some verbs have an irregular future stem.

aller *(to go)*

j'irais	*I would go*	nous irions	*we would go*
tu irais	*you would go*	vous iriez	*you would go*
il/elle irait	*he/she would go*	ils/elles iraient	*they would go*

lire *(to read)*

je lirais	*I would read*	nous lirions	*we would read*
tu lirais	*you would read*	vous liriez	*you would read*
il/elle lirait	*he/she would read*	ils/elles liraient	*they would read*

USES OF THE PRESENT CONDITIONAL

The **conditionnel présent** is used to express a wish or a suggestion. For example:

Je voudrais aller au Japon.	*I would like to go to Japan.*
À ta place, je n'irais pas.	*If I were you, I would not go.*

The **conditionnel présent** is used to make a statement or a request more polite. See the following examples:

Pourriez-vous nous dire où se trouve le Boulevard Victor Hugo?	*Could you tell us where to find the Boulevard Victor Hugo?*
Voudriez-vous vous joindre à nous dimanche?	*Would you like to join us on Sunday?*

The **conditionnel présent** is used when a condition is implied. When the main clause is in the **conditionnel présent,** the **si** clause is in the **imparfait.**

Nous prendrions un taxi si nous étions pressés.	*We would take a cab if we were in a rush.*
Romain monterait une affaire s'il pouvait trouver des associés.	*Romain would start a business if he could find some partners.*

The **conditionnel présent** is also used to express unconfirmed or alleged information. In this case, it is called the **conditionnel journalistique**, most useful to know when reading the press or listening to the news.

Le président se rendrait en Inde mardi.	*The president is reportedly going to India on Tuesday.*
Son voisin serait impliqué dans une affaire louche.	*His neighbor is allegedly involved in a shady business.*

In formal French, **savoir** in the **conditionnel présent** is the equivalent of **pouvoir** in the **présent**.

NOTE: *"Pas" is omitted in this formal usage.*

Je ne saurais vous exprimer ma gratitude.	*I shall never be able to express all my gratitude.*
Je ne saurais vous renseigner.	*I am afraid I can't give you any information.*

Oral Practice

Read the following sentences aloud.

Si j'avais plus de temps, j'aimerais bien aller en Asie.	*If I had more time, I would like to go to Asia.*
S'ils avaient un autre enfant, ils devraient trouver un appartement plus grand.	*If they had another child, they would have to find a larger apartment.*
S'il perdait son passeport, il irait à l'ambassade.	*If he lost his passport, he would go to the embassy.*
Si je vendais mon appartement, je pourrais acheter cette maison.	*If I sold my apartment, I could buy this house.*
Pas du tout! Si je pouvais, je le mettrais à la porte.	*Not at all! If I could, I would fire him.*
Nous serions ravis de la revoir.	*We would be delighted to see her again.*
Si mon ordinateur tombait en panne, je piquerais une crise.	*If my computer broke down, I would have a fit.*

Written Practice 4

Put the first verb into the conditionnel présent and the second verb into the imparfait.

Elle (faire) la cuisine si elle (avoir) le temps.   *Ferait*_____   *avait*_____

1. Nous (être) contents s'il (venir). _____   _____
2. Vous (aller) dans le parc s'il (faire) beau. _____   _____
3. Il (prendre) des vacances s'il (pouvoir). _____   _____
4. Tu (emmener) Sophie à l'opéra si elle (venir) à Paris. _____   _____
5. Il y (avoir) moins de violence si les hommes (être) plus raisonnables. _____   _____

The Past Conditional

The **conditionnel passé** *(past conditional)* expresses what would have happened if another event had taken place or if certain conditions had not been present. It is formed with the present conditional of **être** or **avoir** and the past participle of the main verb. The rules of agreement common to all compound tenses still apply.

aller *(to go)*

je serais allé(e)	*I would have gone*	nous serions allé(e)s	*we would have gone*
tu serais allé(e)	*you would have gone*	vous seriez allé(e)(s)	*you would have gone*
il/elle serait allé(e)	*he/she would have gone*	ils/elles seraient allé(e)s	*they would have gone*

visiter *(to visit)*

j'aurais visité	*I would have visited*	nous aurions visité	*we would have visited*
tu aurais visité	*you would have visited*	vous auriez visité	*you would have visited*
il/elle aurait visité	*he/she would have visited*	ils auraient visité	*they would have visited*

USES OF THE PAST CONDITIONAL

The **conditionnel passé** can express regret or reproach. For example:

Il aurait dû vous mettre au courant.	*He should have informed you.*
J'aurais aimé le rencontrer.	*I would have liked to meet him.*

The **conditionnel passé** is often found with a **si** clause in the **plus-que-parfait**.

Ils auraient fait plus attention si vous les aviez avertis.	*They would have been more careful if you had warned them.*
Elle serait venue si vous le lui aviez demandé.	*She would have come if you had asked her to.*

The **conditionnel passé** is used, like the **conditionnel present**, as a **conditionnel journalistique** to make a statement not confirmed by authorities. In most cases where English uses a qualifier such as *allegedly* or *reportedly*, the conditional will be used in French. See the following examples:

La diphtérie aurait causé la mort de milliers de personnes dans cette région.	*Diphtheria reportedly killed thousands of people in this region.*
Un traité de paix aurait été signé pendant la nuit.	*A peace treaty was supposedly signed during the night.*

The **conditionnel** and **conditionnel passé** are also used with **au cas où** *(in case or if)*.

Au cas où la réunion n'aurait pas lieu cet après-midi, appelez-moi.	*In case the meeting should not take place this afternoon, call me.*
Au cas où il aurait échoué à son examen, il aurait une autre chance dans un mois.	*If he failed his exam, he would have another chance in a month.*

Oral Practice

Read the following sentences aloud.

Si j'avais mieux dormi, je ne serais pas si fatigué.	*If I had slept more, I would not be so tired.*
S'il avait mis de l'écran solaire, il n'aurait pas attrapé de coup de soleil.	*If he had put on sunscreen, he would not have gotten sunburned.*
Il aurait gagné l'élection si son programme avait été plus clair.	*He would have won the election if his program had been clearer.*
Si le président n'avait pas été assassiné, l'avenir aurait pris une tournure différente.	*If the president had not been assassinated, the future would have taken a different turn.*
S'il ne s'était pas gavé de chocolats, il ne serait pas malade.	*If he had not stuffed himself with chocolate, he would not be sick.*
Nous aurions trouvé un remplaçant au cas où il n'aurait pas pu venir.	*We would have found a substitute if he had been unable to come.*

Si j'avais dîné à la Tour d'Argent, j'aurais commandé le fameux canard...	*If I had eaten at the Tour d'Argent, I would have ordered the famous duck . . .*
J'aurais aimé être océanographe.	*I would have liked to be an oceanographer.*

Written Practice 5

Put the first verb into the conditionnel passé and the second verb into the plus-que-parfait.

Je (aller) à la plage s'il (faire) beau. *serais allé(e)* *avait fait*

1. Elle (dîner) avec toi si elle (pouvoir). _____ _____
2. Vous (visiter) ce château si vous (avoir) plus de temps. _____ _____
3. Ils (voir) le film s'il (être) sous-titré. _____ _____
4. Nous (inviter) Mélanie si elle (rentrer) de vacances. _____ _____
5. Il (écrire) un roman s'il (avoir) plus d'imagination. _____ _____

Could, Should, and Would

Could, should, and *would* have different meanings in English and are translated in several ways in French. Every time you come across one of these verbs in English, make sure to examine its nuances before translating it into French.

COULD

When *could* refers to a single, unique action in the past, the **passé composé** of **pouvoir** is used. Note the following example:

Elle n'a pas pu venir. *She could not come.*

When *could* is a description or refers to a habitual action, the **imparfait** of **pouvoir** is used.

À cette époque-là, les femmes ne pouvaient pas porter de pantalon au travail.	*At that time, women could not wear pants at work.*

When *could* refers to an idea of the future, a hypothesis, or a suggestion, the **conditionnel présent** of **pouvoir** is used.

Pourriez-vous aller chercher Maud à l'aéroport?	*Could you pick up Maud at the airport?*

SHOULD

When *should* means *ought to*, the **conditionnel présent** or the **conditionnel passé** is used.

Ils devraient être plus prudents.	*They should be more cautious.*
Vous n'auriez pas dû leur en parler.	*You should not have talked to them about it.*

When *should* refers to a hypothetical situation, the **imparfait** is used. For example:

Si vous aviez besoin de quoi que ce soit, n'hésitez pas à me contacter.	*If you should need anything, do not hesitate to contact me.*

WOULD

When *would* refers to a repeated action in the past, the **imparfait** is used.

Quand il était jeune, il allait à la piscine tous les jeudis.	*When he was young, he would go to the swimming pool every Thursday.*

When *would* is part of a polite request, the **conditionnel** is used.

Voudriez-vous baisser le volume?   *Would you mind turning down the volume?*

When *would* refers to a specific action in the past, the **passé composé** of **vouloir** is used.

Elle lui a demandé d'enlever le col   *She asked him to remove the lace collar;*
en dentelle; il n'a pas voulre.   *he would not do it.*

When *would* refers to an idea of the future, a hypothesis, or a suggestion, the **conditionnel présent** of the main verb is used.

Nous nous inscririons à ce   *We would sign up for this course if there*
cours s'il y avait de la place.   *were some space.*

QUIZ

Put the following sentences into the **futur simple**.

Elle regarde le film. <u>Elle regardera le film.</u>

1. Nous allons en Tunisie en janvier. _____
   Noëlle travaille jusqu'à vingt heures. _____
   Vous faites un voyage en Islande. _____
   Je prends le métro. _____
   Ils sont au Kenya. _____

Put both verbs into the **futur simple**.

Elle (pouvoir) te répondre quand   <u>pourra</u>   <u>seras</u>
tu (être) là.

2. Nous (commencer) quand tout
le monde (être) assis.   _____   _____

Elle (prendre) beaucoup de photos
quand elle (voyager) en Australie.   _____   _____

Il (acheter) du pain quand il (aller)
à la boulangerie.   _____   _____

Quand elle (être) grande, elle
(devenir) professeur.   _____   _____

Dès que vous (arriver), nous vous
(expliquer) la situation.   _____   _____

Put the first verb into the **futur simple** and the second verb into the **futur antérieur**.

Je (venir) quand je (finir) mon travail.   *viendrai*   *j'aurai fini*

3. Nous (préparer) le repas quand tu
(faire) les courses.   _____   _____

Il (écouter) ses messages quand
il (rentrer) à la maison.   _____   _____

Les enfants (manger) le gâteau quand
vous le (couper).   _____   _____

Elle (ranger) ses affaires quand
elle (défaire) sa valise.   _____   _____

On (commencer) quand ils (arriver).   _____   _____

Put the first verb into the conditionnel présent and the second verb into the **imparfait**.

Je (étudier) la musique si je (avoir)
l'oreille musicale.   *J'étudierais*   *j'avais*

4. Il (acheter) un parapluie s'il (pleuvoir).   _____   _____
Je lui (donner) de l'argent s'il en
(avoir) besoin.   _____   _____

Elle (mettre) cette robe si elle (aller)
à une soirée.   _____   _____

Nous (être) ravis si vous nous (inviter).   _____   _____

Il (venir) si vous le lui (demander).   _____   _____

Rewrite these sentences changing the verbs from the **conditionnel présent** to the **conditionnel passé** and from the **imparfait** to the **plus-que-parfait**.

Il prendrait le train s'il pouvait. *Il aurait pris le train s'il avait pu.*

5. L'enfant mangerait s'il avait faim.

_____

Nous assisterions au programme si nous étions en ville.

_____

Vous joueriez au tennis s'il ne pleuvait pas.

_____

Elle vous enverrait un message si elle n'était pas si occupée.

_____

Tu lui expliquerais la décision s'il te contactait.

_____

Translate the following sentences using **vous** and inversion when necessary.

6. What time will they arrive? _____

7. I'll call you when I'm in France. _____

8. Could you help me? _____

9. If had known, I would not have invited them.

_____

10. He should not have told you the end of the film.

CHAPTER 18

_____

Knowing Who Is Who with Relative Pronouns

In this chapter you will learn:

The Relative Pronouns

It is essential to know how to connect ideas together in the same sentence. One way to link ideas back to persons and things already mentioned is by using **les pronoms relatifs** (*relative pronouns*). Relative pronouns relate two sentences, making one dependent on the other. The dependent sentence is called the subordinate clause. Choosing the correct relative pronoun depends on the pronoun's function in the sentence (subject, direct object, or object of a preposition).

The Relative Pronoun *qui*

Let's start with the relative pronoun **qui,** used as a subject. **Qui** may refer to people or things and may mean *who, whom, which, what,* or *that.* See the following examples:

Il remercie le passant qui lui a donné un plan de Paris.	*He thanks the passerby who gave him a Paris map.*
Le guide qui nous a fait visiter le musée Rodin a étudié les beaux-arts.	*The guide who showed us around the musée Rodin studied fine arts.*
Elle a lu le livre qui est exposé dans la vitrine.	*She read the book that is exhibited in the window.*
Le film qui va sortir vendredi a eu d'excellentes critiques.	*The film that will be released on Friday has received excellent reviews.*

The **i** of **qui** is never dropped in front of a vowel sound.

Nous n'avons jamais rencontré le nouveau locataire. Nous ne savons pas qui il est.	*We have never met the new tenant. We don't know who he is.*
Il ne m'a toujours pas dit qui il invitait à la soirée.	*He has not yet told me who(m) he is inviting to the party.*

The verb following **qui** agrees with the noun or pronoun that **qui** replaces.

C'est moi qui lui ai fait la meilleure offre.	*It was I who made the best offer.*

C'est vous qui avez décliné son invitation.	*It's you who declined his invitation.*
C'est toi qui es arrivé en retard.	*It's you who arrived late.*
C'est nous qui sommes coupables.	*We are the ones who are guilty.*

Oral Practice

Ask the following questions and then answer them, aloud.

Qui t'a offert cette bague?	*Who gave you this ring?*
C'est Benoît qui m'a offert cette bague.	*It was Benoît who gave me this ring.*
Tu connais les filles des Clément?	*Do you know the Clements' daughters?*
Je connais celle qui habite à Rennes.	*I know the one who lives in Rennes.*
Tu vas à la séance qui commence à 20h?	*Are you going to the show that starts at 8 P.M.?*
Non, je vais à la séance qui commence à 22h.	*No, I am going to the show that starts at 10 P.M.*
Qu'est-ce que ce tableau représente?	*What does this painting represent?*
Ça représente une île qui est située dans le Pacifique.	*It represents an island that is situated in the Pacific.*
Vous êtes malade?	*Are you sick?*
J'ai dû manger quelque chose qui m'a rendu malade.	*I probably ate something that made me sick.*
Vous êtes allée faire des courses?	*Did you go shopping?*
Oui, j'ai acheté beaucoup de choses qui étaient en solde aujourd'hui.	*Yes, I bought a lot of things that were on sale today.*
Vous avez de la famille au Canada?	*Do you have family in Canada?*
Oui, j'ai une cousine qui habite à Québec.	*Yes, I have a cousin who lives in Quebec City.*
Pourquoi fait-il si froid?	*Why is it so cold?*
Il y avait une fenêtre qui n'était pas fermée.	*There was a window that was not closed.*

Written Practice 1

Make full sentences with the elements below, using the **passé composé**.

moi/ouvrir la porte *C'est moi qui ai ouvert la porte.*

1. lui/gagner le match _____
2. vous/poser la question _____
3. eux/arriver en avance _____
4. toi/recevoir le prix _____
5. moi/découvrir le site _____

The Relative Pronoun *que*

When the clause introduced by a relative pronoun already has a subject, the relative pronoun is the object of the verb of the clause it introduces. In this case, the relative pronoun **que** (*whom, which,* or *that*) is used. **Que** may also refer to people and things.

C'est le conférencier que tout le monde aime entendre.	*He is the lecturer whom everyone loves to hear.*
Voici un professeur que je ne connais pas.	*Here's a teacher whom I do not know.*
Il n'a pas encore lu le livre que tu lui as donné.	*He has not yet read the book you gave him.*
Voici la piscine que les enfants adorent.	*Here is the swimming pool that the children love.*

The **e** of **que** is dropped before a vowel.

C'est la route qu'ils prennent.	*It is the road they take.*
Les secrétaires qu'elle engage viennent de la même agence.	*The secretaries she hires come from the same agency.*

In the **passé composé**, if the direct object is placed before the verb, the past participle agrees in gender and number with the object.

Les restaurants que vous avez recommandés étaient hors pair.	*The restaurants you recommended were outstanding.*
Les lettres qu'elle a retrouvées lui seront très utiles pour son nouveau livre.	*The letters she has found will be most useful for her new book.*

In French, the relative clause is often inserted into the main clause. For example:

Le piano qu'elle a vendu aux enchères le mois dernier appartenait à son arrière-arrière-grand-mère.	*The piano she sold at auction last month belonged to her great-great-grandmother.*
Je ne me souviens pas du remède que le médecin a prescrit l'an passé pour le soulager.	*I don't remember the remedy that the doctor prescribed last year to give him some relief.*

Oral Practice

Read the following sentences aloud.

Ce sont les magazines que Sara a apportés.	*These are the magazines Sara brought.*
C'est votre maison?	*Is this your house?*
Notre maison, c'est celle que vous voyez de l'autre côté du lac.	*Our house is the one you see across the lake.*
Les photos qu'elle a prises en Inde sont magnifiques.	*The pictures she took in India are wonderful.*
C'est la veste qu'il a achetée en Italie.	*It's the jacket he bought in Italy.*
Je ne connais pas le suspect que la police a arrêté.	*I don't know the suspect whom the police arrested.*
J'ai rempli le formulaire jaune que tu m'avais donné.	*I filled out the yellow form you had given me.*
J'ai vérifié les adresses qu'on nous avait communiquées.	*I checked the addresses we had been given.*

Written Practice 2

Complete the sentences with **qui**, **que**, or **qu'**.

Elle ouvre la porte *qui* est fermée.

1. Il aime le parfum _____ tu portes.
2. Nous choisissons les fromages _____ vous préférez.
3. Je ne sais pas _____ il est.
4. Vous aimez la musique _____ il choisit.
5. La voiture _____ est devant la maison est à lui.

Relative Pronouns Following Prepositions

When verbs are followed by prepositions, the relative pronouns **qui, quoi, lequel, laquelle, lesquels,** and **lesquelles** are used. The preposition is placed before the relative pronoun. **Qui** is used to refer to people only, while **lequel, laquelle, lesquels,** and **lesquelles** refer to things. **Lequel, laquelle, lesquels,** and **lesquelles** may also be used for people; this usage, however, is less common. Compare:

C'est le responsable à qui j'ai donné mes documents.	*That is the official to whom I gave my documents.*

Less common in modern French:

C'est le responsable auquel j'ai donné mes documents.	*That is the official to whom I gave my documents.*

Let's see other examples:

Voici le journal auquel je m'abonne.	*Here's the newpaper to which I subscribe.*
C'est la pièce à laquelle elle s'intéresse.	*That's the play she is interested in.*
Nous ignorons à quoi il pense.	*We don't know what he is thinking about.*
C'est l'avocate pour qui je travaille.	*That is the lawyer for whom I work.*
C'est l'organisation caritative pour laquelle il travaille.	*That is the charity he works for.*

Dites-moi avec qui vous viendrez dimanche!	*Tell me with whom you're coming on Sunday!*
L'arrogance avec laquelle il s'exprime est inadmissible.	*The arrogance with which he expresses himself is unacceptable.*

NOTE: *With the preposition **parmi** (among), use **lequel** instead of **qui**.*

Il y avait de nombreux candidats, parmi lesquels une dizaine d'Australiens.	*There were many candidates, among whom there were about ten Australians.*

USING *OÙ*

The relative pronoun **où** often replaces **dans lequel, sur lequel,** or **par lequel.** For example:

La ville où ils habitent est en Dordogne.	*The town where they live is in Dordogne.*
Voici la colline où ils construisent leur maison.	*Here is the hill where they are building their house.*

Où is also used after expressions of time.

Le jour où il ne pleuvra pas, nous irons au jardin botanique.	*On the day (when) it does not rain, we'll go to the botanical garden.*
Le quinze mars, c'est le jour où il est mort.	*March fifteenth is the day (when) he died.*

Oral Practice

Ask the following questions and then answer them, aloud.

Vous connaissez Hervé?	*Do you know Hervé?*
Oui, c'est le jeune homme avec qui Ève s'est mariée.	*Yes, that's the young man whom Ève married.*
Qui sont-ils?	*Who are they?*

Ce sont les musiciens sans qui la fête aurait été un échec.	*They are the musicians without whom the party would have been a flop.*
C'est une vieille chaise, non?	*This is an old chair, isn't it?*
La chaise sur laquelle tu es assis a plus de cent ans.	*The chair you are sitting on is more than a hundred years old.*
Où dînons-nous? Au restaurant?	*Where are we having dinner? In a restaurant?*
Je ne sais pas où nous dînons.	*I don't know where we are having dinner.*
Pour qui travaillez-vous ces jours-ci?	*Whom are you working for these days?*
L'entreprise pour laquelle je travaille est danoise.	*The firm I am working for is Danish.*
Tu sais pour qui elle a voté?	*Do you know whom she voted for?*
Non, je ne sais pas pour qui elle a voté.	*No, I don't know whom she voted for.*
Vous avez lu notre rapport annuel?	*Did you read our annual report?*
Oui, j'ai lu le rapport selon lequel vous avez eu une année remarquable.	*Yes, I read the report according to which you had a remarkable year.*
Cette photo ne te dit rien?	*This picture doesn't ring a bell?*
Non, la photo à laquelle je pense était en noir et blanc.	*No, the picture I am thinking of was in black and white.*

Written Practice 3

Complete the sentences with the appropriate preposition and relative pronoun.

Le stylo _avec lequel_ il écrit est de bonne qualité.

1. L'ami _____ il habite tout le mois de mai est un sculpteur brésilien.
2. Le film _____ je pense n'est pas sous-titré.
3. Le canapé _____ ils sont assis vient de Norvège.
4. Le jour _____ elle a été élue, l'histoire a pris un autre tournant.
5. J'ignore _____ il pense.

The Relative Pronoun *dont*

The relative pronoun **dont** can be used in different ways. The pronoun **dont** acts as an object and can refer to people and things. It is used to refer to objects of verbs or adjectives that are followed by the preposition **de.** The pronoun **dont** takes on different meanings. It can imply possession, as shown here:

Le metteur en scène dont j'ai oublié le nom passera à la télé ce soir.	*The film director whose name I forgot will be on TV tonight.*
Voici la chanteuse d'opéra dont je connais la mère.	*Here is the opera singer whose mother I know.*

The relative pronoun **dont** is used with verbs and adjectives using the preposition **de**.

Le critique a parlé du nouveau film de Michel Audiard.	*The critic spoke about Michel Audiard's new film.*
Le film dont le critique a parlé est de Michel Audiard.	*The film the critic talked about is by Michel Audiard.*
Nous nous approchons du Panthéon.	*We are approaching the Pantheon.*
Le monument dont nous nous approchons est le Panthéon.	*The monument we are approaching is the Pantheon.*
Le metteur en scène est content de son film.	*The director is happy about his film.*
C'est un film dont le metteur en scène est content.	*It is a film the director is happy about.*
L'enfant est fier de son exploit.	*The child is proud of his achievement.*
C'est un exploit dont l'enfant est fier.	*It is an achievement the child is proud of.*

In modern French, **dont** often replaces **duquel, de laquelle, desquels,** and **desquelles.** For example:

La conseillère dont je parle s'appelle Madame Villiers.	*The adviser I am talking about is Madame Villiers.*

The previous example is preferable to:

La conseillère de laquelle je parle s'appelle Madame Villiers.	*The adviser I am talking about is Madame Villiers.*

Oral Practice

Ask the following questions and then answer them, aloud.

Tu as besoin de ces ampoules?	*Do you need these lightbulbs?*
Oui, ce sont de ces ampoules dont j'ai besoin.	*Yes, these are the lightbulbs I need.*
Tu te souviens de notre prof de maths?	*Do you remember our math teacher?*
La seule chose dont je me souviens, c'est de sa méchanceté.	*The only thing I remember is her meanness.*
L'architecte est fier de son travail?	*Is the architect proud of his work?*
L'édifice dont il est le plus fier est l'Opéra de Lyon.	*The building he is the proudest of is the Lyon Opera.*
Tu te sers de ce dictionnaire?	*Are you using this dictionary?*
Non, ce n'est pas de ce dictionnaire dont je me sers.	*No, it is not this dictionary I am using.*
De quoi ont-ils peur?	*What are they afraid of?*
La chose dont ils ont peur, c'est de son refus.	*The thing they are afraid of is his refusal.*
Xavier est amoureux?	*Xavier is in love?*
Oui, mais je ne connais pas la femme dont il est amoureux.	*Yes, but I don't know the woman he is in love with.*
Il y avait des erreurs dans le texte?	*Were there any mistakes in the text?*
La seule erreur dont je me suis aperçu était minuscule.	*The only mistake I noticed was tiny.*
Il a envie de changement?	*Does he want change?*
Ce n'est pas le changement dont il a envie.	*It is not change he wants.*

L'affaire est réglée?

The matter is settled?

Non, c'est une affaire dont le gouvernement s'occupe actuellement.

No, it is a matter the government is presently taking care of.

Written Practice 4

Formulate sentences following the model. Use the present tense.

document/avoir besoin (il) *Voici le document dont il a besoin.*

1. voiture/avoir envie (ils) _____
2. roman/parler (elle) _____
3. conséquences/avoir peur (je) _____
4. choses/se souvenir (elle) _____
5. résultats/être heureux (nous) _____

Using the Antecedent *ce*

When there is no specific word or antecedent for the relative pronoun to refer to, the antecedent **ce** is added. **Ce qui, ce que, ce dont,** and **ce à quoi,** all meaning *what,* refer to ideas, not to persons, and do not have gender or number. Choosing the correct indefinite relative pronoun again depends on the pronoun's function in the sentence (subject, direct object, or object of a preposition).

Ce qui is used as the subject of the dependent clause.

Ce qui est arrivé est incompréhensible.

What happened is incomprehensible.

Je ne comprends pas ce qui se passe.

I don't understand what's happening.

Ce que is used as the direct object of the dependent clause.

Ce que vous dites n'a aucun sens.	*What you are saying makes no sense.*
Elle a l'habitude de dire ce qu'elle pense.	*She is used to saying what's on her mind.*
Ce qu'il fait est merveilleux.	*What he does is wonderful.*

Ce dont is used when verbs take the preposition **de.**

Ce dont elle a l'habitude, c'est de dire ce qu'elle pense.	*What she is used to is saying what's on her mind.*
Nous ne savons pas ce dont ils ont besoin.	*We don't know what they need.*
Ce dont vous parlez est tout nouveau pour nous.	*What you are talking about is all new to us.*

Ce à quoi is used with verbs that take the preposition **à.**

Ils ne comprennent pas ce à quoi il s'oppose.	*They don't understand what he is opposed to.*
Ce n'est pas ce à quoi je m'attendais.	*It is not what I expected.*

Commonly, the indefinite relative pronouns **ce qui, ce que, ce à quoi,** and **ce dont** are placed at the beginning of a sentence to show emphasis. When a verb requires a preposition, it is repeated in the second clause.

Ce qui la fascine, c'est ce phénomène.	*What fascinates her is this phenomenon.*
Ce qu'elle regrette, c'est le manque de transparence.	*What she regrets is the lack of transparency.*
Ce dont ils se plaignent, c'est de la pollution.	*What they are complaining about is pollution.*
Ce à quoi je m'intéresse, c'est à votre nouvelle théorie.	*What I am interested in is your new theory.*

Written Practice 5

Formulate sentences following the model. Use the present tense.

  aimer/cinéma italien (elle) *Ce qu'elle aime, c'est le cinéma italien.*

  1. s'intéresser/musique (il) _____
  2. avoir besoin/ordinateur (tu) _____
  3. comprendre/situation (je) _____
  4. se souvenir/fin du film (vous) _____
  5. parler/fascinant (elle) _____

Indirect Speech

To have an indirect speech, you need, of course, a direct speech. In a direct speech, the question is posed directly. For example:

Est-ce que vous acceptez notre   *Do you accept our offer?*
  offre?

In an indirect speech, the words of one or more people are reported.

Elle lui demande s'il accepte leur   *She asks him whether he accepts their*
  offre.   *offer.*

Let's look at other examples of direct and indirect speech.

Savez-vous si elle sait conduire?   *Do you know whether she can drive?*

Je lui demande si elle sait conduire.   *I ask her whether she knows how to drive.*

Qu'est-ce que vous faites le   *What do you do on weekends?*
  week-end?

Vous lui demandez ce qu'il fait   *You ask him what he does on weekends.*
  le week-end.

De quoi as-tu besoin?   *What do you need?*

Je lui demande ce dont il a besoin.   *I ask him what he needs.*

Où l'a-t-il rencontrée?	*Where did he meet her?*
Je ne sais pas où il l'a rencontrée.	*I don't know where he met her.*

When switching from direct to indirect speech, some changes of tense occur when the verb in the main clause is in the past. If the verb in the main clause is in the past and the action (in the indirect speech) is in the present, the verb in the indirect speech clause is changed into the **imparfait.**

Il fait beau à Paris aujourd'hui.	*The weather is nice in Paris today.*
J'ai entendu dire qu'il faisait beau à Paris aujourd'hui.	*I heard that the weather is nice in Paris today.*
Le président est au Japon.	*The president is in Japan.*
J'ai entendu dire que le président était au Japon.	*I heard that the president was in Japan.*

If the verb in the main clause is in the past and the action (in the indirect speech) is in the past, the verb in the indirect speech clause is changed into the **plus-que-parfait.**

Ils ont déménagé.	*They have moved.*
On m'a dit qu'ils avaient déménagé.	*I heard they'd moved.*
Vous avez démissionné.	*You resigned.*
J'ai entendu dire que vous aviez démissionné.	*I heard you'd resigned.*

If the verb in the main clause is in the past and the action (in the indirect speech) is in the future, the verb in the indirect speech clause is changed into the **conditionnel.**

Victoire ira en Amérique du Sud en mai.	*Victoire will go to South America in May.*
J'ai entendu dire que Victoire irait en Amérique du Sud en mai.	*I heard Victoire would be going to South America in May.*
Ils se marieront l'an prochain.	*They're getting married next year.*
On m'a dit qu'ils se marieraient l'an prochain.	*I heard they would be getting married next year.*

Oral Practice

Read the following sentences aloud.

Je ne sais pas si le magasin est fermé.	*I don't know whether the store is closed.*
J'ignore qui assistera à la cérémonie.	*I don't know who will attend the ceremony.*
Je pense qu'ils habitent en banlieue.	*I think they live in the suburbs.*
Je ne sais pas à quoi rêvent les jeunes filles.	*I don't know what young girls dream of.*
Je voudrais savoir à quelle heure commence la conférence.	*I'd like to know at what time the lecture starts.*
Je ne sais pas chez qui nous dînons vendredi.	*I don't know whose house we are having dinner at on Friday.*
J'ai entendu dire qu'il quitterait Paris pour de bon la semaine prochaine.	*I heard he would leave Paris for good next week.*
On m'a dit qu'elle avait pris sa retraite.	*I heard she had retired.*
J'ai entendu dire qu'il pleuvait à Hanoi aujourd'hui.	*I heard that it was raining in Hanoi today.*
J'ai entendu dire qu'elle se présenterait aux élections.	*I heard that she would be running for election.*
Tu ne devineras jamais ce dont ils ont besoin.	*You'll never guess what they need.*
On m'a dit que Sonia travaillait à Strasbourg.	*I was told Sonia works in Strasbourg.*
On m'a dit qu'il avait vendu sa moto.	*I heard he sold his motorbike.*
On ne sait pas ce qu'ils ont choisi.	*No one knows what they've chosen.*
Je crois savoir ce dont ils ont envie.	*I think I know what they feel like.*

Written Practice 6

Formulate sentences starting with **j'ai entendu dire que**.

> être en Argentine/aujourd'hui (il)
> *J'ai entendu dire qu'il était en Argentine aujourd'hui.*

1. travailler en Chine/en 1998 (vous)

   _____

2. aller en Afrique/dans deux ans (elle)

   _____

3. acheter une maison/le mois dernier (ils)

   _____

4. pleuvoir à Madrid/aujourd'hui (il)

   _____

5. prendre sa retraite/l'année prochaine (il)

   _____

QUIZ

Complete the sentences with **qui**, **que**, or **qu'**.

> La voiture _qui_ est devant la banque est à moi.

1. Le plan de Paris _____ vous m'avez donné est très utile.

   Les photos _____ sont sur la table sont à moi.

   C'est moi _____ ai organisé la fête.

   L'assistant _____ Rémi a engagé a d'excellentes qualifications.

   Je n'aime pas les meubles _____ il a achetés.

Complete these sentences with the appropriate relative pronoun.

La chaise sur _laquelle_ il est assis, est en bois.

2. La revue à _____ je m'abonne est mensuelle.
Leur enfant est né l'année _____ ils se sont installés à Nice.
Le livre _____ je pense doit être à la bibliothèque.
Les ingrédients avec _____ elle prépare le plat sont tous bio-
logiques.
Je vous présente les artistes avec _____ nous allons organiser le
concert.

Formulate sentences following the model. Use the present tense.

acteur/parler (je) _C'est l'acteur dont je parle._

3. chose/se souvenir (il) _____
livre/avoir besoin (je) _____
ordinateur/se servir (ils) _____
affaire/s'occuper (je) _____
projet/être fier (elle) _____
entreprise/parler (il) _____

Complete with **ce qui**, **ce que**, **ce dont**, or **ce à quoi**.

Ce que vous voulez, c'est un peu de tranquillité.

4. _____ nous ne comprenons pas, c'est leur obstination.
_____ est fait, est fait.
_____ nous avons besoin, c'est de vos conseils.
_____ m'étonne, c'est sa réaction.
_____ je m'intéresse, c'est à la science.
_____ nous espérons, c'est son retour.
_____ je demande, c'est le silence.
_____ il pense, c'est au résultat des élections.

_____ tu parles est très grave.

_____ il s'attend, c'est au pire.

Formulate sentences starting with **on m'a dit**. Watch out for tenses.

Il a travaillé en Italie. *On m'a dit qu'il avait travaillé en Italie.*

5. Tu iras à Bruxelles lundi. _____

Il fait beau à Venise aujourd'hui. _____

Ils ont eu des ennuis. _____

Tu déménageras bientôt. _____

Vous êtes un très bon conférencier. _____

Translate the following sentences using the **vous** form when necessary.

6. He does not know what you want. _____

7. What I need is another pen. _____

8. The person he is talking about is my brother. _____

9. I don't know what happened. _____

10. The pictures he took are beautiful. _____

CHAPTER 19

The Subjunctive Mood

In this chapter you will learn:

The Subjunctive
The Present Subjunctive
Uses of the Subjunctive
The Past Subjunctive

The Subjunctive

The subjunctive is a mood, not a tense. The mood of a verb determines how one views an event. You have studied tenses in the indicative mood (**le présent,** **l'imparfait, le futur,** etc.), stating an objective fact; the imperative mood, which

gives commands; and the conditional mood, relating to possibilities. The subjunctive is another mood, which refers to someone's opinion or deals with hypothetical action.

The Present Subjunctive

For most verbs, the present of the subjunctive is formed by adding the subjunctive endings (**e, es, e, ions, iez,** and **ent**) to the stem. The stem for **je, tu, il, elle, ils,** and **elles** is found by dropping the **ent** ending from the third person plural present indicative form.

Let's take the verb **parler** (*to speak*). The third person plural: **ils parlent.** The stem: **parl-.**

je parle	*I speak*
tu parles	*you speak*
il/elle parle	*he/she speaks*
ils/elles parlent	*they speak*

The stem for **nous** and **vous** is found by dropping the **ons** from the first person plural of the present indicative form. For **nous** and **vous**, the present of the subjunctive is identical to the **imparfait.** The first person plural: **nous parlons.** The stem: **parl-.**

nous parlions	*we speak*
vous parliez	*you speak*

Now let's look at **écrire** and **prendre**.

écrire *(to write)*

j'écrive	*I write*	nous écrivions	*we write*
tu écrives	*you write*	vous écriviez	*you write*
il/elle écrive	*he/she writes*	ils/elles écrivent	*they write*

prendre *(to take)*

je prenne	*I take*	nous prenions	*we take*
tu prennes	*you take*	vous preniez	*you take*
il/elle prenne	*he/she takes*	ils/elles prennent	*they take*

Some verbs have an irregular form in the subjunctive. **Être** (*to be*) and **avoir** (*to have*) have both irregular stems and irregular endings.

être

je sois	*I am*	nous soyons	*we are*
tu sois	*you are*	vous soyez	*you are*
il/elle soit	*he/she is*	ils/elles soient	*they are*

avoir

j'aie	*I have*	nous ayons	*we have*
tu aies	*you have*	vous ayez	*you have*
il/elle ait	*he/she has*	ils/elles aient	*they have*

Three verbs have an irregular subjunctive stem but regular endings.

savoir *(to know)*

je sache	*I know*	nous sachions	*we know*
tu saches	*you know*	vous sachiez	*you know*
il/elle sache	*he/she knows*	ils/elles sachent	*they know*

pouvoir *(to be able to)*

je puisse	*I can*	nous puissions	*we can*
tu puisses	*you can*	vous puissiez	*you can*
il/elle puisse	*he/she can*	ils/elles puissent	*they can*

faire *(to do)*

je fasse	*I do*	nous fassions	*we do*
tu fasses	*you do*	vous fassiez	*you do*
il/elle fasse	*he/she does*	ils/elles fassent	*they do*

Aller (*to go*) and **vouloir** (*to want*) are partially irregular.

aller *(to go)*

j'aille	*I go*	nous allions	*we go*
tu ailles	*you go*	vous alliez	*you go*
il/elle aille	*he/she goes*	ils/elles aillent	*they go*

vouloir *(to want)*

je veuille	*I want*	nous voulions	*we want*
tu veuilles	*you want*	vous vouliez	*you want*
il/elle veuille	*he/she wants*	ils/elles veuillent	*they want*

Uses of the Subjunctive

There are three main concepts that require the use of the subjunctive: wish or desire, emotion, and doubt.

THE SUBJUNCTIVE TO EXPRESS A WISH OR DESIRE

The subjunctive is used after verbs expressing the notion of wish or desire. It is used when the subjects of the main and dependent clauses are different. Compare:

Je veux aller à Lyon.	*I want to go to Lyon.*
Je veux que tu ailles à Lyon.	*I want you to go to Lyon.*
Nous souhaitons que vous assistiez à la réunion.	*We wish you to attend the meeting.*

THE SUBJUNCTIVE TO EXPRESS AN EMOTION

The subjunctive is used after expressions of emotion. For example:

Nous sommes ravis que tu puisses te joindre à nous.	*We are delighted you can join us.*
Je suis désolé que Julie ne soit pas là.	*I am sorry Julie is not here.*

THE SUBJUNCTIVE TO EXPRESS DOUBT

The subjunctive is also used after expressions of doubt.

Je doute qu'il sache la réponse.	*I doubt he knows the answer.*
Elle ne croit pas qu'il soit à la hauteur de la tâche.	*She does not think he is up to the task.*

The verbs **penser** (*to think*) and **croire** (*to believe*) in the affirmative form are followed by the indicative mood. However, in the negative and interrogative forms, the subjunctive can be used to underline the uncertainty of the event.

Je ne crois pas que M. Henri est innocent.	*I don't think Mr. Henri is innocent.*

This sentence means that I am actually sure Mr. Henri is guilty.

Je ne crois pas que M. Henri soit innocent.	*I don't think Mr. Henri is innocent.*

Here, there is some doubt about his guilt. The difference will often be detected in the intonation of the voice or through gestures.

Oral Practice

Ask the following questions and then answer them, aloud.

Pourquoi est-il de mauvaise humeur?	*Why is he in a bad mood?*
Il est furieux que vous ne participiez pas à la compétition.	*He is furious that you will not take part in the competition.*
Tu crois qu'il va s'occuper de cette affaire?	*Do you think he'll take care of this matter?*
Je doute qu'il s'occupe de cette affaire.	*I doubt he'll take care of this matter.*
Nous pouvons vous accompagner?	*Can we go along with you?*
Je préfère que vous restiez au bureau aujourd'hui.	*I would prefer for you to stay in the office today.*
Est-ce qu'on peut t'aider à faire la cuisine?	*Can we help you cook?*
J'aimerais mieux que vous mettiez la table.	*I'd rather you set the table.*
Vous avez l'air content.	*You look happy.*
Je suis si content que mon ami Jean aille avec moi à Paris.	*I am so happy my friend Jean is coming with me to Paris.*
On m'a dit que Bertrand démissionnait. C'est vrai?	*I heard Bertrand was resigning. Is it true?*
Oui, et je regrette vraiment qu'il démissionne.	*Yes, and I am really sorry he is resigning.*
Elle a lu le rapport?	*Did she read the report?*

Non. Mais je tiens à ce qu'elle le lise avant lundi.	*No. But I insist she read it before Monday.*
Vous pensez qu'il va remporter les élections?	*Do you think he is going to win the elections?*
J'ai bien peur qu'il n'ait pas assez de voix.	*I am really afraid he won't have enough votes.*
Qu'est-ce qu'il veut vraiment?	*What does he really want?*
Il veut que le projet ait du succès en Asie.	*He wants the project to succeed in Asia.*
Il a l'air déçu.	*He looks disappointed.*
Oui, il est déçu que le programme soit annulé.	*Yes, he is disappointed the program is canceled.*

Written Practice 1

Put the verbs in parentheses into the subjunctive.

Elle voudrait que tu _ailles_____ à Paris avec elle. (aller)

1. Il souhaite que vous lui _____ d'ici vendredi. (répondre)
2. Je suis ravie qu'il _____ venir. (pouvoir)
3. Elle désire que tu _____ le français. (apprendre)
4. Elle doute qu'ils _____ à l'heure. (être)
5. Il est triste que tu _____ ce soir. (ne pas venir)

THE SUBJUNCTIVE AFTER CERTAIN IMPERSONAL EXPRESSIONS

The subjunctive is also used after certain impersonal expressions. Just as some verbs are followed by the indicative and others by the subjunctive, some impersonal expressions are followed by one mood or the other. In most cases, the expressions followed by the subjunctive express will, obligation, necessity, emotion, and doubt. Compare:

Il est évident qu'il fera beau demain. *It is obvious the weather will be nice tomorrow.*

Il est possible qu'il fasse beau demain. *It is possible the weather will be nice tomorrow.*

Here are some impersonal expressions followed by the indicative:

il est certain	*it is certain*	il est sûr	*it is sure*
il est évident	*it is obvious*	il est vrai	*it is true*
il est probable	*it is probable*	il me (lui) semble	*it seems to me (to him/her)*

Here are some impersonal expressions followed by the subjunctive:

cela ne vaut pas la peine	*it is not worth it*	il est normal	*it is normal*
il est bizarre	*it is odd*	il est possible	*it is possible*
il est bon	*it is a good thing*	il est préférable	*it is preferable*
il est dommage	*it is a shame*	il est rare	*it is rare*
il est essentiel	*it is essential*	il est regrettable	*it is unfortunate*
il est étonnant	*it is amazing*	il est souhaitable	*it is desirable*
il est étrange	*it is strange*	il est surprenant	*it is surprising*
il est important	*it is important*	il est triste	*it is sad*
il est indispensable	*it is essential*	il est utile	*it is useful*
il est juste	*it is fair*	il faut	*one must*
il est mauvais	*it is a bad thing*	il se peut	*it may be*
il est naturel	*it is natural*	il vaut mieux	*it is better*

Oral Practice

Repeat aloud the following sentences.

Il faut que je finisse ce roman d'ici la semaine prochaine. *I have to finish this novel by next week.*

Il est rare qu'ils soient en retard. *It is rare for them to be late.*

Il est peu probable qu'il reçoive son diplôme. *It is unlikely he'll get his degree.*

Il est dommage qu'il pleuve. *It is a shame it is raining.*

Il est regrettable qu'il parte si tôt. *It is unfortunate he is leaving so early.*

Il est étonnant que vous acceptiez ces conditions.	*It is surprising for you to accept these conditions.*
Il se peut qu'il n'y ait plus de billets.	*It is possible there are no more tickets.*
Il est triste que vous quittiez l'équipe.	*It is sad you are leaving the team.*
Il est préférable que nous arrivions avant midi.	*It is preferable for us to arrive before noon.*
Il est étrange qu'il se conduise ainsi.	*It is strange for him to behave this way.*
Il est possible que vous gagniez le marathon.	*You may win the marathon.*
Il faut qu'elle sache la vérité.	*She has to know the truth.*
Il est normal que l'enfant fasse encore ces fautes d'orthographe.	*It is normal for the child to still be making these spelling mistakes.*
Il est essentiel que vous leur racontiez cette histoire.	*It is essential that you tell them this story.*
Il est important que tout soit prêt avant l'arrivée de nos invités.	*It is important that everything be ready before our guests' arrival.*

Written Practice 2

Put the following sentences into the subjunctive.

Il est rare qu'il (faire) si froid à cette saison.
Il est rare qu'il fasse si froid à cette saison.

1. Il faut que vous (aller) lui rendre visite.

2. Il est essentiel que tu (connaître) les grandes lignes du projet.

3. Il est incroyable que ce produit (se vendre) si bien.

4. Il est possible que nous (accepter) leur offre.

_____

5. Il est important qu'il (prendre) de longues vacances.

_____

THE SUBJUNCTIVE WITH CONJUNCTIONS

Another instance where you will have to decide to use either the indicative or the subjunctive is when using conjunctions. The conjunctions in this list are followed by the subjunctive mood.

afin que	*so that, in order to*
en attendant que	*while waiting for*
avant que	*before*
bien que	*although*
à condition que	*on the condition that*
de crainte que	*for fear that*
jusqu'à ce que	*until*
à moins que	*unless*
de peur que	*for fear that*
pour que	*so that, in order to*
pourvu que	*provided that*
quoique	*although*
sans que	*without*

For example:

Il arrivera à dix heures à moins que le train ait du retard.	*He will arrive at ten unless the train is late.*
Nous déjeunerons dans le jardin pourvu qu'il ne pleuve pas.	*We'll have lunch in the garden provided it does not rain.*

Certain conjunctions are sometimes replaced by a preposition, which is then followed by an infinitive. This is done when the subject of the main clause and of the dependent clause are the same.

NOTE: *There are no prepositions corresponding to* ***jusqu'à ce que****,* ***bien que****,* ***quoique****, or* ***pourvu que****.*

Je prends mon parapluie de peur d'être mouillé.	*I take my umbrella for fear of getting wet.*
Il consulte son emploi du temps avant de prendre un rendez-vous.	*He checks his schedule before making an appointment.*

Pourvu que takes a different meaning when used in a single clause. It is a very handy expression, also followed by the subjunctive, for expressing a hope.

Pourvu qu'il fasse beau demain!	*Let's hope the weather is nice tomorrow!*
Pourvu qu'ils ne soient pas en retard!	*Let's hope they are not late!*
Pourvu qu'il y ait encore des places!	*Let's hope there are still some seats left!*
Pourvu que vous puissiez assister au vernissage!	*Let's hope you can attend the opening!*

Oral Practice

Repeat aloud the following sentences.

Nous ne prendrons pas de décision avant que vous arriviez.	*We won't make a decision before you arrive.*
Elle est très gentille quoiqu'elle ne soit pas très efficace.	*She is very nice although she is not very efficient.*
Elle répétera l'exercice jusqu'à ce qu'il comprenne.	*She will repeat the exercise until he understands.*
Je te prête ces livres à condition que tu me les rendes.	*I am lending you these books on the condition you return them to me.*

Tout sera prêt avant que vous arriviez.	*Everything will be ready before you arrive.*
Nous les avertirons pour qu'ils ne soient pas surpris.	*We'll warn them so that they are not surprised.*
Nous irons à Paris bien qu'ils ne puissent pas nous accompagner.	*We'll go to Paris even though they can't go with us.*
Je passerai te chercher à moins qu'il y ait un imprévu.	*I'll come and pick you up unless something unexpected crops up.*
Elle enverra un message afin que tout le monde soit au courant.	*She'll send a message so that everyone can be informed.*

Written Practice 3

Put the following sentences into the subjunctive.

Il parle fort afin que vous le (entendre).
Il parle fort afin que vous l'entendiez.

1. Il va t'aider pour que tu (pouvoir) finir à temps.

   _____

2. À moins que cela (être) trop tard, je te retrouve à vingt heures.

   _____

3. Bien qu'il y (avoir) des scènes amusantes, ce film n'est pas très bon.

   _____

4. Dépêche-toi de rentrer avant qu'il (se mettre) à pleuvoir.

   _____

5. Le président a tout fait pour que les citoyens (être) contents.

   _____

THE SUBJUNCTIVE AFTER A SUPERLATIVE

The subjunctive is also used after a superlative or an adjective conveying a superlative idea, such as **premier** (*first*), **dernier** (*last*), **seul** (*only*), or **unique** (*unique*).

C'est la plus belle ville que je connaisse.	*It is the most beautiful city I know.*
C'est la seule personne à qui je puisse faire confiance.	*He/She is the only person I can trust.*

THE SUBJUNCTIVE AFTER INDEFINITE EXPRESSIONS

The present of the subjunctive is used with indefinite expressions meaning *whatever, wherever,* or *whoever.* When the idea of *whatever* is followed by a verb, the neutral **quoi que** is used. For example:

Quoi qu'il fasse, sa mère se plaint.	*Whatever he does, his mother complains.*
Quoi que vous décidiez, je voterai pour vous.	*Whatever you decide, I'll vote for you.*

When the idea of *whatever* is followed by a noun, **quel que** is used. **Quel que** agrees in gender and number with the subject.

Quelle que soit votre opinion, je m'en fiche.	*Whatever your opinion, I don't care.*
Quel que soit ton but, ne le perds pas de vue.	*Whatever your goal, do not lose sight of it.*

See the following examples that express *wherever*:

Où que tu ailles, je te suivrai.	*Wherever you go, I'll follow you.*
Où que vous soyez, appelez-nous.	*Wherever you are, call us.*

The subjunctive is also used to express *whoever.* For example:

Qui que tu sois, tu as les mêmes droits.	*Whoever you are, you have the same rights.*
Qui que vous soyez, aidez-les.	*Whoever you are, help them.*

THE SUBJUNCTIVE AFTER THE RELATIVE PRONOUNS *QUI* AND *QUE*

The relative pronouns **qui** and **que** can sometimes be followed by the subjunctive. If there is a doubt about the existence of someone or the possible realization of something, the subjunctive may be used after the relative pronoun. For example:

Je cherche quelqu'un **qui** puisse résoudre ces équations.
I am looking for someone who might be able to solve these equations.

Connaîtriez-vous des logiciels **qui** nous permettent d'accroître notre rendement?
Would you know some software allowing us to increase our output?

In this case, there is a doubt whether such a person or object even exists and if so, whether the person or object can accomplish the task.

The Past Subjunctive

The past subjunctive is used in the same manner as the present subjunctive. However, the action of the dependent clause is anterior to the action of the main clause. To form the past subjunctive, use the present subjunctive of **avoir** or **être** plus the past participle of the verb.

lire *(to read)*

j'aie lu	*I have read*	nous ayons lu	*we have read*
tu aies lu	*you have read*	vous ayez lu	*you have read*
il/elle ait lu	*he/she has read*	ils/elles aient lu	*they have read*

partir *(to leave)*

je sois parti(e)	*I have left*	nous soyons parti(e)s	*we have left*
tu sois parti(e)	*you have left*	vous soyez parti(e)(s)	*you have left*
il/elle soit parti(e)	*he/she have left*	ils/elles soient parti(e)s	*they have left*

Note the following example sentences:

Je suis désolé que vous n'ayez pas pu venir.
I am sorry you were not able to come.

Nous sommes ravis que vous ayez obtenu ce poste.
We are delighted you got this position.

Oral Practice

Repeat aloud the following sentences.

Je doute qu'il ait compris l'explication.	*I doubt he understood the explanation.*
Nous regrettons qu'elle n'ait pas accepté notre proposition.	*We are sorry she did not accept our offer.*
Il est possible qu'il soit déjà parti.	*He may have already left.*
Je suis surpris qu'elle ne t'ait pas appelé.	*I am surprised she did not call you.*
Elle craint qu'il ait perdu son chemin.	*She fears he lost his way.*
Il est dommage que vous n'ayez pas eu l'occasion de voir ce film.	*It is a shame you did not get a chance to see this film.*
Je ne crois pas qu'elle ait réussi à le joindre.	*I don't think she managed to reach him.*
Il m'a interrompu avant que j'aie pu finir ma phrase.	*He interrupted me before I was able to finish my sentence.*
Il est curieux que vous n'ayez pas eu des ses nouvelles.	*It is strange you have not heard from him.*
Elle est blessée que vous ayez oublié son anniversaire.	*She is crushed you forgot her birthday.*
Ils ont peur que vous n'ayez pas fait le nécessaire.	*They are afraid you did not do what was necessary.*
Il se peut qu'il soit tombé en panne.	*His car may have broken down.*
Ils sont contents que vous ayez acheté cette maison.	*They are happy you bought this house.*
Il est étrange qu'elle n'ait pas laissé de message.	*It is strange she did not leave a note.*

Written Practice 4

Put the verbs in parentheses into the past subjunctive.

Il a peur que vous _ayez pris_____ la décision trop vite. (prendre)

1. Elle regrette que tu _____ le temps de lire cet article. (ne pas avoir)
2. Je crains que vous _____. (se tromper)
3. Il est possible qu'elle _____ le projet. (terminer)
4. Vous êtes content qu'il _____ son diplôme. (obtenir)
5. Tu ne penses pas qu'elle _____ une erreur? (faire)

QUIZ

Put the verbs in parentheses into the subjunctive.

Je regrette que tu _n'ailles pas_____ à Berlin. (ne pas aller)

1. Il préfère que nous _____ demain. (revenir)
   Nous sommes contents que tu _____ prolonger ton séjour. (pouvoir)
   Je ne crois pas que nous _____ à la campagne ce week-end. (aller)
   Tu aimerais mieux qu'il _____ le train? (prendre)
   Il a peur que nous _____. (ne pas réussir)

Put the following sentences into the indicative or subjunctive mood.

Il est essentiel que toute l'équipe (être) là. _Il est essentiel que toute l'équipe soit là. (sub.)_

2. Il est rare qu'il (pleuvoir) dans cette région. _____
   Il est surprenant qu'ils (ne pas venir) demain. _____
   Il est évident qu'elle (avoir) ses propres raisons. _____
   Il me semble que vous (avoir) tort. _____

Il est probable que ça (finir) mal. _____

Il faut que nous (arriver) avant eux. _____

Put the following sentences into the subjunctive.

Il achète des billets pour que nous (pouvoir) assister au spectacle.

Il achète des billets pour que nous puissions assister au spectacle.

3. Il vous écrira jusqu'à ce que vous lui (donner) une réponse positive.

_____

Il prend sa voiture de peur qu'il y (avoir) une grève des transports.

_____

Elle vous contactera avant que vous (quitter) Paris.

_____

Vérifiez les calculs afin qu'on (ne pas trouver) d'erreurs.

_____

Bien qu'il (courir) vite, il ne gagnera pas cette course.

_____

Put the following verbs into the past subjunctive.

Je ne pense pas qu'il (comprendre) sa réaction.

Je ne pense pas qu'il ait compris sa réaction.

4. Je regrette que vous (abandonner) la compétition.

_____

Il est dommage que nous (ne pas rencontrer) Paul plus tôt.

_____

Elle est triste que tu (échouer) à tous tes examens.

_____

Il est étrange qu'ils (ne pas téléphoner).

_____

Nous craignons qu'il (oublier) l'heure de la réunion.

_____

Je voudrais que vous (finir) tout l'article d'ici ce soir.

_____

Translate the following sentences, using the **vous** form when necessary.

5. Whatever she chooses, he is satisfied. _____
6. Wherever you go, I'll travel with you. _____
7. Whatever his opinions, they never agree with him. _____

Translate the following sentences using the subjunctive and, when necessary, the **tu** form.

8. I want you to go to the theater with us. _____
9. He is happy you will be able to attend his opening. _____
10. Go home before it rains. _____

PART FOUR TEST

Replace **avant** with **après** in the following sentences.

Il appelle son ami avant de trouver un emploi.
Il appelle son ami après avoir trouvé un emploi.

1. Je fais la cuisine avant de faire le ménage.

_____

2. Il téléphone à Caroline avant de prendre sa décision.

_____

3. Ils se lavent les mains avant de faire la cuisine.

_____

4. Elle fait ses valises avant de téléphoner à ses amis.

_____

5. Nous parlons à notre client avant de fixer le prix.

_____

Put the verbs in parentheses into the gerund.

Il a rencontré Rémi en *allant* à la poste. (aller)

6. Elle écoute la radio en _____ . (conduire)
7. Il a fait des progrès en _____ tous les soirs. (étudier)
8. Ils se détendent en _____ une promenade. (faire)
9. Ils sont surpris en vous _____ dans la rue. (voir)
10. Elle amuse les enfants en _____ une histoire. (raconter)

Put the following sentences into the **futur simple**.

      Elle regarde le film. _Elle regardera le film._

11. Vincent vient avec nous demain. _____
12. Ils posent beaucoup de questions. _____
13. Tu dois t'inscrire. _____
14. Nous nous reposons dans le jardin. _____
15. Ils dînent sur la terrasse. _____

Put the first verb into the **futur simple** and the second verb into the **futur antérieur**.

      Je (venir) quand je (finir) mon travail.   _Viendrai_   _j'aurai fini_

16. Nous (partir) dès que nous (finir)   _____   _____
    de déjeuner.
17. Elle (vendre) sa voiture quand elle   _____   _____
    (trouver) une moto.
18. Je (payer) quand je (recevoir)   _____   _____
    la commande.
19. Il (réserver) l'hôtel quand vous (choisir)   _____   _____
    les dates.
20. Tu (pouvoir) lire ce livre quand   _____   _____
    je le (lire).

Put the first verb into the **conditionnel présent** and the second verb into the **imparfait**.

      Je (étudier) la musique si je (avoir)   _J'étudierais_   _j'avais_
      l'oreille musicale.

21. Vous (prendre) l'autoroute si vous   _____   _____
    (être) pressés.
22. Je (boire) de l'eau si je (avoir) soif.   _____   _____
23. Tu (conduire) s'il le (falloir).   _____   _____

24. Elles (aller) chez Paul s'il (habiter) _____   _____
    plus près.

25. Nous (se promener) le long de la Seine _____   _____
    s'il (faire) meilleur.

Create sentences changing the verbs from the **conditionnel présent** to the **conditionnel passé** and from the **imparfait** to the **plus-que-parfait**.

> Il prendrait le train s'il pouvait.
> *Il aurait pris le train s'il avait pu.* _____

26. Ils construiraient une maison s'ils avaient un terrain.

    _____

27. Je voterais pour lui s'il avait un programme plus précis.

    _____

28. Ils jetteraient ces documents s'ils n'en avaient pas besoin.

    _____

29. Il irait chez le dentiste s'il avait mal aux dents.

    _____

30. On irait à Paris si on avait le temps.

    _____

Formulate sentences starting with **on m'a dit**. Watch out for tenses.

> Vous avez gagné la compétition. *On m'a dit que vous aviez gagné la*
> *compétition.*

31. Elle a vécu en Russie. _____

32. Il fera le tour du monde. _____

33. Elles jouent très bien au tennis. _____

34. Tu as pris une décision. _____

35. Elle n'assistera pas à la cérémonie. _____

Put the verbs in parentheses into the subjunctive.

> Je regrette que tu (ne pas aller) à Berlin.   *n'ailles pas*

36. Je souhaite que votre séjour (se passer) bien.   _____
37. Elle désire que tu (suivre) cette affaire.   _____
38. Je veux que tu (choisir) la couleur qui te plaît.   _____
39. Il est triste que vous (ne pas être) là.   _____
40. Je doute qu'ils (savoir) résoudre ce problème.   _____

Put the verbs in parentheses into the indicative or subjunctive mood.

> Il est essentiel que toute l'équipe (être) là.   *soit (sub.)*

41. Il faut que nous (arriver) avant eux.   _____
42. Il se peut qu'il (mentir).   _____
43. Il vaudrait mieux que tu (lire) tous les dossiers.   _____
44. Il est possible que nous (ne pas connaître) toute l'histoire.   _____
45. Il est sûr qu'il (être) tout à fait compétent.   _____

Translate the following sentences, using the inversion and the **vous** form when necessary.

46. It is strange they are late. _____
47. Let's hope the weather will be nice tomorrow! _____
48. Could you help us? _____
49. They should have told us the whole story. _____
50. I heard the president is in Japan today. _____

Conjugate the verbs in parentheses in the present tense.

    1. Pourquoi est-ce que vous (devoir) déménager? _____

    2. (Pouvoir)-vous attendre quelques minutes? _____

    3. Est-ce que vous et Olivier (vouloir) aller au cinéma _____
       avec nous?

    4. Je (devoir) conduire les enfants à l'école. _____

    5. Est-ce que vous (pouvoir) venir ce soir? _____

Conjugate the following pronominal verbs in the present tense.

    6. s'amuser (tu) _____

    7. s'écrire (ils) _____

    8. se reposer (nous) _____

    9. s'habiller (il) _____

   10. se promener (nous) _____

Change from the affirmative to the negative form.

    Je vais acheter cette lampe. *Je ne vais pas acheter cette lampe.*

   11. Il va pleuvoir cette nuit. _____

   12. Ils vont vendre leur voiture. _____

   13. Il va maigrir pendant les vacances. _____

   14. Tu vas aller en Italie. _____

   15. Elle va commander la mousse au chocolat. _____

Put both verbs into the future tense.

   16. Je vous (inviter) au restaurant quand vous (venir) à Paris.

    _____

17. Nous (visiter) le château d'Amboise quand nous (être) dans la vallée de la Loire.

_____

18. Tant qu'il (faire) beau, nous (rester) dans le jardin.

_____

19. Elle vous (contacter) dès qu'elle (avoir) plus de détails.

_____

20. Il (regarder) ces films quand il (pouvoir).

_____

Change these sentences from the immediate future to the immediate past.

Il va partir. _Il vient de partir._ _____

21. Nous allons acheter un nouveau dictionnaire. _____
22. Je vais téléphoner à Guillaume. _____
23. Je vais faire le ménage. _____
24. Elle va finir le projet. _____
25. Il va renouveler sa carte d'identité. _____

Replace both the direct and the indirect object with pronouns.

Tu as donné les livres à Marie. _Tu les lui as donnés._ _____

26. Elle a offert ce collier à son amie. _____
27. Ils n'ont pas envoyé les dossiers à Carole. _____
28. J'écris ces cartes postales à mes cousins. _____
29. Vous vendez ces camions à des entreprises indiennes. _____
30. Elle a raconté cette histoire à ses collègues. _____

Answer the questions in the affirmative, using both a direct and an indirect object pronoun.

Il t'a proposé le poste? *Oui, il me l'a proposé.*

31. Elle vous a rendu vos dossiers? _____
32. Il t'a montré son entreprise? _____
33. Vous m'avez faxé l'accord? _____
34. Tu nous recommandes cet agent? _____
35. Vous pouvez me décrire ce paysage? _____

Change the following sentences to the causative **faire** form.

Il nettoie la salle. *Il fait nettoyer la salle.*

36. Il repasse ses chemises. _____
37. Elle classe les photos. _____
38. Nous sortons le chien. _____
39. Je fais une robe. _____
40. Il décore la salle de classe. _____

Put the first verb into the **passé composé** and the second into the **plus-que-parfait**.

Elle (apprécier) ce que vous (dire) la veille.
Elle a apprécié ce que vous aviez dit la veille.

41. Il (recevoir) la carte que vous (envoyer) de Shanghai.

_____

42. On (savoir) que les entreprises (faire faillite).

_____

43. Elle (annuler) car elle (oublier) un rendez-vous important.

_____

44. Il (perdre) le document que vous lui (confier).

_____

45. La réunion (se passer) comme il le (imaginer).

_____

Put the following verbs into the **passé simple**.

      courir (il)   *il courut*_____

46. manger (tu)   _____
47. entendre (je)   _____
48. vivre (il)   _____
49. être (elle)   _____
50. danser (nous) _____

Put the first verb into the **imparfait** and the second into the **passé simple**.

      Elle (lire) quand on (frapper) à la porte.
      *Elle lisait quand on frappa à la porte.*_____

51. Il (faire) le tour du monde quand sa sœur (gagner) le prix Nobel.

_____

52. Nous (danser) quand l'orchestre (s'arrêter).

_____

53. Ils (vivre) à Berlin quand la guerre (éclater).

_____

54. Vous (écouter) de la musique quand elle (entrer).

_____

55. Je (écrire) quand il (sonner) à la porte.

_____

Replace the boldfaced possessive adjective and noun with a possessive pronoun.

Mon bureau est en bois.   *Le mien est en bois.* _____

56. **Nos cousins** sont au Portugal. _____
57. **Votre chaise** est confortable. _____
58. **Notre chien** est vieux. _____
59. **Leurs souvenirs** sont vagues. _____
60. **Mes lunettes** sont bleues. _____

Replace the demonstrative adjectives and the nouns with a demonstrative pronoun.

61. Ce magazine est de gauche. Ce magazine est de droite.

_____

62. Ces voitures sont vieilles. Ces voitures sont neuves.

_____

63. Cette idée est brillante. Cette idée n'est pas raisonnable.

_____

64. Ce coussin est mou. Ce coussin est mœlleux.

_____

65. Ces plats sont légers. Ces plats sont lourds.

_____

Fill in the appropriate relative pronoun.

Les amis chez *qui* _____ nous passons le week-end sont anglais.

66. La table sur _____ se trouve le vase bleu appartenait à mes grands-parents.
67. L'entreprise pour _____ il travaille est suédoise.
68. Je ne sais pas à _____ elle pense.

69. Le village _____ ils habitent est en haut de la colline.
70. Pour _____ prépare-t-il cette fête d'anniversaire?

Answer the following questions.

Depuis combien de temps faites-vous du ski? (dix ans)
Je fais du ski depuis dix ans.

71. Depuis combien de temps fais-tu de la danse? (trois ans)

    _____

72. Depuis combien de temps faites-vous la cuisine pour les Renaud? (trois mois)

    _____

73. Depuis combien de temps faites-vous la queue? (un quart d'heure)

    _____

74. Depuis combien de temps fais-tu réparer ta voiture chez ce garagiste? (deux ans)

    _____

75. Depuis combien de temps fais-tu faire tes costumes? (dix ans)

    _____

Put the following verbs in parentheses into the subjunctive.

Il achète des billets pour que nous *puissions* assister au spectacle. (pouvoir)

76. En attendant que vous en _____ plus, je continue mes recherches. (savoir)
77. Bien que je _____ mal aux pieds, je vais me promener avec vous. (avoir)
78. À moins que cela te _____, nous arriverons vers midi. (déranger)

79. Il arrose les fleurs pour qu'elles _____ pousser. (pouvoir)
80. Quoique cette huile _____ moins chère, je vais prendre l'autre. (être)

Put the following verbs in parentheses into the past subjunctive.

Je ne pense pas qu'il _ait compris_ _____ sa réaction. (comprendre)

81. Je doute qu'elle _____ un nouvel appartement. (trouver)
82. Nous sommes furieux que tu _____ hier soir. (ne pas venir)
83. Il se peut qu'ils _____ . (déménager)
84. Il est étonnant que vous _____ ce restaurant. (ne pas aimer)
85. Je crains qu'il _____ malade. (être)

Put the following verbs in parentheses into the indicative or subjunctive mood.

Il est crucial que tout le monde (être) là. _soit (sub.)_ _____

86. Il est certain qu'ils (venir) ce soir. _____
87. Il est peu probable qu'elles (faire) un si long voyage. _____
88. Il semble qu'ils (avoir) une solution. _____
89. Il est étonnant qu'ils (être) déjà au courant. _____
90. Il est évident que vous (pouvoir) gagner la campagne. _____

Translate the following sentences, using **vous** and inversion when necessary.

91. Can you cook?

_____

92. Do you know this doctor?

_____

93. She can translate this document in an hour.

_____

94. How long have you been living in this apartment?

_____

95. Could you show me the Eiffel Tower on the map?

_____

96. They go to France every year.

_____

97. What time did they leave?

_____

98. Are you going to buy all these books?

_____

99. Do you remember it?

_____

100. Whatever he does, he succeeds.

_____

ENGLISH-FRENCH GLOSSARY

A

according to selon
to admit avouer
to advise conseiller
again encore
ailleurs elsewhere
to aim at viser à
air-conditioned climatisé
alone seul
along le long de
also aussi
always toujours
to amaze étonner
among parmi
ankle cheville (*f.*)
to announce annoncer
to answer répondre à
anything n'importe quoi
anywhere n'importe où
to apologize s'excuser de
to appear apparaître, paraître
April avril
arm bras (*m.*)
at random au hasard
to attend assister à

August août
aunt tante (*f.*)
available disponible

B

bag sac (*m.*)
bakery boulangerie (*f.*)
balcony balcon (*m.*)
ball balle (*f.*)
barn grange (*f.*)
to be able (to) pouvoir
to be informed être au courant
to be right avoir raison
to be wrong avoir tort
beach plage (*f.*)
bean haricot (*m.*)
bed lit (*m.*)
before avant
behind derrière
to believe croire
to belong appartenir
beside à côté
bet pari (*m.*)
bicycle vélo (*m.*)
bill addition (*f.*)

bird oiseau (*m.*)
birthday anniversaire (*m.*)
bitter amer
bitterness amertume (*f.*)
black noir
blackboard tableau (*m.*)
blue bleu
blunder gaffe (*f.*)
boat bateau (*m.*)
body corps (*m.*)
book livre (*m.*)
bookstore librairie (*f.*)
born né
to borrow emprunter
boss patron (*m.*), patronne (*f.*)
bottle bouteille (*f.*)
box boîte (*f.*)
bracelet bracelet (*m.*)
to break casser
to break down tomber en panne
breakfast petit déjeuner (*m.*)
to bring apporter
brother frère (*m.*)
brother-in-law beau-frère (*m.*)
to brush brosser
bucket seau (*m.*)
to build construire
to burn brûler
to burst éclater
bus car (*m.*)
business affaire (*f.*)
but mais
to buy acheter
by heart par cœur

C
cake gâteau (*m.*)
calculator calculette (*f.*)
to cancel annuler
candle bougie (*f.*)

car voiture (*f.*)
to carry porter
castle château (*m.*)
casual décontracté
cat chat (*m.*)
celebration fête (*f.*)
chair chaise (*f.*)
to chat bavarder
cheap bon marché
cheese fromage (*m.*)
cherry cerise (*f.*)
Chinese chinois
choice choix (*m.*)
to choose choisir
clay argile (*f.*)
to clean nettoyer
to climb monter
close (near) près de
to close fermer
closet placard (*m.*)
coast côte (*f.*)
cold froid
collar col (*m.*)
comfortable confortable
to complain se plaindre
to complete achever
computer ordinateur (*m.*)
to congratulate féliciter
to contemplate envisager
to convince convaincre
to cost coûter
to count compter
country pays (*m.*)
couple couple (*m.*)
course cours (*m.*)
to cross traverser
crowded bondé
cup tasse (*f.*)
cushion coussin (*m.*)
to cut couper

D

daily quotidien
to dance danser
to dare oser
dark sombre
daughter fille (*f.*)
dawn aube (*f.*)
day jour (*m.*)
day: the day after tomorrow après-demain
day: the day before yesterday avant-hier
death mort (*f.*)
December décembre
delighted enchanté, ravi
delightful ravissant
to demonstrate manifester
deposit caution (*f.*)
to describe décrire
dessert dessert (*m.*)
to die mourir
digital numérique
to disappoint décevoir
disappointed déçu
to disturb déranger
to dive plonger
to do faire
to do without se passer de
dog chien (*m.*)
door porte (*f.*)
dozen douzaine (*f.*)
to dream rêver
dress robe (*f.*)
to drink boire
to drive conduire
dubbed doublé
duck canard (*m.*)
to dye teindre

E

early tôt
to eat manger

efficient efficace
egg œuf (*m.*)
to elect élire
elevator ascenseur (*m.*)
end fin (*f.*)
English anglais
enough assez
to erase effacer
even même
to exaggerate exagérer
exam examen (*m.*)
exhibition exposition (*f.*)
to expect s'attendre à
expensive cher
to explore explorer
to express exprimer

F

fabric tissu (*m.*)
face visage (*m.*)
to face affronter
factory usine (*f.*)
to fail rater
failure échec (*m.*)
to faint s'évanouir
faith foi (*f.*)
to fall tomber
famous célèbre
far loin
fast rapide
father père (*m.*)
fear peur (*f.*)
to fear craindre
February février
to feel sentir
to feel like avoir envie de
file fichier (*m.*)
to fill remplir
to find trouver
fire feu (*m.*)

first name prénom (*m.*)
fish poisson (*m.*)
flag drapeau (*m.*)
floor étage (*m.*)
flower fleur (*f.*)
to follow suivre
to forbid interdire
to forget oublier
formerly autrefois
fortunately heureusement
free libre
freedom liberté (*f.*)
fresh frais
friend ami(e) (*m., f.*)
future avenir (*m.*)

G
game jeu (*m.*)
garbage can poubelle (*f.*)
garden jardin (*m.*)
gas essence (*f.*)
to get bored s'ennuyer
to get rid of se débarrasser de
to get sick tomber malade
to get used to se faire à
gift cadeau (*m.*)
gifted doué
to give donner
glass verre (*m.*)
to go aller
to go around the world faire le tour du
  monde
good bon, bonne
government gouvernement (*m.*)
grandfather grand-père (*m.*)
grandmother grand-mère (*f.*)
ground floor rez-de-chausée (*m.*)
to grow old vieillir
to grow up grandir
guilty coupable

H
hair cheveux (*m. pl.*)
hair salon salon de coiffure (*m.*)
hairstyle coiffure (*f.*)
half moitié (*f.*)
hand main (*f.*)
handle manche (*m.*)
to hang accrocher
hat chapeau (*m.*)
to hate détester
to have lunch déjeuner
hazelnut noisette (*f.*)
head tête (*f.*)
to heal guérir
to hear entendre
heart cœur (*m.*)
heat chaleur (*f.*)
heating chauffage (*m.*)
hill colline (*f.*)
to hold tenir
to hope espérer
horse cheval (*m.*)
hot chaud
hour heure (*f.*)
house maison (*f.*)
hunger faim (*f.*)
to be hungry avoir faim
to hurry to se dépêcher de
husband mari (*m.*)

I
to improve améliorer
in dans
in front of devant
in love amoureux(euse)
in spite of malgré
in the back of au fond de
to inform prévenir
information renseignement (*m.*)
to injure blesser

inside dedans
to insist on tenir à
to intend avoir l'intention de
intern stagiaire (*m., f.*)
internship stage (*m.*)
island île (*f.*)

J

jacket veste (*f.*)
jam confiture (*f.*)
January janvier
jewel bijou (*m.*)
to join joindre
to joke blaguer, plaisanter
July juillet
to jump sauter
June juin

K

to keep garder
key clé (*f.*)
king roi (*m.*)
to kiss embrasser
kitchen cuisine (*f.*)
knife couteau (*m.*)
to knit tricoter
to know connaître
to know savoir
knowledge connaissance (*f.*)

L

label étiquette (*f.*)
lace dentelle (*f.*)
ladder échelle (*f.*)
lake lac (*m.*)
landscape paysage (*m.*)
language langue (*f.*)
late tard
law loi (*f.*)
lawn pelouse (*f.*)

lawyer avocat (*m.*), avocate (*f.*)
laziness paresse (*f.*)
to lead mener
to leaf through feuilleter
to learn, to show how apprendre
lease bail (*m.*)
leather cuir (*m.*)
to leave laisser
left gauche (*adj., n., f.*)
to lend prêter
letter lettre (*f.*)
to lie mentir
life vie (*f.*)
to lift soulever
light lumière (*f.*)
light léger, légère
to like aimer
linen lin (*m.*)
to listen écouter
little peu
to live habiter
to live vivre
liver foie (*m.*)
to look at regarder
to look for chercher
to lose perdre
to lose weight maigrir
to love aimer
luck chance (*f.*)

M

madly follement
magic magie (*f.*)
man homme (*m.*)
to manage gérer
manor manoir (*m.*)
to manufacture fabriquer
marble marbre (*m.*)
March mars
masterpiece chef-d'œuvre (*m.*)

May mai
meal repas (*m.*)
meat viande (*f.*)
meeting réunion (*f.*)
merger fusion (*f.*)
milk lait (*m.*)
to miss manquer
mistake erreur (*f.*)
to mix mélanger
money argent (*m.*)
month mois (*m.*)
mood humeur (*f.*)
morning matin (*m.*)
mother mère (*f.*)
mountain montagne (*f.*)
to move déménager
music musique (*f.*)

N

near près de
to need avoir besoin de
neighbor voisin (*m.*), voisine (*f.*)
neighborhood quartier (*m.*)
nest nid (*m.*)
new nouveau
news (piece of) nouvelle (*f.*)
newspaper journal (*m.*)
nice sympathique, gentil(le)
nickname surnom (*m.*)
night nuit (*f.*)
noise bruit (*m.*)
nothing rien
novel roman (*m.*)
novelist romancier (*m.*), romancière (*f.*)
November novembre
now maintenant
number nombre (*m.*)

O

object objet (*m.*)
obvious évident

obviously évidemment
October octobre
of course bien sûr
to offer offrir
office bureau (*m.*)
often souvent
oil huile (*f.*)
on top dessus
to open ouvrir
ordinarily d'ordinaire
outside dehors
to own posséder

P

pain douleur (*f.*)
to paint peindre
painting tableau (*m.*)
to park garer
password mot de passe (*m.*)
path chemin (*m.*)
to pay attention to faire attention à
to peel éplucher
pen stylo (*m.*)
people gens (*m. pl.*)
pepper poivre (*m.*)
perfume parfum (*m.*)
permit permis (*m.*)
to pick cueillir
piece morceau (*m.*)
plane avion (*m.*)
plate assiette (*f.*)
play pièce (*f.*)
to play jouer
player joueur (*m.*), joueuse (*f.*)
pleasant plaisant, agréable
to please plaire
to plug in brancher
position poste (*m.*)
post office poste (*f.*)
postcard carte postale (*f.*)
poster affiche (*f.*)

pothole nid de poule (*m.*)
to predict prédire
present actuel(le)
presently actuellement
to pretend to faire semblant de, feindre de
product produit (*m.*)
profit bénéfice (*m.*)
project projet (*m.*)
pumpkin citrouille (*f.*)
to put mettre
to put away ranger
to put on weight grossir
to put out (light) éteindre

R
rain pluie (*f.*)
to rain pleuvoir
to read lire
to realize se rendre compte
to recommend recommander
red rouge
to register s'inscrire
rehearsal répétition (*f.*)
to reimburse rembourser
to remember se souvenir de
to remind rappeler
to remove enlever
to renew renouveler
rent loyer (*m.*)
to rent louer
to repeat répéter
report rapport (*m.*)
to resign démissionner
to resign oneself to se résigner à
to resolve résoudre
to rest se reposer
to reveal révéler
right droite
right: to be right avoir raison
right away tout de suite
ring bague (*f.*)

to ring sonner
roof toit (*m.*)
room chambre (*f.*), pièce (*f.*)
rotten pourri
row rang (*m.*)
to run courir

S
sad triste
sail voile (*f.*)
sailboat voilier (*m.*)
salt sel (*m.*)
same même
satisfied content
scarf foulard (*m.*)
school école (*f.*)
screen écran (*m.*)
sea mer (*f.*)
to seduce séduire
to see voir
to sell vendre
to send envoyer
September septembre
serious sérieux
serve (to) servir
sewing machine machine à coudre (*f.*)
shame honte (*f.*)
to share partager
shelter abri (*m.*)
shoe chaussure (*f.*)
short court
to show montrer
shower douche (*f.*)
shutter volet (*m.*)
sick malade
silk soie (*f.*)
to sing chanter
sister sœur (*f.*)
sister-in-law belle-sœur (*f.*)
to sit s'asseoir
skin peau (*f.*)

sleep sommeil (*m.*)
to sleep dormir
sleeve manche (*f.*)
slowly doucement
small petit
snow neige (*f.*)
to snow neiger
so tellement, si
software logiciel (*m.*)
to solve résoudre
something quelque chose
sometimes parfois, quelquefois
son fils (*m.*)
song chanson (*f.*)
soon bientôt
to speak parler
speech parole (*f.*)
to spell épeler
to spend dépenser
spice épice (*f.*)
spy espion (*m.*)
square carré
stage fright trac (*m.*)
stamp timbre (*m.*)
star vedette (*f.*), étoile (*f.*)
state état (*m.*)
to stop arrêter, cesser de
straw paille (*f.*)
strawberry fraise (*f.*)
to stroll flâner
subtitled sous-titré
suburb banlieue (*f.*)
to succeed in/at réussir à
to suffer souffrir
sugar sucre (*m.*)
suitcase valise (*f.*)
summer été (*m.*)
sun soleil (*m.*)
sunny ensoleillé
sunset coucher de soleil (*m.*)
sure sûr

to swim nager
swimming pool piscine (*f.*)

T

to take prendre
to take advantage of profiter de
to take along emmener
to take care s'occuper de
to take place avoir lieu
to taste goûter
tea thé (*m.*)
to teach enseigner
to tell raconter
to thank remercier
thank you merci
thatch chaume (*f.*)
to think penser, réfléchir
thirst soif (*f.*)
to throw lancer, jeter
ticket billet (*m.*), ticket (*m.*)
tie cravate (*f.*)
to tie ficeler
time fois (*f.*)
today aujourd'hui
tomorrow demain
tongue langue (*f.*)
tooth dent (*f.*)
tower tour (*f.*)
traffic circulation (*f.*)
to translate traduire
to travel voyager
tray plateau (*m.*)
tree arbre (*m.*)
truth vérité (*f.*)
to turn on allumer
turtle tortue (*f.*)

U

umbrella parapluie (*m.*)
uncle oncle (*m.*)
under dessous, sous

to understand comprendre
unfortunately malheureusement
unknown inconnu
to use se servir de
usually d'habitude

V

vacation vacances (*f. pl.*)
vase vase (*m.*)
veil voile (*m.*)
very très
victory victoire (*f.*)
voice voix (*f.*)
voice mail boîte vocale (*f.*)

W

to wake up (se) réveiller
to walk marcher, se balader, se promener
wall mur (*m.*)
wallet portefeuille (*m.*)
war guerre (*f.*)
to warn prévenir
to wash laver
washing machine machine à laver (*f.*)
to waste gaspiller
watch montre (*f.*)
to watch regarder
water eau (*f.*)
wave vague (*f.*)
to wear porter
week semaine (*f.*)

weekly hebdomadaire
when quand
where où
to whip fouetter
white blanc, blanche
why pourquoi
willingly volontiers
windmill moulin à vent (*m.*)
window fenêtre (*f.*)
windowpane vitre (*f.*)
wine vin (*m.*)
wise sage
to wish désirer
with avec
to withdraw retirer
without sans
wood bois (*m.*)
word mot (*m.*)
work travail (*m.*)
to work travailler
world monde (*m.*)
worried inquiet
to worry s'inquiéter
to wrap emballer
to write écrire
wrong: to be wrong avoir tort

Y

yesterday hier
young jeune

FRENCH-ENGLISH GLOSSARY

A

à côté de next to, beside
abri *(m.)* shelter
accrocher to hang (up)
acheter to buy
achever to finish, to complete
actuel(le) present
actuellement currently
addition *(f.)* bill
affaire *(f.)* business
affiche *(f.)* poster
affronter to face
ailleurs elsewhere
aimer to like, to love
aller to go
allumer to turn on
améliorer to improve
amer bitter
amertume *(f.)* bitterness
ami *(m.)* friend
amie *(f.)* friend
amoureux(-euse) in love
anglais English
anniversaire *(m.)* birthday

annoncer to announce
annuler to cancel
août August
appartenir to belong
apporter to bring
apprendre to learn, to show how
après-demain the day after tomorrow
arbre *(m.)* tree
argent *(m.)* money
argile *(f.)* clay
arrêter to stop
ascenseur *(m.)* **elevator**
s'asseoir to sit
assez enough
assiette *(f.)* plate
assister à to atttend
s'attendre à to expect
au fond in the back
au hasard at random
aube *(f.)* dawn
aujourd'hui *(f.)* today
auprès de next to, close to
aussi also
autrefois formerly

avant before
avant-hier the day before yesterday
avec with
avenir *(m.)* future
avion *(m.)* plane
avocat(e) *(m., f.)* lawyer
avoir besoin de to need
avoir envie de to feel like, want
avoir faim to be hungry
avoir l'intention de to intend to
avoir lieu to take place
avoir raison to be right
avoir tort to be wrong
avouer to admit
avril April

B

bague *(f.)* ring
bail *(m.)* lease
se balader to go for a walk
balcon *(m.)* balcony
balle *(f.)* ball
banlieue *(f.)* suburb
bateau *(m.)* boat
bavarder to chat
beau-frère *(m.)* brother-in-law
belle-sœur *(f.)* sister-in-law
bénéfice *(m.)* profit
bien sûr of course
bientôt soon
bijou *(m.)* jewel
billet *(m.)* ticket
blaguer to joke
blanc(he) white
blesser to injure, to hurt
bleu blue
boire to drink
bois *(m.)* wood
boîte *(f.)* box
boîte vocale *(f.)* voice mail

bon(ne) good
bon marché cheap
bondé crowded
bougie *(f.)* candle
boulangerie *(f.)* bakery
bouteille *(f.)* bottle
bracelet *(m.)* bracelet
brancher to plug in
bras *(m.)* arm
brosser to brush
bruit *(m.)* noise
brûler to burn
bureau *(m.)* office; desk

C

cadeau *(m.)* gift
calculette *(f.)* calculator
canard *(m.)* duck
car *(m.)* bus, coach
carré square
carte postale *(f.)* postcard
casser to break
caution *(f.)* deposit
célèbre famous
cerise *(f.)* cherry
cesser de to stop
chaise *(f.)* chair
chaleur *(f.)* heat
chambre *(f.)* bedroom
chance *(f.)* luck
chanter to sing
chapeau *(m.)* hat
chat *(m.)* cat
château *(m.)* castle
chaud hot
chauffage *(m.)* heating (system)
chaume *(f.)* thatch
chaussure *(f.)* shoe
chef-d'œuvre *(m.)* masterpiece
chemin *(m.)* path

cher, chère expensive
chercher to search, to look for
cheval *(m.)* horse
cheveux *(m. pl.)* hair
cheville *(f.)* ankle
chien *(m.)* dog
chinois Chinese
choisir to choose
choix *(m.)* choice
circulation *(f.)* traffic
citrouille *(f.)* pumpkin
clé *(f.)* key
climatisé air-conditioned
cœur *(m.)* heart
coiffure *(f.)* hairstyle
col *(m.)* collar
colline *(f.)* hill
comprendre to understand
compter to intend; to plan to; to
    count on
conduire to drive
confiture *(f.)* jam
confortable comfortable
connaissance *(f.)* knowledge
connaître to know
conseiller to advise
construire to build
content happy, satisfied
convaincre to convince
corps *(m.)* body
côte *(f.)* coast; rib
coucher de soleil *(m.)* sunset
coupable guilty
couper to cut
couple *(m.)* couple
courir to run
cours *(m.)* course
court short
coussin *(m.)* cushion
couteau *(m.)* knife

coûter to cost
craindre to fear
cravate *(f.)* tie
croire to believe
cueillir to pick, to gather
cuir *(m.)* leather
cuisine *(f.)* cooking; kitchen

D
dans in
danser to dance
se débarrasser de to get rid of
décembre December
décevoir to disappoint
décontracté casual
décrire to describe
déçu disappointed
dedans inside
dehors outside
déjeuner to have lunch
demain tomorrow
déménager to move
démissionner to resign
dent *(f.)* tooth
dentelle *(f.)* lace
se dépêcher de to hurry to
dépenser to spend
déranger to disturb
derrière behind
désirer to desire, to wish
dessert *(m.)* dessert
dessous under
dessus on top
détester to hate
devant in front of
d'habitude usually
disponible available
dizaine *(f.)* about ten
donner to give
d'ordinaire ordinarily

dormir to sleep
doublé dubbed
doucement slowly
douche *(f.)* shower
doué gifted
douleur *(f.)* pain
drapeau *(m.)* flag
droite right

E

eau *(f.)* water
échec *(m.)* failure
échelle *(f.)* ladder
éclater to burst, to explode
école *(f.)* school
écouter to listen
écran *(m.)* screen
écrire to write
effacer to erase
efficace efficient
élire to elect
emballer to wrap
embrasser to kiss, hug
emmener to take along
emprunter to borrow
enchanté delighted
encore again
enlever to remove
s'ennuyer to get bored
enseigner to teach
ensoleillé sunny
entendre to hear
envisager to contemplate
envoyer to send
épeler to spell
épice *(f.)* spice
éplucher to peel
erreur *(f.)* mistake
espérer to hope
espion(ne) *(m., f.)* spy
essence *(f.)* essence; gas

étage *(m.)* floor
état *(m.)* state
été *(m.)* summer
éteindre to put out, to extinguish
étiquette *(f.)* label
étonner to surprise, to amaze
être au courant to be informed
s'évanouir to faint
évidemment obviously
évident obvious
exagérer to exaggerate
examen *(m.)* exam
s'excuser to apologize
explorer to explore
exposition *(f.)* exhibition
exprimer to express

F

fabriquer to make; to manufacture
faim *(f.)* hunger
faire to do; to make
se faire à to get used to
faire attention à to pay attention to
faire le tour du monde to go around the
  world
faire semblant de to pretend to
feindre to feign, to pretend
féliciter to congratulate
fenêtre *(f.)* window
fermer to close
fête *(f.)* party, celebration
feu *(m.)* fire
feuilleter to leaf through
février February
ficeler to tie
fichier *(m.)* file
fille *(f.)* daughter
fils *(m.)* son
fin *(f.)* end
flacon *(m.)* bottle
flâner to stroll

fleur *(f.)* flower
foi *(f.)* faith
foie *(m.)* liver
fois *(f.)* time
follement madly
fouetter to whip
foulard *(m.)* scarf
frais, fraîche fresh
fraise *(f.)* strawberry
frère *(m.)* brother
froid cold
fromage *(m.)* cheese
fusion *(f.)* merger

G
gaffe *(f.)* blunder
garder to keep
garer to park
gaspiller to waste
gâteau *(m.)* cake
gauche *(adj.)* left
gens *(m. pl.)* people
gérer to manage
goûter to taste
gouvernement *(m.)* government
grandir to grow up
grand-mère *(f.)* grandmother
grand-père *(m.)* grandfather
grange *(f.)* barn
grossir to put on weight
guérir to heal
guerre *(f.)* war

H
habiter to live
haricot *(m.)* bean
hebdomadaire weekly
heure *(f.)* hour
heureusement fortunately
hier yesterday
homme *(m.)* man

honte *(f.)* shame
huile *(f.)* oil
humeur *(f.)* mood

I
île *(f.)* island
inconnu unknown
inquiet, inquiète worried
s'inquiéter de to worry about
s'inscrire to register
interdire to forbid

J
janvier January
jardin *(m.)* garden
jeter to throw
jeu *(m.)* game
jeune young
joindre to join
jouer to play
joueur, joueuse *(m., f.)* player
jour *(m.)* day
journal *(m.)* newspaper
juillet July
juin June

L
lac *(m.)* lake
laisser to leave
lait *(m.)* milk
lancer to throw
langue *(f.)* language; tongue
laver to wash
le long de along
léger, légère light
lettre *(f.)* letter
liberté *(f.)* freedom
librairie *(f.)* bookstore
libre free
lin *(m.)* linen
lire to read

lit *(m.)* bed
livre *(m.)* book
logiciel *(m.)* software
loi *(f.)* law
loin far
long: le long de along
louer to rent
loyer *(m.)* rent
lumière *(f.)* light

M

machine à coudre *(f.)* sewing machine
magie *(f.)* magic
magique magic
mai May
maigrir to lose weight
main *(f.)* hand
maintenant now
mais but
maison *(f.)* house
malade sick
malgré in spite of
malheureusement unfortunately
manche *(m.)* handle
manche *(f.)* sleeve
manger to eat
manifester to demonstrate
manoir *(m.)* manor
manquer to miss
marbre *(m.)* marble
marcher to walk
mari *(m.)* husband
mars March
matin *(m.)* morning
mélanger to mix
même same, even
mener to lead
mentir to lie
mer *(f.)* sea
merci thank you
mère *(f.)* mother

mettre to put; to put on
mois *(m.)* month
moitié *(f.)* half
monde *(m.)* world
montagne *(f.)* mountain
monter to go up, to climb
montre *(f.)* watch
montrer to show
morceau *(m.)* piece
mort *(f.)* death
mot de passe *(m.)* password
mourir to die
mur *(m.)* wall
musique *(f.)* music

N

nager to swim
naître to be born
né born
neige *(f.)* snow
neiger to snow
nettoyer to clean
nid *(m.)* nest
nid *(m.)* **de poule** pothole
n'importe où anywhere
n'importe quoi anything
noir black
noisette *(f.)* hazelnut
nombre *(m.)* number
nouveau, nouvelle new
nouvelle *(f.)* piece of news
novembre November
nuit *(f.)* night
numérique digital

O

objet *(m.)* object
s'occuper de to take care of
octobre October
œuf *(m.)* egg
offrir to offer

oiseau *(m.)* bird
oncle *(m.)* uncle
ordinateur *(m.)* computer
oser to dare
où where
oublier to forget
ouvrir to open

P

paille *(f.)* straw
par cœur by heart
paraître to appear
parapluie *(m.)* umbrella
paresse *(f.)* laziness
parfois sometimes
parfum *(m.)* perfume
pari *(m.)* bet
parler to speak
parmi among
parole *(f.)* word; speech
partager to share
parti *(m.)* political party
se passer de to do without
patron(ne) *(m., f.)* boss
pays *(m.)* country
paysage *(m.)* landscape
peau *(f.)* skin
peindre to paint
pelouse *(f.)* lawn
penser to think
perdre to lose
père *(m.)* father
permis *(m.)* permit
petit small
petit déjeuner *(m.)* breakfast
peu little; not much
peur *(f.)* fear
pièce *(f.)* room; play
piscine *(f.)* swimming pool
placard *(m.)* closet
plage *(f.)* beach

se plaindre de to complain about
plaire to please; to enjoy
plaisanter to joke
plat *(m.)* dish
plateau *(m.)* tray
pleuvoir to rain
plonger to dive
pluie *(f.)* rain
poisson *(m.)* fish
poivre *(m.)* pepper
porte *(f.)* door
portefeuille *(m.)* wallet
porter to carry; to wear
posséder to own
poste *(f.)* post office
poste *(m.)* position
poubelle *(f.)* garbage can
pourquoi why
pourri rotten
pouvoir can, to be able to
prédire to predict
prendre to take
prénom *(m.)* first name
près de near, close
prêter to lend
prévenir to warn; to inform
produit *(m.)* product
profiter de to take advantage of
projet *(m.)* project

Q

quand when
quartier *(m.)* neighborhood
quelque chose something
quelquefois sometimes
quotidien(ne) daily

R

raconter to tell
rang *(m.)* row
ranger to put away

rapide fast
rappeler to remind
rapport *(m.)* report
rater to fail
ravi delighted
ravissant delightful
recommander to recommend
réfléchir to think, to reflect
regarder to watch, to look (at)
rembourser to reimburse
remercier to thank
remplir to fill
se rendre compte de to realize that
renouveler to renew
renseignement *(m.)* information
repas *(m.)* meal
répéter to repeat
répétition *(f.)* rehearsal
répondre to answer
se reposer to rest
se résigner à to resign oneself to
résoudre to resolve, solve
retirer to withdraw
réunion *(f.)* meeting
réussir à to succeed at/in
se réveiller to wake up
révéler to reveal
rêver to dream
rez-de-chaussée *(m.)* ground floor
rien nothing
robe *(f.)* dress
roi *(m.)* king
roman *(m.)* novel
romancier(-ière) *(m., f.)* novelist
rouge red

S

sac *(m.)* bag
sage wise
salon de coiffure *(m.)* hair salon
sans without

sauter to jump
savoir to know
seau *(m.)* bucket
séduire to seduce
sel *(m.)* salt
selon according to
semaine *(f.)* week
sentir to feel, to think
septembre September
sérieux(-ieuse) serious
servir to serve
se servir de to use
seul alone
sœur *(f.)* sister
soie *(f.)* silk
soif *(f.)* thirst
soleil *(m.)* sun
sombre dark
sommeil *(m.)* sleep
songer à to think of/about
sonner to ring
souffrir to suffer
soulever to lift
sous under
sous-titré subtitled
se souvenir de to remember
souvent often
stage *(m.)* internship
stagiaire *(m., f.)* intern
stylo *(m.)* pen
sucre *(m.)* sugar
suivre to follow
sûr sure
surnom *(m.)* nickname
sympathique pleasant, nice

T

tableau *(m.)* painting; blackboard
tante *(f.)* aunt
tard late
tasse *(f.)* cup

teindre to dye
tellement so much
temps *(m.)* weather; time
tenir to hold
tenir à to insist on, to be eager
  to/for
tête *(f.)* head
thé *(m.)* tea
timbre *(m.)* stamp
tissu *(m.)* fabric
toit *(m.)* roof
tomber to fall
tomber en panne to break down (car)
tomber malade to get sick
tortue *(f.)* turtle
tôt early
toujours always; still
tour *(f.)* tower
tout de suite right away
trac *(m.)* stage fright
traduire to translate
travail *(m.)* work
travailler to work
traverser to cross
très very
tricoter to knit
triste sad
trouver to find

U
usine *(f.)* factory

V
vacances *(f. pl.)* holidays, vacation
vague *(f.)* wave
valise *(f.)* suitcase
vase *(f.)* slime
vase *(m.)* vase
vedette *(f.)* star
vélo *(m.)* bicycle
vendre to sell
vérité *(f.)* truth
verre *(m.)* glass
veste *(f.)* jacket
viande *(f.)* meat
victoire *(f.)* victory
vie *(f.)* life
vieillir to grow old
vin *(m.)* wine
visage *(m.)* face
viser à to aim at
vitre *(f.)* windowpane
vivre to live
voile *(m.)* veil
voile *(f.)* sail
voilier *(m.)* sailboat
voir to see
voisin(e) *(m., f.)* neighbor
voiture *(f.)* car
voix *(f.)* voice
volet *(m.)* shutter
volontiers willingly
voyager to travel

ANSWER KEY

CHAPTER 1

Written Practice
1. The actor is patient.   2. The dinner is delicious.   3. Valérie and Thomas are waiting for the news.   4. The boss is planning a reorganization of the company.   5. Sandrine works at the bookstore.

Oral Practice
1. (*oh-ray-lee-ya*) 4 syllables   2. (*ah-loo-eht*) 3 syllables   3. (*see-yehst*) 2 syllables   4. (*kwee-zeen*) 2 syllables   5. (*brwee*) 1 syllable   6. (*ah-may-ree-ka(n)*) 4 syllables   7. (*ree-tu-ehl*) 3 syllables   8. (*bwar*) 1 syllable

QUIZ
1. b   2. b   3. c   4. a   5. c   6. b   7. c   8. a   9. c   10. a

CHAPTER 2

Written Practice 1
1. le soleil   2. la télévision   3. le gâteau   4. le journal   5. la nature

Written Practice 2
1. la Bretagne   2. l'Allemagne   3. la Virginie   4. la Pologne   5. le Venezuela

Written Practice 3
1. les plats   2. les châteaux   3. les clés   4. les jardins   5. les maisons

Written Practice 4
1. un avion   2. une avocate   3. des maisons   4. une clé   5. des châteaux

Written Practice 5
1. trente-huit   2. onze   3. quarante-deux   4. seize   5. neuf

Written Practice 6
1. Non, c'est la huitième fois.   2. Non, c'est la quatrième fois.   3. Non, c'est la dixième fois.   4. Non, c'est la troisième fois.   5. Non, c'est la première fois.

Written Practice 7
1. jeudi   2. mardi   3. dimanche   4. vendredi   5. mercredi

QUIZ
1. le journal / la culture / la tortue / la nationalité / le compliment   2. une voiture / un sac / une culture / des hôtels / des journaux   3. la Finlande / la Chine / la Caroline du Sud / le Togo / la Colombie   4. les journaux / les maisons / les frères / les voix / les chapeaux   5. la vendeuse / la directrice / la mécanicienne / l'actrice / la Brésilienne   6. L'anniversaire de Marc est dimanche.   7. Appelez Marc lundi.   8. La sœur de Léa est architecte.
9. Le bureau de Léa est au dixième étage.   10. L'anniversaire de Léa est mardi.

CHAPTER 3

Written Practice 1
1. d   2. c   3. e   4. a   5. b

Written Practice 2
1. nous parlons   2. je garde   3. elle porte   4. vous chantez   5. on donne

Written Practice 3
1. Elle achète   2. Nous commençons   3. Tu appelles   4. Ils révèlent
5. Nous voyageons

Written Practice 4
1. d   2. c   3. e   4. b   5. a

Written Practice 5
1. Aimez-vous les voyages?   2. Préfère-t-elle le riz?   3. Commences-tu en décembre?   4. Cherchent-ils un appartement?   5. Regardons-nous le match de base-ball dans le salon?

Written Practice 6
1. Est-ce que j'appelle Samuel?   2. Est-ce que nous remplaçons Jacques et Laurent?   3. Est-ce que tu voyages en Irlande?   4. Est-ce que vous déménagez jeudi?   5. Est-ce qu'elle prononce le mot correctement?

Written Practice 7
1. Vous cherchez la Place de la Bastille?   2. Tu aimes le chocolat?   3. Elle habite à Rome?   4. Il cherche un nouvel emploi?   5. Vous mangez des escargots?

Written Practice 8
1. Qui parle français ici?   2. Où voyagez-vous en janvier?   3. Pourquoi déménage-t-elle?   4. Où habites-tu?   5. Que cherchez-vous?

Written Practice 9
1. Non, je n'aime pas le nouveau film d'Éric Rohmer.   2. Non, elle n'habite pas à La Rochelle.   3. Non, je ne cherche pas Jacques.   4. Non, je n'apporte rien.
5. Non, je ne voyage jamais par le train.   6. Non, je ne chante pas en allemand.
7. Non, je ne travaille jamais le samedi.   8. Non, je n'étudie pas le chinois.
9. Non, je ne joue pas au tennis.   10. Non, je n'écoute pas l'émission *2000 ans d'histoire*.

QUIZ
1. Est-ce que tu joues au tennis?   2. Est-ce que tu parles portugais?   3. nous commençons   4. nous espérons   5. On voyage en Inde en février?   6. On écoute le concert dans le parc?   7. Oui, je regarde le film de Godard ce soir. / Non, je ne regarde pas le film de Godard ce soir.   8. Oui, j'aime le théâtre moderne. / Non, je n'aime pas le théâtre moderne.   9. Elle n'habite pas à Annecy.   10. Je ne parle pas espagnol.

CHAPTER 4

Written Practice 1
1. suis   2. est   3. êtes   4. n'es pas   5. sont

Written Practice 2
1. c   2. a   3. e   4. b   5. d

Written Practice 3
1. Avez-vous soif?   2. A-t-elle chaud?   3. Ont-ils froid?   4. As-tu peur?
5. A-t-il raison?

Written Practice 4
1. Vous allez à la librairie ce matin.   2. Adèle va à Paris en août.   3. Je vais à Dublin avec Flore.   4. Nous allons au cinéma ce soir.   5. Tu vas à la plage dimanche.

Written Practice 5
1. Anne a peu de chance.   2. Mélanie a trop de documents.   3. Vincent a beaucoup de travail.   4. Valérie a assez de papier.   5. Bruno a tant de problèmes.

Written Practice 6
1. Il y a une bouteille d'eau sur la table.   2. Il y a une tasse de café sur la table.
3. Il y a un litre de lait sur la table.   4. Il y a une demi-livre de champignons sur la table.   5. Il y a une boîte de sardines sur la table.

Written Practice 7

1. b / d   2. a   3. e   4. c   5. b / d

Written Practice 8

1. b / d   2. e   3. b / d   4. a / c   5. a / c

QUIZ

1. Oui, je suis canadien.   2. Oui, j'ai des animaux domestiques.   3. Oui, elle a un appartement dans le treizième arrondissement.   4. Non, je n'aime pas la musique folk.   5. Non, je n'ai pas d'ordinateur.   6. Je vais bien.   7. La cousine de Germain va bien.   8. **62:** soixante-deux **77:** soixante-dix-sept **100:** cent **87:** quatre-vingt-sept **315:** trois cent quinze **10 000:** dix mille   9. Il y a beaucoup de livres sur la table.   10. Est-ce que tu es anglais?

CHAPTER 5

Written Practice 1

1. vous choisissez   2. nous servons   3. elles partent   4. nous remplissons 5. vous sortez

Written Practice 2

1. c   2. e   3. a / d   4. b   5. a / d

Written Practice 3

1. Achète une demi-livre de beurre!   2. Allons au théâtre!   3. Prenez une salade verte!   4. Sois à l'heure!   5. Aie un peu de patience!

Written Practice 4

1. vieilles   2. gentil   3. fascinant   4. intéressant   5. noire

Written Practice 5

1. Justine est gentille.   2. Justine est intelligente.   3. Justine est généreuse. 4. Justine est belle.   5. Justine est créative.

Written Practice 6

1. Céleste est moins efficace que Marion.   2. Agnès est aussi amusante qu'Antoine.   3. Alexandre est moins sportif que Mélissa.   4. Laure est plus créative que José.   5. Emmanuel est aussi doué que son frère.

QUIZ

1. vous prenez   2. elles finissent   3. nous partons   4. Prenez une semaine de vacances!   5. Finis le rapport!   6. Elle est espagnole.   7. Elle est brésilienne.   8. Paolo est moins efficace que Karim.   9. Ce magasin est plus cher que cette boutique.   10. Ce vieil homme est aussi sympathique que ce jeune homme.

PART ONE TEST

1. la tortue   2. la grenouille   3. le chocolat   4. le courage   5. la naissance   6. une montre   7. une propriété   8. une division   9. un homme   10. des peintures   11. l'Indonésie   12. le Maroc   13. le Pérou   14. la Floride   15. le Liban   16. les bijoux   17. les écoles   18. les nez   19. les chevaux   20. les mois   21. Est-ce que tu commandes une salade?   22. Est-ce que tu achètes des tomates?   23. Est-ce que tu habites à Paris?   24. Est-ce que tu remplaces Juliette?   25. Est-ce que tu déménages à Toulouse?   26. On partage un dessert?   27. On achète des fleurs pour Sonia?   28. On apporte un gâteau à Jean?   29. On appelle Mathieu?   30. On déjeune sur la terrasse?   31. Oui, je suis content de mon nouveau travail.   32. Oui, ils ont un dictionnaire français-anglais.   33. Oui, j'ai des lunettes de soleil.   34. Oui, ce restaurant est cher.   35. Oui, ils ont peur des résultats.   36. Les Dubois vont bien.   37. Sylvain va bien.   38. Je vais bien.   39. Mon frère va bien.   40. Mes parents vont bien.   41. Elle est japonaise.   42. Elle est vietnamienne.   43. Elle est africaine.   44. Elle est capricieuse.   45. Elle est naïve.   46. Son ancien patron habite à Paris.   47. La qualité de ce tissu est meilleure.   48. Combien de personnes habitent dans la maison bleue?   49. Aimez-vous Paris?   50. Pourquoi étudie-t-elle l'anglais?

CHAPTER 6

Written Practice 1

1. onze heures et quart du matin   2. quatre heures moins vingt-cinq de l'après-midi   3. sept heures moins le quart du matin   4. quatre heures moins dix de l'après-midi   5. cinq heures et demie du matin

Written Practice 2

1. dix-neuf heures trente   2. quinze heures   3. vingt-trois heures quinze   4. dix-sept heures quarante-cinq   5. dix heures quinze

Written Practice 3

1. Aujourd'hui est le premier jour du printemps.   2. Il voyage rarement.   3. Elle est toujours à l'heure.   4. Ils partent très tôt.   5. Son anniversaire est la semaine prochaine.

Written Practice 4

1. Je vois des erreurs partout.   2. Ce soir, nous dînons dehors.   3. Ils habitent ici mais ils travaillent ailleurs.   4. Mettez votre chapeau dessus.   5. Il habite trop loin.

Written Practice 5

1. André apprend le chinois depuis quatre ans. 2. Céline parle au téléphone depuis une heure. 3. Tu regardes la télé depuis cet après-midi. 4. Ils vont à l'opéra depuis leur enfance. 5. Nous réfléchissons à la question depuis ce matin.

Written Practice 6

1. Il y a une demi-heure qu'elle travaille. 2. Il y a un mois qu'Alex a un nouvel ordinateur. 3. Il y a des semaines qu'elle cherche un emploi. 4. Il y a trois jours que nous sommes en vacances. 5. Il y a des années qu'Agnès étudie la musique.

Written Practice 7

1. Patrice va en Afrique en novembre. 2. Christian va à Rome en hiver. 3. Gérard va en Californie en mars. 4. Géraldine va aux États-Unis en avril. 5. Akiko va au Portugal en automne.

QUIZ

1. Je pars à cinq heures et demie (de l'après-midi). / La séance finit à une heure. / Ce magasin ouvre à neuf heures. / Je reviens à quatre heures et quart. 2. **5:15** P.M.: dix-sept heures quinze 1:10 A.M.: une heure dix 4:55 P.M.: seize heures cinquante-cinq 7:23 A.M.: sept heures vingt-trois 3. Non, je prends le train à vingt heures. / Non, je commence le projet ce matin. / Non, je pars en vacances après-demain. / Non, il déménage dans une semaine. / Non, je prends ce médicament un jour sur deux. 4. Je suis dans ce club depuis deux ans. / Ils sont mariés depuis cinq ans. 5. Frank habite à La Nouvelle-Orléans, aux États-Unis. / Noémie habite à Venise, en Italie. / Ali habite à Ouagadougou, au Burkina Faso. 6. Le palais de Buckingham est en Angleterre. / Le château de Versailles est en France. / La tour de Pise est en Italie. / Le temple d'Angkor Vat est au Cambodge. / Le parc national de Yosemite est aux États-Unis. 7. Quelle heure est-il? 8. Allez-vous en vacances en Tunisie? 9. Depuis quand habitez-vous ici? 10. La réunion commence à midi.

CHAPTER 7

Written Practice 1

1. c 2. e 3. a 4. d 5. b

Written Practice 2

1. pouvons 2. veux 3. veut 4. peux 5. ne peuvent pas

Written Practice 3

1. voyez 2. reçoit 3. pleut 4. aperçoivent 5. sais

Written Practice 4

1. Est-ce qu'il a de la patience? 2. Est-ce que tu manges du poulet? 3. Est-ce qu'ils passent des vacances en France? 4. Est-ce que vous prenez du café?
5. Est-ce que tu achètes de l'eau?

Written Practice 5

1. c 2. e 3. d 4. b 5. a

QUIZ

1. doit 2. veulent 3. devons 4. peut 5. veux 6. la cerise: d /
la tante: e / le musicien: a / le manteau: g / la maison: h / le cristal: i / le vendeur: c
/ le commencement: j / le tableau: b / l'exposition: f 7. Clarisse ne peut pas
travailler aujourd'hui. 8. Voulez-vous aller à Nice en novembre? 9. Toc toc
toc! Est-ce que nous pouvons entrer? 10. L'avion doit arriver à neuf heures (du
matin).

CHAPTER 8

Written Practice 1

1. sais 2. sait 3. savons 4. savent 5. sais

Written Practice 2

1. connaissez 2. connais 3. connaissons 4. connaît 5. connaissent

Written Practice 3

1. savez 2. connais 3. connaissent 4. savons 5. sais

Written Practice 4

1. b 2. d 3. e 4. a 5. c

Written Practice 5

1. d 2. c 3. b 4. e 5. a

Written Practice 6

1. dans 2. dans 3. en 4. en 5. dans

Written Practice 7

1. c 2. e 3. b 4. a 5. d

QUIZ

1. ils connaissent / je sais / nous savons / tu connais / elle connaît / elles savent /
vous savez / nous connaissons / il sait / vous connaissez 2. sais 3. connais
4. sais 5. sais 6. connaissez 7. Je ne sais pas pourquoi la banque est
fermée aujourd'hui. 8. Vous devez décongeler ces légumes. 9. Connaît-elle
Jérôme? 10. Fais-tu tes valises?

CHAPTER 9

Written Practice 1

1. Nous allons prendre des photos.   2. Tu vas inviter tes amis.   3. Ils vont danser toute la soirée.   4. Vous allez finir le roman.   5. Je vais acheter ce stylo.

Written Practice 2

1. Elle ne va pas choisir le menu.   2. Vous n'allez pas prendre le train de dix heures.   3. Je ne vais pas téléphoner à Laurent.   4. Ils ne vont pas accepter l'offre.   5. Tu ne vas pas arriver à l'heure.

Written Practice 3

1. Nous venons de prendre des vacances.   2. Elle vient de répondre à la lettre.
3. Ils viennent de changer de voiture.   4. Je viens de parler au directeur.
5. Il vient d'envoyer une lettre.

Written Practice 4

1. d   2. a   3. e   4. c   5. b

Written Practice 5

1. d   2. e   3. b   4. a   5. c

Written Practice 6

1. Tu fais écrire l'article.   2. Elle fait faire le ménage.   3. Il fait réparer la télévision.   4. Vous faites envoyer le paquet.   5. Elles font préparer le dîner.

QUIZ

1. Elles vont parler. / Il va danser. / Nous allons partir. / Vous allez regarder. / Elle va commencer.   2. Vous n'allez pas envoyer ce document. / Tu ne vas pas finir la nouvelle. / Je ne vais pas appeler Julie. / Nous n'allons pas déménager vendredi. / Elle ne va pas sortir ce soir.   3. Je viens de remplir le réservoir. / Elles viennent de passer des vacances en Finlande. / Elle vient de répondre à la lettre. / Nous venons de faire les courses. / Il vient de prendre une décision.   4. Il fait du yoga depuis six mois. / Elle fait les courses dans ce magasin depuis un an. / Ils font des randonnées depuis vingt ans. / Il fait beau dans la region depuis deux jours. / Il fait froid sur la Côte d'Azur depuis une semaine.   5. Tu fais envoyer des fleurs. / Elle fait arroser les plantes. / Nous faisons écrire la lettre. / Vous faites preparer les documents. / Je fais faire un gâteau au chocolat.   6. Allez-vous inviter Grégoire?   7. Elle fait laver sa voiture chaque semaine.   8. Il fait bouillir de l'eau.   9. Fait-elle la cuisine ce soir?   10. Il vient de déménager.

CHAPTER 10

Written Practice 1
1. Elles se réveillent à huit heures.   2. Nous nous reposons le dimanche.
3. Tu t'habilles pour la fête.   4. Il s'appelle Fabio.   5. Vous vous amusez à la soirée.

Written Practice 2
1. c   2. d   3. e   4. a   5. b

Written Practice 3
1. e   2. a   3. d   4. c   5. b

Written Practice 4
1. lui   2. elle   3. eux   4. elles   5. lui

Written Practice 5
1. C'est à moi.   2. C'est à elle.   3. C'est à nous.   4. C'est à toi.
5. C'est à eux.

QUIZ
1. tu te plains / vous vous dépêchez / ils s'écrivent / je me souviens / nous nous disputons   2. se coucher: e / s'habiller: d / s'aimer: b / s'amuser: c / se réveiller: a   3. Il s'assoit dans le fauteuil car il est fatigué. / Ils s'habillent si élégamment car ils vont à une soirée. / Je me lève si tôt car j'ai une réunion à huit heures. / Elle se lève tard le dimanche car elle aime faire la grasse matinée. / Je me repose cet après-midi car je chante à l'opéra ce soir.   4. Nous allons au cinéma avec eux. / Elle travaille avec lui depuis longtemps. / Ils montent cette affaire avec toi? / Je préfère travailler chez moi. / C'est lui qui va vous faire visiter l'usine.   5. —J'aime le café. —Moi aussi.   6. Elle s'habille pour le carnaval.   7. Il se brosse les dents.   8. À quelle heure est-ce que tu te lèves?   9. Selon lui, il y a encore beaucoup de problèmes.   10. Il n'est pas d'accord avec moi.

PART TWO TEST
1. Le cours de français se termine à onze heures moins dix (du soir).   2. Ce soir, je dîne/nous dînons à sept heures et demie.   3. Son train arrive à six heures moins le quart (de l'après-midi).   4. Ce restaurant ferme à minuit.
5. La surprise-party commence à dix heures (du soir).   6. Je ne vais jamais au cinéma.   7. En général, Édouard arrive tard.   8. Maud téléphone rarement à sa tante.   9. Je vais/Nous allons de temps en temps au jardin botanique.
10. Mon anniversaire, c'est aujourd'hui.   11. J'attends une réponse depuis dix jours.   12. J'étudie la calligraphie depuis trois mois.   13. Je cherche un bureau depuis un mois.   14. J'ai des animaux domestiques depuis mon enfance.
15. Elle travaille à Dijon depuis quatre ans.   16. Karim habite au Caire, en Égypte.   17. Anne habite à Dakar, au Sénégal.   18. Marie habite à Istanbul, en Turquie.   19. Marc habite à Hanoi, au Vietnam.   20. Lorraine habite à

Port-au-Prince, en Haïti.   21. d / Rabat est au Maroc.   22. c / Le Caire est en
Égypte.   23. e / Oulan-Bator est en Mongolie.   24. a / Abidjan est en Côte-
d'Ivoire.   25. b / Santiago est au Chili.   26. Russie   27. Tibet
28. Espagne   29. Égypte   30. Grèce   31. connaît   32. savez   33. sait
34. connais   35. sait   36. vont prendre   37. allons choisir   38. va
acheter   39. allez finir   40. vont rester   41. Moi   42. eux   43. toi
44. nous   45. eux   46. Je ne sais pas pourquoi la banque est fermée
aujourd'hui.   47. Il porte un costume bleu foncé.   48. Ils font la queue depuis
une heure.   49. À quelle heure est-ce que vous vous levez?   50. L'avion part
dans cinq minutes.

CHAPTER 11

Written Practice 1
1. Oui, je la regarde.   2. Oui, je le cherche.   3. Oui, je l'apprends.   4. Oui,
je le finis.   5. Oui, je la connais.

Written Practice 2
1. Non, je ne vais pas les faire.   2. Non, ils ne les ont pas réservés.   3. Non,
elle ne l'a pas trouvée.   4. Non, je ne vais pas la prendre.   5. Non, il ne l'a pas
vue.

Written Practice 3
1. Oui, je lui ai répondu.   2. Oui, il leur a écrit.   3. Oui, je t'ai envoyé le plan
de Paris.   4. Oui, ils me font des cadeaux.   5. Oui, elle leur raconte des
histoires.

Written Practice 4
1. Elle y a répondu.   2. Je m'y intéresse.   3. J'y crois.   4. Il y a goûté.
5. J'y fais attention.

Written Practice 5
1. Je ne m'en souviens pas.   2. Elle n'en a pas l'intention.   3. Je n'en ai pas
peur.   4. Il n s'en est pas occupé.   5. Je n'en ai pas envie.

Written Practice 6
1. Oui, je vous l'envoie.   2. Oui, je vous les laisse.   3. Oui, ils la lui
expliquent.   4. Oui, elle me la donne.   5. Oui, il les lui a écrits.

QUIZ
1. Oui, elle les préfère. / Oui, je le contacte. / Oui, je t'invite. / Oui, il l'a regardé. /
Oui, elles l'écoutent. / Oui, je l'ai engagé.   2. Je leur pose des questions. / Je
leur prête mes livres. / Elle lui a raconté son voyage. / Il leur donne de bons
conseils. / Je lui ai envoyé un guide Michelin.   3. Elle le lui a offert. / Ils ne les
lui ont pas envoyés. / Je les leur écris. / Vous les leur vendez. / Elle la leur a

racontée.   4. Oui, elle me les a rendus. / Oui, il m'en a parlé. / Oui, je vous l'ai/
nous vous l'avons faxé. / Oui, je vous le recommande. / Oui, je peux/nous pouvons
vous le décrire.   5. Elle s'y habitue. / Ils en profitent. / Elle y a réfléchi. / Je
m'en souviens. / Je m'y intéresse. / J'y ai goûté.   6. Donnez-lui ces lunettes!
7. Est-ce que je peux l'emprunter?   8. Elle s'y intéresse.   9. Est-ce que vous
allez l'acheter?   10. Ils s'y habituent.

CHAPTER 12

Written Practice 1
1. Il a habité à Rome.   2. Vous avez parlé au directeur.   3. Tu as participé à
la conférence.   4. Nous avons joué au tennis.   5. J'ai préparé un couscous.

Written Practice 2
1. Elle a choisi un restaurant.   2. Ils ont servi les invités.   3. Vous avez
répondu au message.   4. Elle a fini son travail.   5. Il a perdu ses clés.

Written Practice 3
1. Tu as pris une photo.   2. Elle a eu de la chance.   3. Vous avez mis un
pull. 4. Ils ont reçu un document.   5. Nous avons bu un thé glacé.

Written Practice 4
1. Elle est allée au théâtre.   2. Nous sommes partis à neuf heures.   3. Je suis
arrivé avant Ludovic.   4. Ils sont venus avec leurs enfants.   5. Il est monté au
sommet de la montagne.

Written Practice 5
1. Elle a passé des vacances formidables.   2. Tu as sorti les géraniums sur la
terrasse.   3. Nous sommes retournés en Turquie.   4. Vous avez monté les
valises au premier étage.   5. Ils sont passés devant le casino.

Written Practice 6
1. Elle s'est levée tôt.   2. Il s'est occupé de cette affaire.   3. Je me suis
promené dans le parc.   4. Elles se sont écrit pendant les vacances.   5. Elle
s'est réveillée à l'aube.

Written Practice 7
1. Elle a souvent voyagé en France.   2. On a bien dîné.   3. Ils ont beaucoup
dansé.   4. Ils ont toujours écrit des poèmes.   5. Ils n'ont pas assez lu.

QUIZ
1. nous avons mangé / tu as regardé / ils ont téléphone / vous avez dîné / nous
avons partagé / elles ont écouté / nous avons joué / il a étudié / nous avons visité
2. il a bu / elle a pris / j'ai su / vous avez dit / il a plu / vous avez choisi / j'ai eu /
nous avons perdu / ils se sont mariés / nous avons appris   3. Pendant les
vacances, nous (a.) sommes allés en Bretagne. Nous (b.) avons visité la ville

fortifiée de Saint-Malo. Nous (c.) nous sommes promenés sur les remparts et nous (d.) avons admiré les vieilles maisons. Nous (e.) avons nagé dans la mer et nous (f.) nous sommes reposés sur la plage. Nous (g.) avons fait du vélo et nous (h.) avons pris beaucoup de photos. Nous (i.) avons bien mangé et nous (j.) nous sommes bien amusés. Nous (k.) avons dormi dans un hôtel au bord de la mer. Nous (l.) nous sommes levés tard le matin. Il (m.) a plu seulement un jour. Nous (n.) avons rencontré des gens très sympathiques. Nous (o.) sommes revenus à la maison très contents de nos vacances.   4. Ils sont montés en haut de la Tour Eiffel. / Je suis sorti avec mes amis hier soir. / Ils sont passés devant le musée d'Orsay. / Il a retourné le bifteck. / Elle a monté l'enfant dans ses bras. / Nous sommes retournés en Chine. / Tu as descendu les valises au rez-de-chaussée. / Nous avons passé une semaine en Martinique. / Il a sorti son chien. / Elle est descendue par l'escalator.   5. Elle est allée en Angleterre.   6. Est-ce que vous avez compris l'explication?   7. Il s'est occupé des enfants de sa sœur pendant l'été.   8. Elle est tombée amoureuse de Laurent.   9. Ils ont vendu leur maison.   10. Elle a passé une semaine à Parìs.

CHAPTER 13

Written Practice 1
1. J'étais enthousiaste.   2. Nous étions en réunion.   3. Il faisait froid.
4. Il pleuvait.   5. Vous aviez peur.

Written Practice 2
1. Vous travailliez le samedi.   2. Ils portaient un uniforme.   3. Nous buvions du cidre.   4. Je faisais du yoga.   5. Tu voyais tes amis le week-end.

Written Practice 3
1. Paul dînait quand Marie est entrée.   2. Vous vous reposiez quand on a frappé à la porte.   3. Tu te promenais quand tu as vu un lapin.   4. Elle faisait le ménage quand sa sœur a sonné.   5. Nous regardions le film quand Julie a posé une question.

Written Practice 4
1. Si on allait au parc?   2. Si on jouait aux échecs?   3. Si on se levait tôt?
4. Si on téléphonait à Noémie?   5. Si on faisait une promenade?

Written Practice 5
1. il venait d'arriver à Paris   2. je venais de m'arrêter   3. nous venions de nous installer   4. elle venait de signer le contrat   5. vous veniez de déménager

QUIZ

1. vous saviez / je pensais / tu finissais / il était / nous dînions / elle vendait / vous buviez / nous avions / tu choisissais / vous alliez   2. Je lisais beaucoup. / Je jouais au volley-ball. / Je chantais dans une chorale. / Je voyais beaucoup de films. / Je sortais le samedi soir. / J'apprenais le chinois. / Je me levais tard. / J'avais un correspondant. / Je m'habillais de façon décontractée. / J'étais sportif/sportive. 3. Les tableaux de l'exposition étaient magnifiques. / Tous les jours, elle allait à la piscine. / Je lisais quand le téléphone a sonné. / Ils connaissaient bien la région. / Il était célèbre à vingt ans. / Ses parents avaient deux chiens. / Il faisait la cuisine lorsque son frère est arrivé. / Tu adorais regarder les films muets. / Elle finissait un projet quand sa collègue est entrée. / J'ignorais son état de santé.   4. Elle venait de partir. / Ils venaient d'acheter cet appartement. / Je venais de lui laisser un message. / Nous venions d'arriver. / Il venait de gagner le match. / Elle venait de s'installer. / Je venais d'être promu. / Nous venions de prendre une décision. / Elle venait d'apprendre la nouvelle. / Ils venaient de me contacter.   5. Si on invitait nos voisins? / Si on servait un gigot d'agneau? / Si on plantait des légumes? / Si on prenait des photos? / Si on se réconciliait?   6. Est-ce que vous travailliez quand j'ai téléphoné?   7. Il regardait la télévision quand elle est entrée.   8. Je parlais au téléphone quand le chat a sauté sur la table.   9. Elle venait de finir la lettre quand il a téléphoné.   10. La bibliothèque était-elle ouverte?

CHAPTER 14

Written Practice 1

1. Elle préfère rester à la maison.   2. Nous savons dessiner.   3. Ils doivent partir tôt.   4. Vous désirez aller en Inde.   5. Nous espérons gagner le match.

Written Practice 2

1. de   2. à   3. de   4. à   5. de

Written Practice 3

1. par   2. de   3. sur   4. à   5. d'

Written Practice 4

1. vers   2. chez   3. Selon   4. à   5. sous

QUIZ

1. Elle sait danser. / Nous préférons nous reposer. / Elles souhaitent partir. / Ils vont réussir. / Vous aimez vous promener. / Il avoue avoir tort. / Elles peuvent convaincre. / Ils osent protester. / Nous devons accepter. / Vous désirez démissionner.   2. d' / à / par / de / d' / de / à / à / de / à   3. à / de / aux / Chez / devant / contre / par / à / sous / aux   4. Essaie de l'appeler!   5. J'ai oublié d'apporter un cadeau.   6. Joues-tu au tennis?   7. À quoi penses-tu?   8. Ils

ont décidé d'acheter une nouvelle voiture.   9. Aidez-moi à écrire cette lettre!
10. Il lui a demandé d'inviter sa belle-sœur.

CHAPTER 15

Written Practice 1
1. vous aviez écouté   2. ils s'étaient amusés   3. elle était partie   4. nous
avions dîné   5. tu avais fini

Written Practice 2
1. tu mis   2. elles vinrent   3. je fis   4. elle fut   5. il but

Written Practice 3
1. la sienne   2. le leur   3. les miens   4. la nôtre   5. les miennes

Written Practice 4
1. Celle-ci est petite. Celle-là est grande.   2. Ceux-ci sont chers. Ceux-là sont
bon marché.   3. Celui-ci est français. Celui-là est anglais.   4. Celle-ci est en
rayonne. Celle-là est en soie.   5. Celui-ci est mécanicien. Celui-là est
électricien.

QUIZ
1. vous aviez pris / il était allé / elles s'étaient promenées / nous avions trouvé / tu
avais déjeuné / ils avaient invité / elle était arrivée / j'avais compris / tu avais cru /
nous avions reçu   2. a reçu; avions envoyé / avez compris; avait expliqué / a
pensé; avais oublié / me suis rendu compte; s'étaient trompés / ont obtenu; avaient
demandé. / a appris; avaient fusionné   3. elle voyagea / je fis / il mit / nous
parlâmes / ils sortirent / tu mangeas / j'entendis / il vécut / elle fut / nous dansâmes
4. dînaient; entendirent / conduisait; se mit / discutions; arrivèrent / dormais;
sonna / écrivait; sauta   5. Le sien est près de chez lui. / Le leur est tout neuf. /
La tienne est très agréable. / La mienne est dans le salon. / La sienne est
trépidante. / Les nôtres sont en vacances. / Le vôtre est confortable. / Le nôtre
donne sur la Seine. / Les leurs sont en cuir. / Les miennes sont en couleur.
6. Celui-ci est de gauche. Celui-là est de droite. / Celles-ci sont vieilles. Celles-là
sont neuves. / Celle-ci est japonaise. Celle-là est coréenne. / Celui-ci est sombre.
Celui-là est ensoleillé. / Ceux-ci sont fragiles. Ceux-là sont incassables. / Celui-ci
est inconnu. Celui-là est célèbre.   7. Est-ce que votre appartement est plus grand
que le sien?   8. Est-ce que vous aimez celui-ci ou celui-là?   9. Je n'avais pas
compris le problème.   10. —Est-ce que c'est le vôtre? —Oui, c'est le mien.

PART THREE TEST
1. Oui, je l'ai engagé.   2. Oui, je les entends.   3. Oui, elles l'ont acceptée.
4. Oui, je l'ai vu.   5. Oui, il l'a annulée.   6. Oui, je vais lui offrir ces fleurs.
7. Oui, il leur rend souvent visite.   8. Oui, je lui transmets tes amitiés.

9. Oui, il lui a présenté ses excuses.   10. Oui, je lui ai téléphoné.   11. Oui, j'en ai envie.   12. Oui, j'y pense.   13. Oui, elle s'en occupe.   14. Oui, il y a fait attention.   15. Oui, j'en ai l'intention.   16. il a appris   17. elle a lu   18. j'ai cru   19. nous avons fini   20. tu as dit   21. ont sorti   22. sommes passé   23. a sorti   24. as retourné   25. J'ai rentré   26. nous regardions la télévision   27. tu prenais des photos   28. elle était photographe   29. ils dînaient dans ce restaurant   30. vous aviez un chien   31. Nous venions de faire un voyage en Asie.   32. Vous veniez d'apprendre l'espagnol.   33. Elles venaient de dîner sur la terrasse.   34. Tu venais d'arroser le jardin.   35. Il venait de suivre des cours de danse.   36. à   37. d'   38. de   39. à   40. de   41. nous avions appris   42. ils avaient dû   43. il avait bu   44. elles avaient dit   45. je m'étais demandé   46. Vous n'aviez pas compris le problème.   47. À quoi est-ce qu'ils pensent?   48. Ils ont décidé d'acheter une nouvelle maison.   49. Si on lisait ce roman indien?   50. Chloé est partie à minuit.

CHAPTER 16

Written Practice 1
1. Il passe sa vie à dormir.   2. Je passe ma vie à jouer de la guitare.   3. Ils passent leur vie à visiter les musées.   4. Vous passez votre vie à faire des courses.   5. Tu passes ta vie à inventer des histoires.

Written Practice 2
1. Elle fait son jogging après être allée au supermarché.   2. Tu écoutes de la musique après avoir écrit la lettre.   3. Nous faisons une promenade après avoir dîné.   4. Je lis le journal après avoir emmené les enfants à l'école.   5. Vous appelez Xavier après avoir invité Quentin.

Written Practice 3
1. Nous écoutons de la musique en travaillant.   2. Elle fait de l'exercice en regardant la télé.   3. Ils écrivent en parlant.   4. Il fait le ménage en écoutant la radio.   5. Vous racontez une histoire en conduisant.

Written Practice 4
1. La porte a été fermée.   2. La lettre est écrite.   3. Le problème a été résolu.   4. Un employé a été engagé.   5. Une décision est prise.

QUIZ
1. Vous passez votre temps à travailler. / Elle est allongée à regarder le film. / Il est debout à chanter. / Ils passent leurs vacances à visiter les musées. / Il est accroupi à jardiner.   2. Elle enregistre de la musique après être partie en vacances. / Tu as écrit l'article après être allé à Paris. / Vous avez lu le livre après

avoir vu le film.   3. traversant   4. sachant   5. étant   6. La décision a été prise.   7. Le pont a été construit par le roi du Maroc.   8. Ici, on parle anglais. 9. Voyager est amusant.   10. Pourquoi faire ça?

CHAPTER 17

Written Practice 1
1. Nous irons en Chine.   2. Tu arriveras à l'heure.   3. Elle posera des questions.   4. Vous aurez de la chance.   5. Ils dîneront chez Hervé.

Written Practice 2
1. suivra / aura   2. irons / pourrons   3. téléphoneront / arriveront 4. contacteras / seras   5. verra / visitera

Written Practice 3
1. ferez / aurez gagné   2. applaudira / aura terminé   3. se sentira / auront atterri   4. regarderons / auront dîné   5. enverra / aurez fini

Written Practice 4
1. serions / venait   2. iriez / faisait   3. prendrait / pouvait   4. emmènerais / venait   5. aurait / étaient

Written Practice 5
1. aurait dîné / avait pu   2. auriez visité / aviez eu   3. auraient vu / avait été 4. aurions invité / était rentrée   5. aurait écrit / avait eu

QUIZ
1. Nous irons en Tunisie en janvier. / Noëlle travaillera jusqu'à vingt heures. / Vous ferez un voyage en Islande. / Je prendrai le métro. / Ils seront au Kenya. 2. commencerons; sera / prendra; voyagera / achètera; ira / sera; deviendra / arriverez; expliquerons   3. préparerons; auras fait / écoutera; sera rentré / mangeront; l'aurez coupé / rangera; aura défait / commencera; seront arrivés 4. achèterait; pleuvait / donnerais; avait / mettrait; allait / serions; invitiez / viendrait; demandiez   5. L'enfant aurait mangé s'il avait eu faim. / Nous aurions assisté au programme si nous avions été en ville. / Vous auriez joué au tennis s'il n'avait pas plu. / Elle vous aurait envoyé un message si elle n'avait pas été si occupée. / Tu lui aurais expliqué la décision s'il t'avait contacté.   6. À quelle heure est-ce qu'ils arriveront?   7. Je vous téléphonerai quand je serai en France. 8. Pourriez-vous m'aider?   9. Si j'avais su, je ne les aurais pas invités.   10. Il n'aurait pas dû te raconter la fin du film.

CHAPTER 18

Written Practice 1
1. C'est lui qui a gagné le match.   2. C'est vous qui avez posé la question.
3. C'est eux qui sont arrivés en avance.   4. C'est toi qui as reçu le prix.
5. C'est moi qui a découvert le site.

Written Practice 2
1. que   2. que   3. qui   4. qu'   5. qui

Written Practice 3
1. chez qui   2. auquel   3. sur lequel   4. où   5. à quoi

Written Practice 4
1. Voici la voiture dont ils ont envie.   2. Voici le roman dont elle parle.
3. Voici les conséquences dont j'ai peur.   4. Voici les choses dont elle se
souvient.   5. Voici les résultats dont nous sommes heureux.

Written Practice 5
1. Ce à quoi il s'intéresse, c'est à la musique.   2. Ce dont tu as besoin, c'est d'un
ordinateur.   3. Ce que je comprends, c'est la situation.   4. Ce dont vous vous
souvenez, c'est de la fin du film.   5. Ce dont elle parle, c'est fascinant.

Written Practice 6
1. J'ai entendu dire que vous aviez travaillé en Chine en 1998.   2. J'ai entendu
dire qu'elle irait en Afrique dans deux ans.   3. J'ai entendu dire qu'ils avaient
acheté une maison le mois dernier.   4. J'ai entendu dire qu'il pleuvait à Madrid
aujourd'hui.   5. J'ai entendu dire qu'il prendrait sa retraite l'année prochaine.

QUIZ
1. que / qui / qui / que / qu'   2. laquelle / où / auquel / lesquels / qui   3. C'est
la chose dont il se souvient. / C'est le livre dont j'ai besoin. / C'est l'ordinateur dont
ils se servent. / C'est l'affaire dont je m'occupe. / C'est le projet dont elle est fière. /
C'est l'entreprise dont il parle.   4. Ce que / Ce qui / Ce dont / Ce qui / Ce à quoi
/ Ce que / Ce que / Ce à quoi / Ce dont / Ce à quoi   5. On m'a dit que tu irais à
Bruxelles lundi. / On m'a dit qu'il faisait beau à Venise aujourd'hui. / On m'a dit
qu'ils avaient eu des ennuis. / On m'a dit que tu déménagerais bientôt. / On m'a dit
que vous étiez un très bon conférencier.   6. Il ne sait pas ce que vous voulez.
7. Ce dont j'ai besoin, c'est d'un autre stylo.   8. La personne dont il parle est
mon frère.   9. Je ne sais pas ce qui s'est passé.   10. Les photos qu'il a prises
sont belles.

CHAPTER 19

Written Practice 1

1. répondiez   2. puisse   3. apprennes   4. soient   5. ne viennes pas

Written Practice 2

1. Il faut que vous alliez lui rendre visite.   2. Il est essentiel que tu connaisses les grandes lignes du projet.   3. Il est incroyable que ce produit se vende si bien. 4. Il est possible que nous acceptions leur offre.   5. Il est important qu'il prenne de longues vacances.

Written Practice 3

1. Il va t'aider pour que tu puisses finir à temps.   2. À moins que cela soit trop tard, je te retrouve à vingt heures.   3. Bien qu'il y ait des scènes amusantes, ce film n'est pas très bon.   4. Dépêche-toi de rentrer avant qu'il se mette à pleuvoir. 5. Le président a tout fait pour que les citoyens soient contents.

Written Practice 4

1. n'aies pas eu   2. vous soyez trompé   3. ait terminé   4. ait obtenu
5. ait fait

QUIZ

1. revenions / puisses / allions / prenne / ne réussissions pas   2. Il est rare qu'il pleuve dans cette région. (sub.) / Il est surprenant qu'ils ne viennent pas demain. (sub.) / Il est évident qu'elle a ses propres raisons. (ind.) / Il me semble que vous avez tort. (ind.) / Il est probable que ça finira mal. (ind.) / Il faut que nous arrivions avant eux. (sub.)   3. Il vous écrira jusqu'à ce que vous lui donniez une réponse positive. / Il prend la voiture de peur qu'il y ait une grève des transports. / Elle vous contactera avant que vous quittiez Paris. / Vérifiez les calculs afin qu'on ne trouve pas d'erreurs. / Bien qu'il coure vite, il ne gagnera pas cette course.   4. Je regrette que vous ayez abandonné la compétition. / Il est dommage que nous n'ayons pas rencontré Paul plus tôt. / Elle est triste que tu aies échoué à tous tes examens. / Il est étrange qu'ils n'aient pas téléphoné. / Nous craignons qu'il ait oublié l'heure de la réunion. / Je voudrais que vous ayez fini tout l'article d'ici ce soir.   5. Quoi qu'elle choisisse, il est satisfait.   6. Où que vous alliez, je voyagerai avec vous.   7. Quelles que soient ses opinions, ils ne seront jamais d'accord avec lui.   8. Je veux que tu ailles au théâtre avec nous.   9. Il est content que tu puisses assister à son vernissage.   10. Rentre à la maison avant qu'il pleuve.

PART FOUR TEST

1. Je fais la cuisine après avoir fait le ménage.   2. Il téléphone à Caroline après avoir pris sa décision.   3. Ils se lavent les mains après avoir fait la cuisine. 4. Elle fait ses valises après avoir téléphoné à ses amis.   5. Nous parlons à notre client après avoir fixé le prix.   6. conduisant   7. étudiant   8. faisant

9. voyant   10. racontant   11. Vincent viendra avec nous demain.   12. Ils poseront beaucoup de questions.   13. Tu devras t'inscrire.   14. Nous nous reposerons dans le jardin.   15. Ils dîneront sur la terrasse.   16. partirons / aurons fini   17. vendra / aura trouvé   18. paierai / j'aurai reçu   19. réservera / aurez choisi   20. pourras / l'aurai lu   21. prendriez / étiez   22. boirais / j'avais   23. conduirais / fallait   24. iraient / habitait   25. nous promènerions / faisait   26. Ils auraient construit une maison s'ils avaient eu un terrain.   27. J'aurais voté pour lui s'il avait eu un programme plus précis.   28. Ils auraient jeté ces documents s'ils n'en avaient pas eu besoin.   29. Il serait allé chez le dentiste s'il avait eu mal aux dents.   30. On serait allé(s) à Paris si on avait eu le temps.   31. On m'a dit qu'elle avait vécu en Russie.   32. On m'a dit qu'il ferait le tour du monde.   33. On m'a dit qu'elles jouaient très bien au tennis.   34. On m'a dit que tu avais pris une décision.   35. On m'a dit qu'elle n'assisterait pas à la cérémonie.   36. se passe   37. suives   38. choisisses   39. ne soyez pas   40. sachent   41. arrivions (sub.)   42. mente (sub.)   43. lises (sub.)   44. ne connaissions pas (sub.)   45. est (ind.)   46. Il est bizarre qu'ils soient en retard.   47. Pourvu qu'il fasse beau demain!   48. Pourriez-vous nous aider?   49. Ils auraient dû nous raconter toute l'histoire.   50. On m'a dit que le président était au Japon aujourd'hui.

FINAL EXAM

1. devez   2. Pouvez   3. veulent   4. dois   5. pouvez   6. tu t'amuses   7. ils s'écrivent   8. nous nous reposons   9. il s'habille   10. nous nous promenons   11. Il ne va pas pleuvoir cette nuit.   12. Ils ne vont pas vendre leur voiture.   13. Il ne va pas maigrir pendant les vacances.   14. Tu ne vas pas aller en Italie.   15. Elle ne va pas commander la mousse au chocolat.   16. Je vous inviterai au restaurant quand vous viendrez à Paris.   17. Nous visiterons le château d'Amboise quand nous serons dans la vallée de la Loire.   18. Tant qu'il fera beau, nous resterons dans le jardin.   19. Elle vous contactera dès qu'elle aura plus de détails.   20. Il regardera ces films quand il pourra.   21. Nous venons d'acheter un nouveau dictionnaire.   22. Je viens de téléphoner à Guillaume.   23. Je viens de faire le ménage.   24. Elle vient de finir le projet.   25. Il vient de renouveler sa carte d'identité.   26. Elle le lui a offert.   27. Ils ne les lui ont pas envoyés.   28. Je les leur écris.   29. Vous les leur vendez.   30. Elle la leur a racontée.   31. Oui, elle me les a rendus.   32. Oui, il me l'a montrée.   33. Oui, je vous l'ai faxé.   34. Oui, je vous le recommande.   35. Oui, je peux vous le décrire.   36. Il fait repasser ses chemises.   37. Elle fait classer les photos.   38. Nous faisons sortir le chien.   39. Je fais faire une robe.   40. Il fait décorer la salle de classe.   41. Il a reçu la carte que vous aviez envoyée de Shanghai.   42. On a su que les entreprises avaient fait faillite.   43. Elle a annulé car elle avait oublié un rendez-vous

important.   44. Il a perdu le document que vous lui aviez confié.   45. La réunion s'est passée comme il l'avait imaginé.   46. tu mangeas   47. j'entendis 48. il vécut   49. elle fut   50. nous dansâmes   51. Il faisait le tour du monde quand sa sœur gagna le prix Nobel.   52. Nous dansions quand l'orchestre s'arrêta.   53. Ils vivaient à Berlin quand la guerre éclata.   54. Vous écoutiez de la musique quand elle entra.   55. J'écrivais quand il sonna à la porte.   56. Les nôtres sont au Portugal.   57. Le vôtre est confortable. 58. Le nôtre est vieux.   59. Les leurs sont vagues.   60. Les miennes sont bleues.   61. Celui-ci est de gauche. Celui-là est de droite.   62. Celles-ci sont vieilles. Celles-là sont neuves.   63. Celle-ci est brillante. Celle-là n'est pas raisonnable.   64. Celui-ci est mou. Celui-là est moelleux.   65. Ceux-ci sont légers. Ceux-là sont lourds.   66. laquelle   67. laquelle   68. qui/quoi 69. où   70. qui   71. Je fais de la danse depuis trois ans.   72. Je fais la cuisine pour les Renaud depuis trois mois.   73. Je fais la queue depuis un quart d'heure.   74. Je fais réparer ma voiture chez ce garagiste depuis deux ans. 75. Je fais faire mes costumes depuis dix ans.   76. sachiez   77. j'aie 78. dérange   79. puissent   80. soit   81. ait trouvé   82. ne sois pas venu(e)   83. ils aient déménagé   84. n'ayez pas aimé   85. ait été 86. viendront (ind.)   87. fassent (sub.)   88. aient (sub.)   89. soient (sub.) 90. pouvez (ind.)   91. Savez-vous faire la cuisine?   92. Connaissez-vous ce médecin?   93. Elle peut traduire ce document en une heure.   94. Depuis combien de temps habitez-vous (dans) cet appartement?   95. Pourriez-vous me montrer la Tour Eiffel sur le plan?   96. Ils vont en France chaque année. 97. À quelle heure sont-ils partis?   98. Allez-vous acheter tous ces livres? 99. Vous en souvenez-vous?   100. Quoi qu'il fasse, il réussit.

INDEX

ABOUT THE AUTHOR

Annie Heminway, a native of France, is a French teacher at the Alliance Française in New York. She also has taught at Rutgers University and Arizona State University. Heminway is the author of more than ten books on the French language, including *Practice Makes Perfect: French Pronouns and Prepositions* (McGraw-Hill, 2006), and the upcoming *Practice Makes Perfect: Complete French Grammar*, also from McGraw-Hill.